Grow Native

Bringing Natural Beauty to Your Garden

Quarto is the authority on a wide range of topics.

Quarto educates, entertains and enriches the lives of
our readers—enthusiasts and lovers of hands-on living.

www.quartoknows.com

First published in 2016 by Cool Springs Press, an imprint of Quarto Publishing Group
USA Inc., 400 First Avenue North, Suite 400, Minneapolis, MN 55401 USA.
Telephone: (612) 344-8100 Fax: (612) 344-8692

quartoknows.com
Visit our blogs at quartoknows.com

Cool Springs Press titles are also available at discounts in bulk quantity for industrial or
sales-promotional use. For details contact the Special Sales Manager at Quarto Publishing
Group USA Inc., 400 First Avenue North, Suite 400, Minneapolis, MN 55401 USA.

10 9 8 7 6 5 4 3 2 1

ISBN: 978-1-59186-655-8

Library of Congress Cataloging-in-Publication Data

Names: Steiner, Lynn M., 1958- author.
Title: Grow native : bringing natural beauty to your garden / Lynn M. Steiner.
Other titles: Bringing natural beauty to your garden
Description: Minneapolis, MN : Cool Springs Press, 2016. | Includes index.
Identifiers: LCCN 2015044029 | ISBN 9781591866558 (sc)
Subjects: LCSH: Native plant gardening--United States. | Native plants for
    cultivation--United States.
Classification: LCC SB439 .S82 2016 | DDC 635.9/6760973--dc23
LC record available at http://lccn.loc.gov/2015044029

Acquiring Editor: Billie Brownell
Project Manager: Alyssa Bluhm
Senior Art Director: Brad Springer
Cover Designer: Diana Boger
Interior Design: Rob Johnson
Layout: Laurie Young

Printed in China

AUGUST 2016

Grow Native

Bringing Natural Beauty to Your Garden

Lynn M. Steiner

COOL
SPRINGS
PRESS
Home and Garden Experts™

MINNEAPOLIS, MINNESOTA

Acknowledgments

Thank you to the many gardeners who always and generously say yes when I ask if I can visit and photograph their gardens. Native-plant gardeners are truly the most sharing of all gardeners as they know how important it is to get others "on the bandwagon." People whose gardens are included in this book are Jeremy Mayberg and Amy-Ann Greenspan, Diane Hilscher, Veronika Phillips, Jan Hayman, Jackie Metalak, Fred and Marcy Schram, Roger Miller, Connie Taillon, Amy Welch, Barbara Burgum, Sharon and Fred Remund, Dick and Marsha Krueger, Marge Hols, Robert and Marlene Olsen, Erik Olsen, Gary Britton, Kent Peterson, Bonnie Blodgett, Deb Revier, and Pat Neuman.

Thank you to the many public gardens I visit across the country, where I find inspiration as well as photographic opportunities. Some of the photographs used in this book were taken at Minnesota Landscape Arboretum, Chanhassen, Minnesota; Mt. Cuba Center, Hockessin, Delaware; Bowman's Hill Wildflower Preserve, New Hope, Pennsylvania; Morton Arboretum, Lisle, Illinois; Garden in the Woods, Framington, Massachusetts; Longwood Gardens, Kennet Square, Pennsylvania; Shaw Nature Reserve, Gray Summit, Missouri; Carpenter Nature Center, Hastings, Minnesota; Bartram's Garden, Philadelphia, Pennsylvania; Ambler Arboretum, Ambler, Pennsylvania; Birmingham Botanic Garden, Birmingham, Alabama; Missouri Botanic Garden, St. Louis, Missouri; Tyler Arboretum, Media, Pennsylvania; Morris Arboretum, Philadelphia, Pennsylvania; Olbrich Botanic Garden, Madison, Wisconsin; Cornell Plantation, Ithaca, New York; and High Line Trail, New York, New York.

Thank you to Billie Brownell for thinking of me for this project and working hard to make sure it came to fruition, and to Alyssa Bluhm and the rest of the staff at Cool Springs Press.

Thank you to my friend and neighbor, Larry Swanson, for sharing his beautiful photographs of butterflies, insects, and hummingbirds on native plants. As always, thanks to my husband, Ted, for supporting my gardening efforts—sometimes successful, sometimes not—as well as my writing, photography, and travel.

Contents

Introduction

There are many things we can do as gardeners that greatly enhance the natural world and the creatures we share it with. I call it "responsible gardening." At the top of the list is using native plants. As a responsible, native-plant gardener, your goal should be to combine your love of plants and the joy you get from tending them in your own yard with what you know about our natural plant heritage and your desire to avoid contributing to its further destruction and possible extinction. The result should be a place where you derive much personal enjoyment but cause as little damage as possible to the natural world. Ideally, your garden will enhance the benefits to native ecosystems as it provides a haven for native plant species facing elimination from their natural habitats as well as a much-needed sources of pollen, food, and shelter for native fauna.

I have evolved quite a bit since my early days of gardening, well over 30 years ago. One of the most important lessons I have learned along the way is that we can't separate our gardens from the natural world.

What happens in our gardens has ramifications well beyond our property boundaries. The plants we choose don't always stay in our gardens. And the plants that we bring into our gardens from other areas of the country and the world can have serious effects on our natural areas and our native pollinators, birds, and other fauna. The chemicals and fossil fuels (for mowing, fertilizing, and so forth) often used in traditional gardening are also cause for alarm. The bottom line is, gardening isn't always such a "green" hobby.

The good news is that native plants can be used in any designed landscape the same way nonnative plants can be used. In the past, native plants were relegated to naturalistic landscapes and in large prairie and woodland gardens. But as people become more aware of the benefits of using native plants, they are discovering that they do extremely well in traditional landscapes as well. Whether you want a cottage garden, a modern-looking landscape, or a mixed border with season-long interest, there are native plants that will fit the bill.

Nothing says "Midwestern" like a prairie garden. Lynn's garden in Minnesota includes blanket flower, wild onion, purple coneflower, wild petunia (*Ruellia humilis*), and prairie coneflower.

Diversity Reigns

Just as North America is made up of many different types of people, it is also made up of many different native plant communities, ranging from forests to grasslands to bogs to xeric landscapes, determined by the physical environment of an area as well as the climate. These communities are home to not only a great diversity of plants but also many species of birds, mammals, and insects. We should draw on our natural plant heritage as we develop our own landscapes and gardens, helping to perpetuate these amazing habitats that are becoming lost at an alarming rate.

A well-functioning native landscape should be based on a natural plant community, preferably one that would have been found in your area. Use the map at go.grolier.com/atlas?id=mtlr054, which provides a general look at the original plant provinces of North America. Within each community there are many subgroups, including wetlands and waterways and open areas in forested areas. Use these communities as a starting point when choosing plants for your own landscape. Obviously, plants that evolved in the same conditions as you have will do well in your gardens. However, it is still important to base your final plant selections on your existing conditions. If you live within the Eastern Deciduous Forest province but have a yard without any trees, you will not be able to replicate that shady woodland habitat. You will need to stick with plants that evolved in sunnier habitats.

A Look Inside This Book

Grow Native is all about celebrating the native plants of North America and learning how to include and enjoy them in your own garden. The goal is to help you design native plant gardens and grow more native plants in your landscape while creating gardens that you enjoy. Fortunately, there are *many* beautiful native plants available to help you achieve this goal!

NATIVE BUZZ

Monarch Butterfly
Danaus plexippus

Adults migrate August through October, flying thousands of miles south to hibernate along the California coast and in central Mexico. A few overwinter along the Gulf coast or south Atlantic coast. Along the way, monarchs stop to feed on flower nectar and to roost together at night.

Range: Southern Canada south through all of the United States, Central America, and most of South America.

Habitat: Many open habitats, including fields, meadows, weedy areas, marshes, and roadsides.

Larval Food: Most people are aware of the important relationship between monarch butterfly caterpillars and members of the milkweed family (*Asclepiadaceae*), but it bears repeating: without milkweeds, there will be no monarchs. Females lay eggs singly under the host leaves; caterpillars eat leaves and flowers.

Adult Food: Nectar from all milkweeds. Many other natives, including dogbanes (*Apocynum* species), goldenrods, blazing stars, ironweeds (*Vernonia* species), and tickseeds.

In this book you will find native plants suitable for traditional gardens and learn how to effectively and acceptably incorporate them into your landscape. The end result should be a garden or landscape that reflects a sense of our natural plant communities as well as a setting where you can tend native plants and enjoy their seasonal changes and the wildlife they attract.

Chapter 1 provides the background you need to understand what native plants are and why they should be considered for garden use.

Chapter 2 covers the practical aspects of selecting and planting native plants based on your site conditions.

In Chapter 3 you'll learn how to use native plants in ways that are aesthetically pleasing as well as acceptable to neighbors and city officials. You'll learn how to blend native plants with traditional landscape plants, what plants do best in small spaces and formal landscapes, and what plants to use for special situations, such as boulevards, shady spots, and rain gardens. This chapter also covers appropriate plants for attracting birds, butterflies, and other wildlife.

Chapter 4 is devoted to maintaining native plants and gardens, including weed control, grooming, and dealing with possible pests. You'll also find basic gardening information tailored to native plants.

Chapter 5 is a comprehensive Plant Profiles section. It provides the information you need to choose appropriate natives to include in your garden. I carefully selected the plants to feature those that tend to do better in traditional landscape settings, avoiding those that are too aggressive, hard to grow, or difficult to locate in the nursery trade. I included a good variety of sun and shade plants and a cross-section of plants native to the major biomes of the US. To the many wonderful plants that didn't make my cut—I apologize.

Inspiration Gallery

For inspiration on how to pull it all together, take a look at the photographs throughout the book. They illustrate how gardeners throughout the country have created native plant gardens and landscapes. Above all, I encourage you to learn from nature itself: Take lots of walks in our many parks and natural areas for inspiration.

Spring in the Pacific Northwest is prime time for shade gardens. This Seattle entry garden includes natives red-flowering currant (*Ribes sanguineum*) and false lily-of-the-valley (*Maianthemum dilatatum*).

Mark Turner

NATIVE BUZZ

Eastern Tiger Swallowtail Butterfly
Papilio glaucus

First-hatched caterpillars look like bird poop, a good camouflage. Older caterpillars turn green, with a large head and bright eyespots, which are there to fool predators.

Range: Eastern North America from Ontario south to the Gulf Coast, west to Colorado plains and central Texas.

Habitat: Deciduous broadleaf woods, forest edges, river valleys, gardens, parks, and suburbs.

Larval Food: Leaves of various plants, including wild cherries (*Prunus* species), magnolias, basswood, tulip tree (*Liriodendron tulipifera*), red maple, spicebush, birches, ashes (*Fraxinus* species), cottonwoods (*Populus* species), mountain ashes (*Sorbus* species), and willows (*Salix* species).

Adult Food: Nectar of flowers from a variety of plants, including wild cherries, milkweeds, purple coneflowers, and Joe-pye weeds.

Mark Turner

Gardening with native plants will help you become a responsible and sustainable gardener so you can complement your natural surroundings rather than cause further harm to them. Priority is put on choosing the right plant for the right place so you can reduce or eliminate your need for artificial fertilizers, pesticides, and watering; choosing plants that are beneficial to native pollinating insects and birds are a priority as well. This xeriscaped garden in southwestern Washington state includes California poppy (*Eschscholzia californica*), buckwheats (*Eriogonum* species), and beardtongues.

Catriona Erler

The key to creating a successful home landscape with native plants is to understand the natural plant communities that once covered your part of the country and work toward successfully incorporating them into your gardens and landscape. Nature is truly the best garden designer, and you will never go wrong if you attempt to imitate it. This garden in Texas includes 'Henry Deulberg' blue salvia, Turk's cap (*Malvaviscus arboreus* var. *drummondii*), redflower false yucca (*Hesperaloe parviflora*), big muhly grass (*Muhlenbergia lindheimer*), little bluestem, and blackfoot daisy (*Melampodium leucanthum*).

INTRODUCTION

11

The vast Eastern Deciduous Forest once covered much of the eastern US. This woodland garden at Longwood Gardens in Delaware includes a good representation of the plants that can be found in this province: oaks, mayapples (*Podophyllum peltatum*), foamflowers, woodland phlox 'Sherwood Purple', and sedges.

In California, it is imperative that landscape plants get by on little or no supplemental water. In this front yard, turfgrasses are replaced with drought-tolerant native shrubs, grasses, and perennials, including California poppy (*Eschscholzia californica*), 'Blue Springs' beard-tongue, Douglas iris (*Iris douglasiana*), red fescue (*Festuca rubra*), and Cleveland sage (*Salvia clevelandii*).

13

NATIVE BUZZ

Mourning Cloak Butterfly
Nymphalis antiopa

One of the first butterflies seen in spring because it does not migrate; instead, it overwinters as an adult in loose tree bark and tree cavities. Adding host trees to your landscape will increase your chances of seeing these spring beauties.

Range: All of North America.

Habitat: Anywhere host plants occur, including woods, open spaces, parks, and suburbs; especially in riparian areas.

Larval Food: Birches, elms (*Ulmus* species), hackberry, poplars, cottonwood, willows.

Adult Food: Tree sap (especially oaks) in spring, followed by flower nectar and rotting fruits in summer.

NATIVE BUZZ

Red Admiral Butterfly
Vanessa atalanta

• •

This butterfly has a very erratic, rapid flight. Males perch on ridge-tops, if available, in the afternoon to wait for females, who lay eggs singly on the tops of host plant leaves. Young caterpillars eat and live within a shelter of folded leaves; older caterpillars make a nest of leaves tied together with silk.

Range: Guatemala north through Mexico and the United States to northern Canada. Cannot survive very cold winters; most of North America must be recolonized each spring by southern migrants.

Habitat: Moist woods, yards, parks, marshes, seeps, moist fields. During migrations, it is found in almost any habitat from tundra to subtropics.

Larval Food: Plants of the nettle family, including stinging nettle (*Urtica dioica*), tall wild nettle (*U. gracilis*), wood nettle (*Laportea canadensis*), and false nettle (*Boehmeria cylindrica*), and possibly hops *(Humulus)*.

Adult Food: Prefer sap flows on trees, fermenting fruit, and bird droppings, visiting flowers only when these are not available. Then they will nectar at common milkweed, purple coneflower, red clover, aster, and alfalfa, among others.

14

In the southeastern US, sandy beach habitats were once prevalent. This Florida landscape includes natives false rosemary (*Conradina canescens*) and myrtle oak (*Quercus myrtifolia*). Garden design by Randy Harelson.

Dency Kane

Mark Turner

You can often tell where a person comes from by the way they dress, speak, or act. You can also often tell where a plant comes from by how it looks and grows. This native-plant landscape in Tucson, Arizona, includes saguaro (*Carnegia gigantea*), yuccas, blackfoot daisy (*Melampodium leucanthum*), and Mexican sage (*Salvia leucantha*).

CHAPTER ONE

What Are Native Plants & Why Should We Use Them?

16

Just what *is* a native plant? Most people consider a North American native plant to be one that grows naturally without human intervention and was here before European settlement. Some people only consider a plant native if it is indigenous to within a certain radius (a range of 50 to 200 miles) of its location. Other people allow a more expansive definition, which may include any plant that would have been found in their state or even all of North America.

By and large, the indigenous peoples lived in harmony with the plants and animals of an area without drastically altering the natural ecosystems. European settlers, on the other hand, had a major impact on the landscape as they cut down large stands of trees, plowed up acres of prairies, suppressed natural fires, and introduced plants from their homelands and other parts of this continent.

Unlike most introduced plants, though, a native plant fully integrates itself into a biotic community, establishing complex relationships with other local plants and animals. Not only does a native plant depend on the organisms with which it has evolved, but the other organisms also depend on it, creating a true web of life. This natural system of checks and balances ensures that native plants seldom grow out of control in their natural habitats.

The word "wildflower" is a commonly used term, but it does not necessarily mean a native plant, since not all wildflowers are native to an area. Wildflowers include introduced plants that have escaped cultivation and grow wild in certain areas. Examples are Queen Anne's lace (*Daucus carota*) and chicory (*Chicorium intybus*), two common roadside plants, neither of which is native to any area of the United States.

The prairie ecosystem once covered over 200 million acres in the middle United States and south-central Canada. Today, less than one percent of our native prairies remain. A good way to experience this species-rich habitat is to visit a restored prairie such as the Schulenberg Prairie at the Morton Arboretum in Lisle, Illinois.

WHAT ARE NATIVE PLANTS & WHY SHOULD WE USE THEM?

Giant Swallowtail Butterfly
Papilio cresphontes

. . . .

This is a fairly large butterfly, with wingspans reaching over 6 inches. Males patrol for receptive females. Females lay single eggs on host leaves and twigs. Caterpillars resemble bird droppings.

Range: Throughout eastern North America west to the Rocky Mountains, south through the desert, southwest to South America.

Habitat: Many locales, including rocky and sandy hillsides near streams or gullies in the North; pine flats, towns, and citrus groves in the South.

Larval Food: Trees and herbs of the citrus family (*Rutaceae*), including *Citrus* species, prickly ash (*Zanthoxylum americanum*), hop tree (*Ptelea trifoliata*), and common rue (*Ruta graveolens*).

Adult Food: Nectar from many flowers, including azaleas, goldenrods, and swamp milkweed.

Larry E. Swanson

18

The Name Game: Classifying Native Plants

Learning Latin names can be frustrating, but it is important, especially with native plants. Many have more than one common name, many share the same or similar common names, and many common names vary from one section of the country to another. So it's easy to end up with the wrong plant—one that may not even be native. A prime example is the common name "cedar." This can refer to arborvitae, cypress, false cypress, juniper, and sequoia, all of which are different plants.

The fundamental taxonomic plant category is the species, a group of genetically similar plants within a genus, a larger botanical division. Genus and species names are commonly Latin and italicized; the genus name is capitalized and comes first followed by the species in lowercase. Within a species, there are also subspecies (abbreviated as "ssp."), varieties ("var."), and forma ("f.").

A subspecies has a characteristic that isn't quite different enough to make it a separate species. This characteristic may occur over a wide range or in a geographically isolated area. Varieties and forma have minor recognizable variations from the species, such

Latin names often offer clues on how to identify a plant. For example, knowing that *tomentosus* means "downy" and *laevis* means "smooth" will help you remember what a plant looks like. And in this case, *Actaea rubra* ("red") helps you remember this species has red fruits.

As an example of natural variation within a species, the typical form of *Ratibida columnifera* has yellow ray flowers, but *forma pulcherrima* (which translates to "very beautiful") has maroon rays.

as flower color or leaf size, but are not distinct enough to be labeled subspecies. An example is found in *Cypripedium calceolus* (yellow lady's slipper), which is further differentiated into var. *pubescens* (large yellow lady's slipper), var. *makasin* (greater yellow lady's slipper), and var. *parviflorum* (small yellow lady's slipper). The latter variety is shorter and has a slightly different flower shape and color than the other two, but without seeing the plants side by side, it can be difficult to tell which one you are looking at.

A cultivar is a "cultivated variety" that retains its distinguishing features when reproduced by humans. A clone is a type of cultivar propagated vegetatively (i.e., asexually by such means as cuttings, grafting, budding, tissue culture, or layering) from a single selected parent, making each plant exactly alike. Many horticultural landscape plants are propagated by cloning to retain their desirable characteristics. These plants may become trademarked and be given yet another name by the propagator, indicated by a ® or ™. Seed-strain cultivars are propagated from seed and may show some variation from plant to plant. A hybrid cultivar is produced by crossing two or more species or cultivars and the name is preceded by an "x." A hybrid cultivar can be naturally occurring or be developed by plant breeders.

Regional tradition can give different names to the same species. They are all names for the same plant.

Common names: Red maple, rock maple, scarlet maple, soft maple, swamp maple, water maple
Latin name: *Acer rubrum*
Cultivar: 'Franksred'
Trademark name: Red Sunset™

Coral Hairstreak Butterfly
Satyrium titus

Larry E. Swanson

Males perch on shrubs, especially in late afternoon, to watch for females. Females lay eggs singly on host twigs or in litter at the base of plants. Caterpillars hide in litter during the day and emerge at night to feed on leaves and fruits.

Range: Central Canada south to eastern California; east across southern Canada to New England; south to central New Mexico, central Texas, northern Arkansas, and central Georgia.

Habitat: Shrubby areas, brushlands, openings in woodlands, neglected pastures, streamsides, barrens, chaparral, and brushlands.

Larval Food: Black cherry, wild plum, and chokecherry (*Prunus* species) in the rose family (Rosaceae).

Adult Food: Nectar from many flowers, including butterfly weed, New Jersey tea (*Ceanothus americanus*), dogbane (*Apocynum* species), and sulphur flower (*Eriogonum*).

Using Cultivars of Native Plants: Cautions

As native plants become more popular, many are being selectively cultivated to produce different varieties. These cultivars, sometimes called "nativars," are usually chosen for certain characteristics such as larger or double flowers, leaf color, compact growth, or flower color.

Native plant purists will argue that cultivars are not truly native and should not be used in native landscaping. Because they are usually vegetatively propagated (clones), and each plant is exactly alike, they do not contribute to genetic diversity like seed-grown plants. They may also lose some of their attractiveness to native fauna. Pollinating insects may no longer be attracted to a new flower shape or color and chewing insects may not feed on leaves if the leaf chemistry has been changed. These cultivars also run the risk of escaping from landscapes and contaminating natural stands of natives, where they can alter the genetic makeup of the original species.

In most cases, cultivars retain most of the characteristics of the native species and are fine choices for landscape use. However, if you are doing land restoration work or creating a large habitat garden, stick with the true species or even the subspecies or variety native

Dropmore scarlet trumpet honeysuckle (*Lonicera* x *brownii* 'Dropmore Scarlet') is a cultivar selected from a hybrid cross of two native species: *Lonicera sempervirens* and *L. hirsuta*. The crossing of the two species resulted in a nice garden plant with greater winter hardiness and improved flowering and fragrance.

to your area to maintain the true genetic diversity you'll only get from the native species. That means you need to source plants *very locally*.

In some cases, plant breeding has led to cultivars that are extremely changed from their native species, and these plants often do *not* provide the same ecological benefits as the native species. A drastic change in leaf color can confuse insects, and fruits that are enlarged in size may no longer be edible to birds and other wildlife. Some flowers are sterile, thereby denying goldfinches and other small birds of the seeds for food. Some cultivars have double flowers, which are unusable by native pollinators who can't get to the pollen and nectar. A prime example is the wide array of (bizarre) *Echinacea purpurea* cultivars that are available, many of which retain very little of their native heritage.

A responsible gardener will choose a locally sourced, seed-grown plant whenever practical. But using cultivars that have characteristics similar to the species in a landscape setting is still far better than using nonnative plants. Try to stay away from cultivars labeled "insect resistant," because chances are low that it will provide any benefits to native insects, birds, and butterflies.

Misconceptions about Native Plants

Despite the increased interest and promotion of native plants, many people hesitate to use them due to some common misconceptions.

Some people think native plants are colorless and dull, which is simply not true. Once you learn about the wide variety of natives and how to use them properly, you will discover that they have much to offer—not only colorful flowers but also interesting textures, colorful fruits, and year-round interest. They may not all be as bright and showy as many introduced plants, but their subtle beauty can be just as effective in landscaping. When given proper conditions and room to grow in a garden or landscape setting, most native plants produce larger and better flowers than they do when growing in the wild.

Unfortunately, native plants often have a reputation of being the source of allergies. Goldenrods are especially burdened by this misconception. The truth is, most native plants are insect pollinated rather than wind pollinated. Kentucky bluegrass has the potential to produce more allergens than any native plant.

Most native plants are no more invasive than many other garden plants. Most plants that become aggressively

Double bloodroot (*Sanguinaria canadensis* 'Multiplex') is a beautiful, longer-blooming selection, but the double flowers are sterile and don't produce nectar or seeds, so it is best used sparingly in the landscape, leaving the true species for habitat gardens and restorations.

Pink-edged Sulphur Butterfly
Colias interior

Larry E. Swanson

This is a northern butterfly, preferring woods over open areas. Males patrol, with a slow flight, for females. Eggs are laid in mid-summer on blueberry leaves and young caterpillars overwinter. Most feeding occurs the following spring.

Range: From British Columbia and eastern Oregon east through the Great Lakes area to northern New England. Isolated populations in central Appalachians of northeast Pennsylvania, western Maryland, eastern West Virginia, and northwest Virginia.

Habitat: Shrubby openings in woods, bogs, or scrub areas where plants of the heath family (Ericaceae) grow; often in burned or logged sites.

Larval Food: Various blueberry plants (*Vaccinium* species).

Adult Food: Nectar from flowers, including bristly sarsaparilla (*Aralia hispida*) and orange hawkweed (*Hieracium aurantiacum*).

invasive are imported from other countries or from another part of the United States. Keep in mind that any plant can become invasive if it is given the right conditions—a site more conducive to rampant growth than its preferred habitat and a lack of the native insect predators that help keep it in check.

The misconception that native plants are hard to grow comes from the fact that some, such as lady's slippers, have evolved in a rather specific habitat, one that is often hard to recreate in a garden setting. Once you learn about the different plant communities and their soil and sunlight requirements and determine which plants are best for your conditions, you will find that most native plants are easier to grow than their cultivated counterparts because they have evolved in similar climatic and soil conditions as are found in your area.

Some people think native-plant landscapes are messy. Well, nature is "messy." It's full of fallen logs, recycling plant parts, and plants that weave together rather than lay out in straight lines. Once you understand and appreciate this, native plants will no longer appear unattractive. As

you'll learn in Chapter 3, there are many things you can do to make a native landscape look neater, such as incorporating small patches of lawn grasses, creating paths and neat edges, and cutting back certain plants when they are done blooming.

Some people avoid native plants because they think they are hard to find in the nursery trade. Once you learn which plants are native, you will be surprised how many are available at local nurseries. In every part of the country you will find nurseries that specialize in native plants, and many of them offer mail order.

Reasons to Use Native Plants

There are many reasons to use native plants, some more tangible than others. For many gardeners, the initial attraction comes from native plants' reputation of being lower maintenance than a manicured lawn and exotic shrubs. For the most part this is true—provided native plants are given landscape situations that match their cultural requirements. Because they have evolved and adapted to their surroundings, native plants tend to be

Think native plants aren't as showy as nonnative plants? This garden at Mt. Cuba Center in Delaware, which features columbine, woodland phlox, three-leaved stonecrop (*Sedum ternatum*), and green and gold (*Chrysogonum virginianum*), blows that misconception out of the water.

tolerant of tough conditions such as drought and poor soil. Native plants are better adapted to local climatic conditions and better able to resist the effects of native insects and diseases. Their reduced maintenance results in less dependence on fossil fuels and reduced noise pollution from lawn mowers and other types of equipment.

One very important benefit of using native plants is their importance to native insects, birds, and other wildlife, which are critical to the survival of our planet. Creating native ecosystems in our landscapes provides a substitute for the natural habitats that are rapidly being destroyed. And why not plant a garden that is attractive to insects, birds, and other types of wildlife rather than repellant to them? Native plants are best choices for these ecosystems. They are recognized by native birds and insects and known to be palatable, unlike nonnative plants, which have not evolved with native fauna.

Growing native plants gives you peace of mind that you are not further contributing to the degradation of natural habitats. Many traditional landscape plants have the potential to become invasive and weedy when grown in conditions without the natural checks and balances that keep it under control. When a native species moves into a natural area from a garden bed, it usually just becomes a part of the ecosystem. When an alien species move in, it often grows faster and reproduces more successfully. The result is a monoculture that displaces native species and provides little or no habitat for native fauna.

Gardening with native plants will help you create a sense of place rather than just a cookie-cutter landscape.

Goldenrods suffer from a bad rap because they bloom about the same time as ragweed, a major sources of allergens. But as this photo shows, goldenrod is avidly pollinated by insects, not by wind.

Many bees, butterflies, and other insects rely on native plants, like prairie coneflower, for nectar and pollen.

Your yard will be unique among the long line of mown grass and clipped shrubs in your neighborhood, yet still be as attractive or more attractive than other traditional landscapes. You will get an enormous sense of satisfaction from helping re-establish what once grew naturally in your area. You will see an increase in wildlife, including birds, butterflies, and pollinating insects, making your garden a livelier place. (See Chapter 3 for more about designing with natives.)

On a broader scale, using native plants helps preserve the natural heritage of an area. Genetic diversity promotes the mixing of genes to form new combinations, the key to adaptability and survival of all life. Once a species becomes extinct, it is gone forever, as are its genes and any future contribution that it might have made.

A less tangible—but possibly more important—side of using native plants is the connection you make with nature. Gardening with natives instills an understanding of our natural world—its cycles, changes, and history. Communing with nature has a positive, healing effect on human beings. Learning how to work with instead of against nature will do wonders for your spiritual health. By observing native plants throughout the year, a gardener gains insight into seasonal rhythms and life cycles. You will experience intellectual rewards that are somehow missing if you only grow petunias or marigolds.

Common periwinkle (*Vinca minor*) and Spanish bluebell (*Hyacinthoides hispanica*) are two nonnative garden plants that readily adapt to natural woodlands and rapidly grow into large colonies that displace native species.

WHAT ARE NATIVE PLANTS & WHY SHOULD WE USE THEM?

INVASIVE AND WEEDY LANDSCAPE PLANTS & SUGGESTED REPLACEMENTS

While many introduced plants are well-behaved, beautiful additions to gardens, some become harmful invaders of local native habitats. The Invasive Plant Atlas of the United States (www.invasiveplantatlas.org) does a great job of monitoring invasive and potentially invasive species. It is a good idea to consult this site before adding a lot of new plants to your landscape. The following is a list of some of the many traditional landscape plants that have the potential to become weedy invasives in certain areas of the country. Also listed are some native plants that have similar cultural requirements and/or physical traits that make them good substitutes. For a complete list of potentially invasive plants, see the Invasive Plant Atlas.

Flowers, Groundcovers & Grasses

INSTEAD OF THIS	PLANT THIS	
Aegopodium podagraria (goutweed)	• Iris cristata (dwarf crested iris) • Mitella diphylla (bishop's cap) • Pachysandra procumbens (Allegheny spurge)	• Phlox stolonifera (creeping phlox) • Tiarella cordifolia (foamflower)
Campanula rapunculoides (creeping bellflower)	• Agastache foeniculum (anise hyssop) • Campanula rotundifolia (harebell) • Baptisia australis (blue false indigo) • Geranium maculatum (wild geranium)	• Mertensia virginica (Virginia bluebells) • Monarda species (bee balms) • Verbena stricta (hoary vervain)
Convallaria majalis (lily of the valley)	• Adiantum pedatum (maidenhair fern) • Asarum species (wild gingers) • Iris cristata (dwarf crested iris) • Mitella diphylla (bishop's cap)	• Pachysandra procumbens (Allegheny spurge) • Phlox stolonifera (creeping phlox) • Tiarella cordifolia (foamflower)
Daucus carota (Queen Anne's lace)	• Asclepias incarnata (swamp milkweed) • Baptisia alba (white false indigo) • Dalea candida (white prairie clover)	• Penstemon digitalis (beardtongue) • Phlox paniculata (garden phlox) • Phlox maculata (wild sweet William)
Glechoma hederacea (creeping Charlie)	• Asarum species (wild gingers) • Fragaria species (wild strawberries) • Mitella diphylla (bishop's cap) • Pachysandra procumbens (Allegheny spurge)	• Sedum ternatum (stonecrop) • Tiarella cordifolia (foamflower) • Waldsteinia fragarioides (barren strawberry)
Hemerocallis fulva (tawny daylily)	• Asclepias tuberosa (butterfly milkweed) • Echinacea species (purple coneflowers) • Gaillardia species (blanket flowers) • Heliopsis helianthoides (oxeye)	• Rudbeckia species (black-eyed Susans) • Salvia coccinea (scarlet sage) • Silene regia (royal catchfly)

Flowers, Groundcovers & Grasses

INSTEAD OF THIS	PLANT THIS	
Hesperis matronalis (dame's rocket)	• Agastache foeniculum (anise hyssop) • Amsonia species (blue stars) • Aquilegia species (columbines) • Dalea purpurea (purple prairie clover)	• Geranium maculatum (wild geranium) • Penstemon digitalis (beardtongue) • Phlox Carolina (Carolina phlox) • P. paniculata (garden phlox)
Iris pseudacorus (yellow flag)	• Asclepias incarnata (swamp milkweed) • Chelone species (turtleheads)	• Eutrochium species (Joe-pye weeds) • Iris versicolor (blue flag iris)
Leucanthemum vulgare (oxeye daisy)	• Baptisia alba (white false indigo) • Dalea candida (white prairie clover) • Parthenium integrifolium (wild quinine) • Penstemon digitalis (beardtongue)	• Phlox maculata (wild sweet William) • Phlox paniculata (garden phlox) • Pycnanthemum virginianum (Virginia mountain mint)
Lysimachia nummularia (creeping Jenny)	• Asarum species (wild gingers) • Fragaria species (wild strawberries) • Iris cristata (dwarf crested iris) • Mitella diphylla (bishop's cap) • Pachysandra procumbens (Allegheny spurge)	• Phlox stolonifera (creeping phlox) • Sedum ternatum (stonecrop) • Tiarella cordifolia (foamflower) • Waldsteinia fragarioides (barren strawberry)
Lythrum salicaria (purple loosestrife)	• Agastache foeniculum (anise hyssop) • Echinacea species (purple coneflowers) • Eutrochium species (Joe-pye weeds)	• Liatris species (blazing stars) • Monarda species (bee balms) • Verbena species (vervains)
Miscanthus sinensis (maiden grass)	• Panicum virgatum (switchgrass) • Spartina pectinata (prairie cordgrass)	• Sorghastrum nutans (Indian grass)
Phalaris arundinacea (reed canary grass)	• Chasmanthium latifolium (northern sea oats) • Deschampsia cespitosa (tufted hair grass) • Muhlenbergia capillaris (pink muhly grass)	• Schizachyrium scoparium (little bluestem) • Sporobolus heterolepis (prairie dropseed)
Tanacetum vulgare (common tansy)	• Asclepias tuberosa (butterfly milkweed) • Gaillardia species (blanket flowers) • Helenium autumnale (sneezeweed)	• Heliopsis helianthoides (oxeye) • Rudbeckia species (black-eyed Susans)
Vinca minor (common periwinkle)	• Asarum species (wild gingers) • Iris cristata (dwarf crested iris) • Mitella diphylla (bishop's cap) • Pachysandra procumbens (Allegheny spurge)	• Phlox stolonifera (creeping phlox) • Tiarella cordifolia (foamflower) • Waldsteinia fragarioides (barren strawberry)

27

continued on page 28

Shrubs, Vines & Trees

INSTEAD OF THIS	PLANT THIS	
Acer ginnala (Amur maple)	• *Acer circinatum* (vine maple) • *Acer glabrum* (Rocky Mountain maple) • *Amelanchier* species (serviceberries) • *Carpinus caroliniana* (American hornbeam) • *Chionanthus virginicus* (fringetree)	• *Cornus alternifolia* (pagoda dogwood) • *Hamamelis virginiana* (witch hazel) • *Ptelea trifoliata* (hop tree) • *Viburnum* species (viburnums)
Acer platanoides (Norway maple)	• *Acer rubrum* (red maple) • *A. saccharum* (sugar maple) • *Cladrastis kentukea* (yellowwood) • *Gymnocladus dioicus* (Kentucky coffee tree)	• *Magnolia acuminata* (cucumber magnolia) • *Quercus* species (oaks) • *Tilia americana* (basswood)
Ailanthus altissima (tree of heaven)	• *Amelanchier* species (serviceberries) • *Cladrastis kentukea* (yellowwood) • *Gymnocladus dioicus* (Kentucky coffee tree)	• *Ostrya virginiana* (ironwood) • *Rhus typhina* (staghorn sumac)
Albizia julibrissin (mimosa)	• *Carpinus caroliniana* (American hornbeam) • *Cercis canadensis* (redbud)	• *Gymnocladus dioicus* (Kentucky coffee tree) • *Ostrya virginiana* (ironwood)
Ampelopsis brevipedunculata (porcelain berry)	• *Clematis virginiana* (virgin's bower) • *Gelsemium sempervirens* (Carolina jessamine)	• *Lonicera sempervirens* (trumpet honeysuckle) • *Parthenocissus quinquefolia* (woodbine)
Berberis thunbergii, B. vulgaris (barberries)	• *Dasiphora fruticosa* (potentilla) • *Diervilla* species (bush honeysuckles) • *Ilex* species (hollies, winterberry) • *Juniperus* species (junipers)	• *Photinia* species (chokeberries) • *Physocarpus opulifolius* (ninebark) • *Thuja* species (cedars)
Buddleia davidii (butterfly bush)	• *Callicarpa americana* (American beautyberry) • *Ceanothus americanus* (New Jersey tea) • *Cephalanthus occidentalis* (buttonbush)	• *Diervilla* species (bush honeysuckles) • *Rhododendron* species (azaleas, rhododendrons) • *Viburnum* species (viburnums)
Caragana arborescens (Siberian peashrub)	• *Diervilla* species (bush honeysuckles) • *Ribes aureum* (clove currant)	• *Thuja* species (cedars)
Celastrus orbiculatus (Oriental bittersweet)	• *Celastrus scandens* (American bittersweet) • *Clematis virginiana* (virgin's bower)	• *Lonicera sempervirens* (trumpet honeysuckle)
Elaeagnus angustifolia (Russian olive)	• *Chionanthus virginicus* (fringetree) • *Elaeagnus commutata* (silverberry) • *Salix sericea* (silky willow)	• *Shepherdia argentea* (buffaloberry) • *Viburnum prunifolium* (blackhaw)
Euonymus alatus (winged burning bush)	• *Cornus racemosa* (gray dogwood) • *Ilex* species (hollies, winterberry) • *Lindera benzoin* (spicebush)	• *Physocarpus pulifolius* (ninebark) • *Photinia* species (chokeberries) • *Rhus typhina* (staghorn sumac)

Shrubs, Vines & Trees

INSTEAD OF THIS	PLANT THIS	
Euonymus fortunei (winter creeper)	• *Arctostaphylos uva-ursi* (bearberry) • *Juniperus* species (junipers)	• *Mahonia repens* (creeping mahonia)
Hedera helix (English ivy)	• *Asarum* species (wild gingers) • *Mahonia repens* (creeping mahonia) • *Pachysandra procumbens* (Allegheny spurge)	• *Tiarella cordifolia* (foamflower) • *Waldsteinia fragarioides* (barren strawberry)
Ligustrum vulgare (common privet)	• *Ilex* species (hollies, winterberry) • *Photinia* species (chokeberries)	• *Thuja* species (cedars) • *Viburnum prunifolium* (blackhaw)
Lonicera japonica (Japanese honeysuckle)	• *Celastrus scandens* (American bittersweet) • *Clematis virginiana* (virgin's bower)	• *Lonicera sempervirens* (trumpet honeysuckle)
Lonicera tatarica (Tatarian honeysuckle)	• *Amelanchier* species (serviceberries) • *Cornus racemosa* (gray dogwood) • *Diervilla* species (bush honeysuckles) • *Lindera benzoin* (spicebush) • *Photinia* species (chokeberries)	• *Physocarpus opulifolius* (ninebark) • *Rhododendron* species (azaleas, rhododendrons) • *Viburnum* species (viburnums)
Paulownia tomentosa (princess tree)	• *Asimina triloba* (pawpaw) • *Catalpa* species (catalpas) • *Chionanthus virginicus* (fringetree)	• *Magnolia acuminata* and *M. macrophylla* (magnolias)
Pyrus calleryana (Bradford pear)	• *Amelanchier laevis* and *A. × grandiflora* (serviceberries) • *Cercis canadensis* (redbud)	• *Chionanthus virginicus* (fringetree) • *Halesia diptera* (silverbell)
Rhamnus cathartica (common buckthorn)	• *Cornus racemosa* (gray dogwood) • *Hamamelis virginiana* (witch hazel) • *Photinia* species (chokeberries)	• *Thuja* species (cedars) • *Viburnum* species (viburnums)
Robinia pseudoacacia (black locust)	• *Acer rubrum* (red maple) • *Cladrastis kentukea* (yellowwood) • *Gymnocladus dioicus* (Kentucky coffee tree)	• *Magnolia acuminata* (cucumber magnolia) • *Quercus* species (oaks) • *Tilia americana* (basswood)
Rosa multiflora (multiflora rose)	• *Rosa setigera, R. carolina, R. virginiana, R. acicularis* (wild roses)	
Sorbus aucuparia (European mountain ash)	• *Acer rubrum* (red maple) • *Cladrastis kentukea* (yellowwood) • *Gymnocladus dioicus* (Kentucky coffee tree)	• *Magnolia acuminata* (cucumber magnolia) • *Sorbus americana* (American mountain ash)
Ulmus pumila (Siberian elm)	• *Celtis laevigata* (sugarberry) • *Celtis occidentalis* (hackberry)	• *Quercus* species (oaks) • *Tilia americana* (basswood)
Viburnum opulus (European cranberry bush)	• *Ilex* species (hollies, winterberry) • *Hydrangea* species (hydrangeas) • *Photinia* species (chokeberries)	• *Viburnum trilobum* (highbush cranberry)
Wisteria floribunda, W. sinensis (wisterias)	• *Wisteria frutescens, W. macrostachya* (native wisterias)	

29

Dame's rocket, creeping Charlie, and goutweed are all aggressive, nonnative plants that can easily be replaced by native plants with similar characteristics.

Native Plant Conservation

Once you've been convinced of the benefits of growing native plants, it's time to temper that recommendation by saying it's important to use them properly and responsibly.

Native-plant gardeners face moral and ethical considerations that traditional gardeners do not. You must be sure that the native plants you buy are propagated by a nursery and not collected in the wild. You want to purchase plants that were "nursery propagated," not just "nursery grown." Reputable nurseries will readily volunteer information on the origin of their plants, so evasiveness or ambiguous answers from nursery owners should trigger caution.

Never dig up plants growing in their native habitats for garden use unless the plants are facing imminent destruction from development. It is always preferable to try to preserve or restore a natural habitat rather than destroy it, but sometimes this just isn't possible. If you have permission to collect seeds from a stand of native plants, take only what you need. Collect only a few seeds from several plants in the stand; never take all of the seeds from one plant. Do not collect underground plant parts. Collecting must never endanger a plant population.

The rapid destruction of native habitats in the last century means many native plants and animals are threatened with extinction. You should become aware of these plants, since in many states it is illegal to gather, take, buy, or sell plants listed as endangered or threatened. A safeguard for endangered native species is the Federal Endangered Species Act of 1973. This law applies only to federal lands, however. Protection of endangered plants on other public and private lands is left up to individual states, and each state has its own list of endangered, threatened, and special-concern plants.

In addition to any local native-plant nurseries, a good place to purchase native plants is at a botanic garden or arboretum plant sale such as this one at Bowman's Hill Wildflower Preserve in Pennsylvania.

CHAPTER TWO

Garden Basics: Selecting & Planting Native Plants

32

I f you are new to the world of natives, you may find it overwhelming trying to decide what to grow. It is *definitely* worth the time to educate yourself before you choose which native plants to include in your gardens and where to place them. Find out about a plant's characteristics, and don't plant it unless you are sure it is going to work on your site and fit your desired level of maintenance.

Gardening with native plants focuses more on your existing site conditions and matching plants to them rather than selecting plants first and finding a place to put them later—a holistic approach rather than thinking in terms of individual plants. By grouping plants with similar soil, water, and light requirements, you'll end up with combinations that work well together naturally. That said, even with all the information geared toward choosing the

right plant for the right place, don't be afraid to try a few things that intrigue you, even if odds are against survival. Make a point of growing something new each year. Even if it doesn't survive, you'll gain confidence and skill from the experience.

This chapter covers the importance of good soil and how to amend or alter yours, if needed. As with all types of gardening, to be successful with native plants it is essential that you understand the basics of gardening in your climate. You should know your hardiness zone, frost dates, and average rainfall (which can be researched online). You must also have a good understanding of your site, including sunlight amounts and existing soil conditions. Knowing these things will help you choose the best plants for your conditions, which is the first step in creating a healthy, long-lived native-plant landscape.

This well-designed entry garden containing a mixture of prairie grasses and forbs is perfectly suited to the prairie-style architecture of the home.

Soil & pH

You may think this section doesn't have anything to do with *selecting* plants. But it does. It's especially important when selecting natives—even more than it is in traditional gardening—to *match the plant to the site*. Good soil is *the* most important factor in any type of gardening, but especially with natives. If you provide plants with suitable soil, the rest is a piece of cake. Native plants will soon establish themselves and become almost maintenance-free. It is definitely worth taking some time to get to know your soil. A good place to start is to have it tested by a soil-testing laboratory; check with your local university Extension Service office for labs in your area. A soil test will provide you with information on existing soil texture and fertility, along with recommendations on what to add to improve it.

Soils typically have four basic components: sand, silt, clay, and organic matter. The proportions of these ingredients largely determine the soil texture, which in turn determines other soil properties such as fertility, porosity, and water retention. Heavier soils hold more moisture; sandy soils drain faster.

Organic matter, also known as humus, is decomposing plant or animal material. Organic matter determines a soil's capacity to produce nitrogen, supports a community of soil microorganisms crucial to plant life, and retains bacterial byproducts such as water and carbon dioxide. It also creates a moist, slightly acidic environment critical for the transfer of minerals from soil particles to plants.

Soil acidity and alkalinity are measured in terms of pH on a scale from 1 to 14. A reading of 7 on the scale indicates the soil is neutral in pH. Lower than 7, the soil is increasingly acidic; higher than 7, it is increasingly alkaline. Soil pH is important because it affects the availability of nutrients necessary for plant growth. Most nutrients are most soluble at a pH between 6 and 7. That is why most plants grow best in "slightly acidic soil." Iron chlorosis, yellowing foliage caused by lack of available iron, can be a problem on alkaline soils.

Most native plants tolerate a range of soil pH, but some survive only within a narrow window. Plants within a native community have often evolved to grow best with a similar soil pH. By growing these native plants

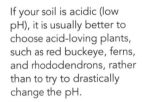

If your soil is acidic (low pH), it is usually better to choose acid-loving plants, such as red buckeye, ferns, and rhododendrons, rather than to try to drastically change the pH.

Adding organic matter is the best thing you can do to improve your soil. Find a spot on your site where you can compost leaves, grass clippings, and other organic materials.

together in a certain area of your garden, you'll be able to base your mulch choices and soil amendments on the pH needs of the entire group. It is possible to change the soil pH around just one or two plants, however, by regularly working in the appropriate pH-altering soil amendments.

Even though many natives tolerate tough conditions, most—including sun-loving, dry-soil plants—grow better in a garden setting if the soil has been amended with organic matter. In the natural world, native plants recycle *themselves*, creating abundant organic matter. If you can follow this principle in your own landscape— great. However, for city and suburban gardeners it's not always practical to allow all fallen leaves to stay on the ground or compost all plants back into the garden.

Adding organic matter is the key to improving soil texture, fertility, and pH. It is difficult to add too much organic matter, especially if it's partly decomposed. Organic matter increases the aeration of clay soils and improves the moisture and nutrient retention of sandy soils. It adds valuable nutrients at a slow and steady pace, and it has a buffering affect on soil pH. The best source of organic matter for gardeners is compost. Composting materials such as cow or horse manure, peat moss, grass clippings, and leaves ensures they will be in optimum condition to be worked into the soil.

Whenever possible, add organic matter to the soil before planting. Dig the garden bed as deeply as possible and incorporate 3 to 4 inches of organic matter—well-rotted manure, compost, shredded leaves, or ground pine bark. Some plants require nitrogen-fixing bacteria, which can be incorporated into the soil in the form of a commercially available inoculant. If your soil is very "heavy" (high in clay), add 2 inches of sharp builder's sand along with the compost or manure. Sand alone will only make matters worse, but when it is added with organic matter, it does help loosen heavy soil.

Deciding What to Grow

When choosing which natives to grow, it is usually best to start with what is native in your area. There are many resources; a good place to look is The Ladybird Wildflower Center website (www.wildflower.org). It has

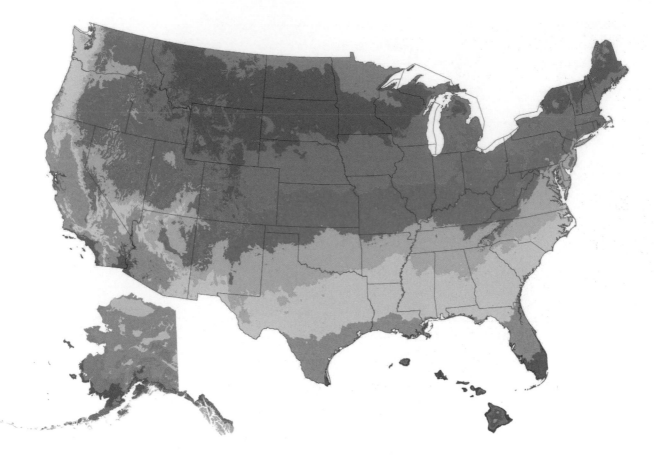

Hardiness zones indicate the severity of winter temperatures. The lower the number, the more severe (colder) the winter climate based on temperatures. This book uses the most common system, the United States Department of Agriculture (USDA) Hardiness Zones, which are based on average annual minimum winter temperatures. While it is important to know your hardiness zone, don't live and die by it. Use it as a guideline. A plant's ability to survive winter is affected by many factors, such as snow cover, soil moisture, the plant's age, and winter mulching. Keep in mind that just because a plant is native in your state, it doesn't mean it will be hardy where you live. Plants evolve in ecological conditions, which rarely follow state boundaries.

Average Annual Extreme Minimum Temperature 1976-2005

Temp (F)	Zone	Temp (C)
-60 to -50	1	-51.1 to -45.6
-50 to -40	2	-45.6 to -40
-40 to -30	3	-40 to -34.4
-30 to -20	4	-34.4 to -28.9
-20 to -10	5	-28.9 to -23.3
-10 to 0	6	-23.3 to -17.8
0 to 10	7	-17.8 to -12.2
10 to 20	8	-12.2 to -6.7
20 to 30	9	-6.7 to -1.1
30 to 40	10	-1.1 to 4.4
40 to 50	11	4.4 to 10
50 to 60	12	10 to 15.6
60 to 70	13	15.6 to 21.1

a searchable database of North American native plants. You can find out which plants have been native to your state and also narrow your search by plant type, growing conditions, and plant characteristics. The site also has a Recommended Species page that lists plants by state and a list of suppliers in each state. Another good resource is the USDA Plants Database (www.plants.usda.gov). Its searchable database provides a list of plants native to your state and even lets you dial in to what's native at a county level!

The next step is to select plants that will do well on your site, provide habitat for local fauna (if that is a priority for you), and fit your level of maintenance. That is where this book comes into play. Take the time to learn a plant's characteristics, preferred growing conditions, and growth habits. There are native plants to fit any landscape situation, but they may not all be indigenous to your area. You will have to decide if you only want to include species within your providence or if you are willing to expand your palette to include any North American native plant.

After you have a list of appropriate plants, you can bring in more aesthetic considerations. Choose plants with varying bloom times, both concurrent and consecutive, to ensure that there is something happening in your landscape year-round. Evergreens are essential to winter landscapes, but many other woody ornamentals offer interesting bark and colorful fruits that last through winter. The dried flower heads of prairie plants provide visual interest, as well as food for birds. Prolong the growing season by including fall-blooming perennials that survive several degrees of frost and plants that are up early in spring, providing interest from flowers or emerging foliage.

Choose plants that appeal to all the senses: pick a variety of colors, shapes, and textures to see; fragrant blossoms and foliage to smell; fruit to taste; soft, hairy foliage, smooth bark, and silky seedheads to touch; leaves that whisper and rustle in the wind to hear. Plant fragrant species close to seating areas or under windows where they can be fully appreciated. Texture comes from foliage as well as bark and stems, stone walls, and pathways.

In general, it is best to make sure your landscape has a wide variety of species—both within it and compared to all the other trees and shrubs on the street. Monocultures can lead to big problems in the landscape, as we saw with the American elm and green ash. Go for diversity, especially with woody plants.

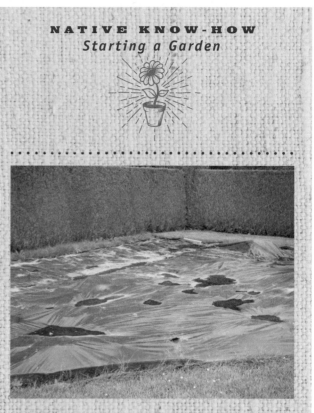

One option for getting rid of existing vegetation on a new garden is to cover the soil with plastic for several months before planting.

Some people believe that native plants are so tough that all you have to do is scatter seeds or add an abundance of plants, and they will take over an area and thrive. This misconception couldn't be further from the truth. Native plants establish themselves in an area over hundreds of years; they can't simply be planted and expected to grow in landscapes—especially if the soil is unlike that in its natural habitat and/or is covered with aggressive nonnative plants—that is, weeds.

Proper site preparation is key to success with native plants. If you are starting a new bed, take the time to get rid of existing vegetation and improve the soil before you start putting plants in the ground. This preparation will pay significant dividends in the end.

Many oaks, including swamp white oak, have leaves that persist well into winter and bring color to a snow-covered landscape.

In some cases, you may actually want to "fight the site." If you plant aggressive plants in unsuitable habitats, they will not do as well and consequently be better behaved. The most common way to do this is to plant things that like a moister soil in dry soil conditions.

Flowers, Ferns & Groundcovers

Native flowers, ferns, and groundcovers are the most fun aspect of gardening. Their showy blooms, various sizes and forms, and interesting leaves bring color, interest, and texture to a landscape. Many are attractive to butterflies, birds, and bees, and some are good for cutting. Others are more functional, offering erosion control on a slope, or they offer attractive ways to deal with a low area in the lawn or dry shade under large trees.

Flowers Many native flowers are well suited to garden and landscape use. Some you may already know and grow. Monarda, butterfly weed, Joe-pye weed, asters, and

Jack-in-the-pulpit (*Arisaema triphyllum*) is a beautiful native that can become quite prolific when grown in its preferred moist, rich soil. Growing it in drier, less-fertile soil will help keep it in check.

Many native flowers, such as black-eyed Susans, purple coneflower, and monarda, are already common sights in perennial borders.

SPECIAL-USE NATIVES
Spring Ephemerals/Summer Dormants

• •

Allium tricoccum (wild leek/ramps)
Anemone quinquefolia (wood anemone)
Caltha palustris (marsh marigold)
Camassia species (camas)*
Cardamine concatenata/Dentaria species (toothworts)
Claytonia species (spring beauties)
Delphinium species (larkspurs)*
Dicentra canadensis (squirrel corn)
Dicentra cucullaria (Dutchman's breeches)
Dodecatheon species (shooting stars)*
Enemion biternatum (false rue anemone)
Erythronium species (trout lilies)
Lewisia rediviva (bitterroot)
Mertensia species (bluebells)*
Podophyllum peltatum (mayapple)*
Pulsatilla patens (pasque flower)*
Sanguinaria canadensis (bloodroot)*
Stylophorum diphyllum (Celandine poppy)
Symplocarpus foetidus (skunk cabbage)
Thalictrum thalictroides (rue anemone)
Trientalis borealis (starflower)
Trillium species (trilliums)
Uvularia species (bellworts)*

* indicates plants that may go dormant in summer

black-eyed Susan are all commonly grown in perennial beds and mixed borders, and wild ginger, bloodroot, and blue phlox are common in shade gardens. Although some flowers can be used as single specimen plants, most flowers look best in groups of three, five, seven or more, as they are in nature.

Some native flowers are ephemeral in nature, meaning they are up early in spring, bloom, set seed, and then go dormant before summer's heat. While they are very welcome sights in early spring, keep in mind that they'll leave bare spots in the garden. They should be placed with plants such as wild ginger, ferns, and heucheras that will cover the bare ground when the ephemerals disappear. Once spring ephemerals are gone, be careful not to accidentally dig up their dormant clumps. If you will be cultivating that area of the garden, you may want to add plant markers in late spring so you don't disturb their roots in summer or fall.

Shooting stars, Virginia bluebells, and camas are among the later-blooming flowers that often go dormant

If you are growing spring ephemerals such as large-flowered trillium (*Trillium grandiflorum*) in a woodland garden, be sure to include plants with persistent foliage nearby.

Most ferns have two different shapes of fronds—sterile and fertile—but not all are as showy as on cinnamon fern (*Osmundastrum cinnamomea*).

before the end of summer, especially when grown without supplemental watering. Plan accordingly and place them where later-blooming plants will fill in.

Ferns Ferns evoke the essence of American forests, where most native ferns grow in moist, rich, acidic soil in part to full shade. However, they are actually a conspicuous part of the country's vegetation in all but the driest prairie ecosystems. Many adapt well to shady landscape situations where their foliage provides interesting textural contrasts to other plants. They add visual buoyancy, lightening the garden with their wide assortment of foliage shapes and varying shades of green. With adequate soil and moisture, fern foliage will be attractive until fall frost kills them back or winter snow covers them.

Ferns are typically used in shade gardens, where they are excellent background plantings, fillers, blenders,

groundcovers, or focal points. Although the small fiddleheads appear fairly early in spring, the leaves do not fully mature for quite awhile. This growth pattern makes ferns good companions for many of the early flowering ephemerals that die back in early summer. Some ferns can be used in foundation plantings, and some of the sun-tolerant types can be used in mixed borders. They look good around water gardens, and some of the smaller types can be used in shady rock gardens. Ferns also can be used to create a soft boundary between one section of a garden and another.

Groundcovers The term "groundcover" is subjective, but it is typically used to refer to spreading plants that stay under a foot tall. They are usually herbaceous plants, but some low-growing shrubs such as bearberry (*Arctostaphylos uva-ursi*) and creeping junipers can be used as groundcovers. Some can take light foot traffic.

Some have showy flowers, but for most the attractive foliage is the highlight.

Groundcovers are often used in tough sites where other plants, especially traditional lawn grasses, don't do well, such as in heavy shade or on steep slopes. But groundcovers can also become design elements; a mass planting often has a clean, contemporary look. You can combine several different groundcovers with similar cultural requirements to create a tapestry effect.

Grasses & Sedges

Native grasses bring both practical and aesthetic benefits to the landscape. On the practical side, they are nearly no maintenance. They are very adaptable, grow in poorer soils than most garden plants, and once established they require very little care beyond annual cutting back. They rarely need watering or fertilizing and are seldom bothered by insects, diseases, or deer. On the aesthetic side, grasses come in a wide range of heights, colors, and textures, and offer more than one season of interest. They also bring movement and sound to the landscape, two elements lacking in most plants. Most grasses are tolerant of wind and can be used in open, exposed areas where other plants would be damaged.

Native grasses are often classified according to their main growth periods: warm season or cool season. Cool-season grasses grow best in spring. They like ample

Groundcovers don't need to be planted as a monoculture. Here *Sedum ternatum* and dwarf crested iris mingle to create an interesting mosaic of textures and colors.

water and may turn brown during times of drought. Warm-season grasses don't really come into their own until midsummer, and then they take center stage right through winter. They tend to be drought tolerant.

Grasses are also classified according to their growth habits: clump forming or rhizome forming. Clump-forming grasses grow in nice, neat mounds, increasing in width

41

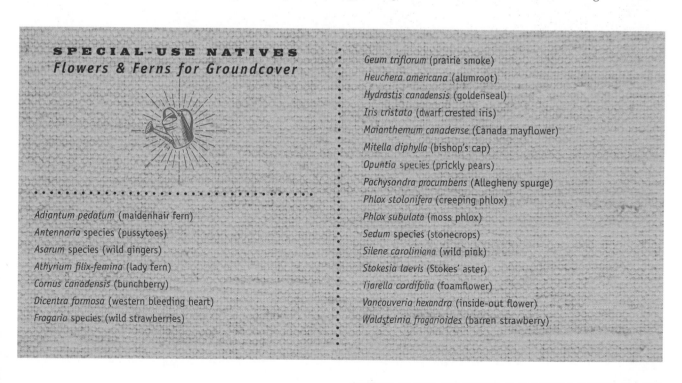

SPECIAL-USE NATIVES
Flowers & Ferns for Groundcover

Adiantum pedatum (maidenhair fern)
Antennaria species (pussytoes)
Asarum species (wild gingers)
Athyrium filix-femina (lady fern)
Cornus canadensis (bunchberry)
Dicentra formosa (western bleeding heart)
Fragaria species (wild strawberries)

Geum triflorum (prairie smoke)
Heuchera americana (alumroot)
Hydrastis canadensis (goldenseal)
Iris cristata (dwarf crested iris)
Maianthemum canadense (Canada mayflower)
Mitella diphylla (bishop's cap)
Opuntia species (prickly pears)
Pachysandra procumbens (Allegheny spurge)
Phlox stolonifera (creeping phlox)
Phlox subulata (moss phlox)
Sedum species (stonecrops)
Silene caroliniana (wild pink)
Stokesia laevis (Stokes' aster)
Tiarella cordifolia (foamflower)
Vancouveria hexandra (inside-out flower)
Waldsteinia fragarioides (barren strawberry)

slowly over time and rarely becoming invasive. Rhizome-forming grasses spread by underground stems and can become invasive. These grasses have their place (many make excellent groundcovers on tough sites), but it usually isn't in a formal landscape situation. Obviously, it's important to know the characteristics of each grass before you install them in your landscape.

Being wind-pollinated, grasses don't need brightly colored flowers to attract insects: they release their pollen into the air to float from flower head to flower head. This doesn't mean their flowers aren't attractive, however. They can be lacy panicles, stiff brushes, or waving plumes, often with beautiful fall color. Most grasses flower from late summer into fall, but some flower earlier.

Native grasses can be used as accent or specimen plants, ground covers, and screens. Many of the clump-forming types mix well in perennial borders, and they are essential in prairie gardens and natural landscapes. Most grasses, especially those with delicate, airy seedheads, look best against a dark background and placed where they can catch morning or evening light.

Fine-textured but tough, Pennsylvania sedge is worth considering as a substitute for traditional lawn grasses on shady sites.

Native clumping grasses such as prairie dropseed make wonderful landscape plants, even in the middle of Manhattan along the Highline Trail.

Nothing says "tended landscape" more than a carpet of turf-grass. And, truth be told, mowable lawn grasses are usually the most practical choice for certain areas such as play or pet areas. But keep in mind that these areas are monocultures with little to offer the environment. It is best to think of lawn areas as part of the hardscape. Give a lawn the same consideration you give a patio or deck and consider its high maintenance costs, both to you and to the environment.

Remember that "lawn" doesn't necessarily have to be made up of high-maintenance Kentucky bluegrass or bentgrass. There are some native grasses and sedges that withstand occasional mowing and can be used as substitutes for traditional turfgrasses. These grasses can't take weekly mowing like traditional turf-grasses, but they do make environmentally friendly groundcovers in areas where the main objective is to cover the ground with

'Mo-Buff' buffalograss (*Bouteloua dactyloides*) is used as a lower-maintenance turfgrass at Shaw Nature Reserve in Missouri.

something that can withstand use by people and pets. This list includes *Bouteloua* species (grama grasses, buffalograss), *Carex pensylvanica* (Pennsylvania sedge), and *Schizachyrium scoparium* (little bluestem).

43

Grasses have a pure, abstract quality that blends well with modern architectures, and their shapes, colors, and textures contrast nicely with wood, stone, and other hard structural surfaces. Some people choose to create entire gardens of grasses. Beyond their landscape value, many are valuable sources of food and cover for birds, and the mature seedheads are prized for dried arrangements.

Sedges are grasslike plants, but they're not true grasses. They can be distinguished from grasses by their solid, three-angled flower stems (grasses have round, hollow flower stems). Most sedges form dense, compact clumps of bright green foliage, great in a landscape. Some are even quite shade tolerant.

Shrubs, Small Trees & Vines

Shrubs A shrub is generally considered to be a woody plant with multiple stems that is usually less than 15 feet tall when mature. It can be deciduous or evergreen. Shrubs are an important design element in landscapes. Not only do they provide structure, they also add form

Tiger Eyes sumac is a striking shrub that makes a nice accent plant.

Gray dogwood (*Cornus racemosa*) is a shrub that is easily pruned into a small and attractive multi-stemmed tree.

and texture and are often relied on to provide a backdrop for showier flowering plants. They often have ornamental characteristics that carry them through more than one season, sometimes throughout the year. Some shrubs are grown for their flowers or fruit, but many are grown for the foliage color and form, which brings structure to a landscape.

Many small- to medium-sized shrubs work well in the mixed border, where they complement herbaceous perennials and provide season-long interest. Many shrubs have fruits that provide winter interest as well as attract birds and other wildlife. In shade and woodland gardens, shrubs and small trees provide that middle layer that ties together full-sized shade trees and the flowers and groundcovers growing beneath them. Evergreen shrubs are great for providing year-round interest, either as part of a border, in foundation plantings, or as well-grown specimen plants. Shrubs are

Grape honeysuckle (*Lonicera reticulata*) is a twining vine that is often left unsupported and grown more as a dense shrub.

valuable for hedges and massing, and some can even be used as large-scale groundcovers.

Small trees are those that usually stay under 25 feet tall or large shrubs that can be easily pruned to a single stem or multiple stems. Small trees are often used as specimen plantings, where the beauty of their flowers, bark, and foliage can really shine. They are good choices for providing shade in small yards, where traditional shade trees grow too big. Small trees are important for adding height to entry and patio gardens, and many make nice lawn trees in small yards.

Vines are woody plants with long stems that can be trained to a support structure. They serve both ornamental and functional roles in the landscape. Vines are a good way to bring the dimension of height to areas not suitable for trees, such as in tight courtyards or next to buildings. Their verdant covering softens arbors and trellises, often providing shade for areas underneath. They also serve as screening, covering unsightly landscape elements such as chain-link fences or compost and storage structures.

To use vines correctly, you must understand their climbing characteristics. *Clinging vines* use aerial roots or small sucker pads to attach themselves to their support structure. These vines climb almost anything, including smooth walls, and they can eventually mar the surface of their support. *Twining vines* wind their stems around anything they can reach. They will climb on thin, vertical supports such as strings or poles. *Vines with tendrils*

Evergreens are usually planted to provide interest in the dormant season, when most plants are bare of leaves and flowers. While they do excel in this regard, they are also valuable for the many other benefits they bring to a landscape. Their evergreen foliage provides a dark backdrop for flowering and fruiting herbaceous plants. They provide year-round screening, and many make good hedges. Some can be used in foundation plantings, where they offer a certain stability, and they offer interest and texture in mixed-shrub borders. Most provide shelter for birds and other forms of wildlife, and some provide food as well.

Most people would agree that mature evergreens are a real asset when it comes to property value. However, their value quickly goes down if they are diseased or improperly pruned, which is often the case. It is so easy to fall in love with cute little "button" or pyramidal evergreens, but keep in mind that they grow into tall or spreading shrubs that aren't easy to keep small with pruning, and they are more susceptible to insect and disease problems when they are growing in a contained space. Most evergreens look best when they are allowed to grow naturally, without a lot of shaping. If you want an evergreen to stay within a certain size range, look for a dwarf or compact cultivar rather than trying to restrict the growth of full-sized species.

Consider natives such as this willow oak when choosing a shade tree. No other group of plants supports more species of butterflies, and therefore birds, than these stately trees.

(which are actually modified leaves) coil them around their support structure. These vines need slender supports such as wire or lath, since their tendrils can't usually encircle anything larger than a couple inches diameter.

Trees

A tree is a woody plant that grows over 25 feet when mature. It is usually a single-trunked plant, but it can have multiple trunks. Some trees retain branches and leaves all the way to the ground, but most develop a canopy that you can walk under. Trees may be deciduous or evergreen and they come in various forms: pyramidal, weeping, columnar, roundheaded, vase-shaped, and arching.

Large trees are valued for their beauty as well as for the shade they provide. But they have a lot more to offer landscapes. They provide structure with their weight and form. The overhead leafy canopy of a spreading tree frames the elements and the view below it. Trees are home to many types of birds and also provide habitat for

Paper birch makes a nice clumping tree. It will do well in land-scapes as long as its roots are cool and shaded.

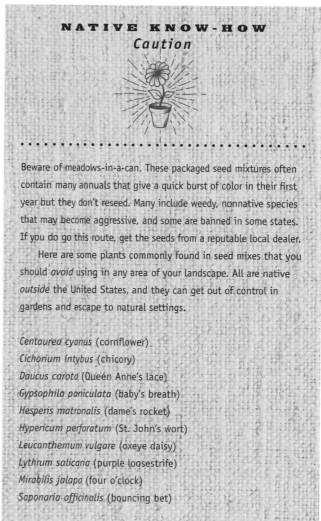

butterflies and beneficial insects. Many provide beautiful fall color when their foliage turns shades of red, yellow, and orange. And don't forget the benefits at eye level, especially in the dormant season: many trees have bark with interesting texture and color.

The trees you plant will become major elements in your landscape. Keep the mature size in mind and make sure the tree you select will be in scale with your home. Don't make the mistake of planting a tiny oak seedling 10 feet from your front door or a basswood under a power line. The canopy of a large tree will complement a two-story home, but many shade trees are too large for small lots and one-story homes. There are many trees in the 40-foot-range that provide ample shade and are in better scale with homes. These smaller species are also good choices if you will be planting under an obstruction such as a power line or near a sidewalk or driveway.

Another thing to keep in mind is species diversity. While it isn't usually a good idea to plant a hodgepodge of many different types of trees, you should avoid planting all one species, especially if there are already a lot of that species in your neighborhood. Serious disease and insect problems on trees, which can be devastating to neighborhoods, are often associated with overplanting of a species.

Certain trees are more tolerant of typical urban conditions than others. They're able to handle atmospheric pollutants from industry and cars, compacted soil, poor drainage, lighting, and salt spray from snow plows. If these conditions exist where you are planting, select trees that can tolerate these situations. Finally, some trees can be messy, dropping leaves, flowers, nuts, fruits, or twigs. They may be fine as yard trees, but you wouldn't want to plant one over your deck or driveway.

Aggressive reseeders such as Queen Anne's lace can wreak havoc in native plantings.

Planting

The best time to plant most plants is spring, which gives them ample time to become established before they have to endure their first winter in the ground. Rainfall is also usually more abundant in spring. Plant or transplant early-blooming and spring-ephemeral species after they flower, usually in late spring but before they "disappear" for summer. Summer- and fall-blooming flowers, ferns, grasses, and most woody plants can be planted in spring or fall—actually, all season long if they are container grown. However, planting in the high temperatures of midsummer means you will have to be diligent about providing adequate water. You may also need to provide shelter from the sun for a few weeks.

Fall planting should be finished at least 6 weeks before hard-freezing weather occurs. In cold climates, it is a good idea to put down a winter mulch of weed-free straw or leaves after the ground has frozen. This helps ensure that the new plants will remain firmly planted in the soil through winter freeze-thaw cycles.

Seeds take longer to produce a showy end product, but they are less expensive, and there are often more choices available than with container plants. Many woodland plants have specific moisture and temperature requirements for germination and are difficult for beginners to grow from seeds. Most grassland plants, however, are relatively easy to start from seeds. If you will be seeding a large area, you may want to consider a seed mixture. However, be sure to purchase one from a reputable native-plant propagator in your area. Avoid any nationally available "meadow in a can."

Shrubs, vines, and trees are typically sold as container plants, balled-and-burlapped, or bare root. (A fourth way to plant a tree is with a tree spade—a large, tractor-carried device which can plant larger trees, but it's usually a much more expensive option.) Bare-root plants are the most wallet-friendly, but you must plant them before they start growing in spring. Container-grown plants are the most popular and most flexible with regard to planting times. Balled-and-burlapped specimens are large and fill out a garden quicker, but they are also more expensive. Whenever possible, buy woody plants grown locally; they have a better chance of surviving in your garden. And buying locally reduces the high costs and fossil fuel inputs associated with transport.

Container-grown plants are the most popular way to go. They can be planted anytime during the growing season, but the cooler, wetter weather in spring and fall usually gives the best results. And the fewer or smaller the leaves are on a tree, the faster it will recover from transplanting. Bare-root shrubs should only be planted in spring when they are just coming out of their dormancy. Balled-and-burlapped shrubs are usually quite large and challenging to plant. They should be planted in spring or fall as soon as possible after purchase.

Before planting woody plants, amend the soil with a good amount of organic matter such as compost, peat moss, or well-rotted manure. Mix this organic matter thoroughly with the planting-hole soil. Place a potted plant at the same depth it was growing in the container. Bare-root plants should be planted so that the crown is level with the ground level. Newly planted trees should not need additional fertilizer.

In most cases, newly planted trees should not be staked. It is better to allow them a little movement to encourage stronger trunks and healthy root systems. However, trees planted on a very windy, exposed site may benefit from staking for their first season or two, especially if they are top-heavy. String the staking wire through a section of garden hose to protect the bark from injury. The wire should hold the tree firmly without putting undue pressure on the trunk. The staked tree should still be able to sway somewhat in the wind. Any stakes should be removed as soon as the tree has rooted well, usually after the first year.

Now that you've learned how to prepare your garden beds and choose the best plants for your landscape, the fun begins with garden design. The next chapter will help you place these plants in well-designed garden beds that are attractive as well as good for the environment.

Native shrubs are usually sold as container plants, which can be planted at any time during the growing season.

CHAPTER THREE

Native Plants in Gardens & Landscapes

50

Landscape design is the process of creating beautiful, useful spaces that you will enjoy being in. Your landscape should be a reflection of your lifestyle, including spaces for things you and your family enjoy doing, as well as space in which to entertain and relax. Base your landscape decisions on practical considerations such as current conditions, future use, and maintenance issues, but don't forget to have fun and make it a place you'll truly enjoy.

A properly planted native-plant landscape should reflect your own preferences for color, style, and plants. If you have a Colonial style house in the suburbs and prefer a formal entryway with clipped hedges, there are native plants that will fit the bill. If you're a plant lover who can't resist the hodgepodge of a collector's garden, that's fine too. No matter how many natives you use

or in which way you use them, you will be helping to counteract the tragedy of habitat destruction and the reduction in native-plant populations that is occurring around the world. And, on a more personal note, you won't have to leave home to enjoy nature. It will be right at your doorstep.

In this chapter, you'll learn how to create an effective landscape using all or some native plants. A native landscape can come under great scrutiny from uneducated neighbors, so it's important that your gardens be well tended. Many design tips are included to help you make native plants work in more-traditional settings. You'll learn which plants are especially good for attracting butterflies, birds, and bees. This chapter also covers practical aspects of using native plants in places such as rain gardens, boulevard strips, xeriscaping, and shade.

This well-designed and maintained entry garden includes Missouri evening primroses (*Oenothera macrocarpa*), rock-roses (*Helianthemum nummularium*), western serviceberry, and nonnative lavender (*Lavandula angustifolia*).

Mark Turner

NATIVE PLANTS IN GARDENS & LANDSCAPES

Landscape Designs Using Native Plants

Basically, there are three ways to use native plants in a landscape: integration, habitat gardening, and restoration.

On one end of the spectrum is *restoration*, where you only grow plants that were once indigenous to your region in habits that would have been original to your area. This is a wonderful way to preserve and enjoy the beauty of individual plants and also to preserve entire ecosystems or plant communities.

For people who live in cities and suburban areas, restoring a prairie or recreating an authentic woodland garden are not usually practical options, even if you have a large property. Because our landscapes have been altered so much by human activity, it is difficult to go back to the point where you can successfully grow only native plants without investing quite a bit of time and effort in plant

eradication and site preparation. If you truly want to establish a *pure* stand of plants that once grew naturally in your area, you should get help from a professional specializing in native-plant restorations.

People who have a strong interest in growing native plants will get immense pleasure from the creation of *habitat gardens* within their landscape. The goal is to recreate a natural habitat that would have once been found in your area. A working habitat garden should include all or almost all native plants, and should be allowed to evolve and grow in a naturalistic way, ultimately forming a working community. It will provide food and shelter for native insects and birds, which in turn bring added benefits to the garden as well as the gardener.

To create an effective habitat garden, start by assessing the different areas of your landscape and

A prairie restoration is a wonderful way to experience how native plants interact with native fauna and reduce your maintenance.

This shady spot alongside a house is a perfect place for a woodland habitat garden that includes large-flowered bellwort, Virginia bluebells, Solomon's seal, and celandine poppy (*Stylophorum diphyllum*).

Native camas integrated beautifully into a traditional garden border at Longwood Gardens in Pennsylvania.

determining which native habitats would be best suited to the conditions. If you are tired of fighting with grass under large shade trees, remove the grass and begin creating a woodland garden. If you have a large open lawn area in full sun that is just a drain on your lawn mower and time, consider a prairie or meadow garden. By establishing large areas of native-plant communities, you will help preserve natural ecosystems that once flourished in your area *and* have an attractive, easy-to-tend garden filled with plants with similar cultural requirements. You will get to experience firsthand the intricacies of a natural plant community.

For most gardeners, though, the most practical way to use native plants is to *integrate* them with nonnative, traditional landscape plants that have proven to be noninvasive and adaptable to your area. This can be as simple as mixing natives in with your plantings or replacing traditional plants with natives. You may already be doing this without realizing it. If your mixed borders include blazing star, butterfly weed, or black-eyed Susans, or if your shade garden is home to wild ginger, dogwoods, or maidenhair fern, you are already well on your way to using native plants. Once you see which natives work well for your site, you can replace more nonnative plants, increasing the value your landscape offers our native fauna.

Creating a Well-Tended Native Landscape

When it comes to landscape design, most garden books will overwhelm you with design lingo about form, texture, color, and so on. While you should keep these things in mind, nature has already made these decisions for you. If you follow its lead, you'll naturally end up with a landscape full of interesting textures, colors, and plant forms without much effort. Plants found growing together in the wild will usually combine nicely in a garden setting, creating a multi-season habitat that is pleasing to the eye as well as attractive to beneficial insects and birds.

There is really no right or wrong way to use native plants, as long as it makes you happy. That being said, there are some design techniques you will want to consider to make your native-plant landscape suitable for your situation. Even with all the benefits of using native plants, there are still people who have a hard time appreciating them in traditional landscape settings. If this describes your situation, or if you just like a more traditional-looking landscape, there are several

53

American Lady Butterfly
Vanessa virginiensis

During the afternoon, males perch on hilltops or on low vegetation if there are no hills. Females lay eggs singly on the top of host plant leaves. Caterpillars are solitary, living and feeding in a nest of leaves tied with silk.

Range: Southern United States, Mexico, and Central America south to Colombia. Migrates to and temporarily colonizes the northern United States and southern Canada.

Habitat: Open places with low vegetation, including dunes, meadows, parks, vacant lots, and forest edges.

Larval Food: Plants in the sunflower family, including everlasting (*Gnaphalium obtusifolium*), pearly everlasting (*Anaphalis margaritacea*), pussytoes (*Antennaria plantaginifolia*), wormwoods (*Artemisia* species), and ironweeds (*Vernonia* species).

Adult Food: Flower nectar almost exclusively, including dogbane, purple coneflowers, asters, goldenrods, marigolds, common milkweed, and vetches.

Larry E. Swanson

things you can do to help your landscape look more tended and cared for.

While most natives adapt best to naturalistic designs, they can be used in formal settings. You'll just have to put a little more thought into plant selection and planting design. Start by using traditional planting and design methods. Plant in groups of three, five, or seven plants as this is more typical of nonnative landscapes. In small spaces, limit the number of species and maybe consider a simple planting of one species, such as a contained bed devoted to little bluestem or prairie dropseed.

There is a misconception that natural landscapes are chaotic and lack perceptible patterns. In relatively undisturbed, naturally evolving landscapes, patterns are ever-present—not in the form of orchard-like grids of trees, but in the subtle arrangements of plants. Nature tends to mass similar forms together and accent them with contrasting forms. Take a cue and plant in drifts of color rather than in straight rows. Drifts can consist of several of the same plants, which have the added advantage of being extra attractive to pollinating insects, or

This front-yard urban garden employs several strategies to keep it looking well-tended: a small area of turfgrass, a limited number of species, and traditional mulch.

SPECIAL-USE NATIVES
Container Gardening

As a rule, most native plants don't adapt well to container growing. Many have taproots (a long root that grows vertically downward) or a limited bloom time. If you do want to use native plants in containers, group several large pots that contain mixes of grasses and perennials that will provide interest throughout the season, rather than individual pots that contain just one plant.

This well-designed container garden at Mt. Cuba Center in Delaware features cultivars of native plants: *Heuchera* 'Georgia Peach' and 'Citronelle', *Polemonium reptans* 'Stairway to Heaven', *Phlox divaricata* 'Blue Moon', and *Rhododendron vaseyi*.

Flowers & Ferns
Adiantum pedatum (maidenhair fern)
Agastache species (hyssops)
Allium species (wild onions)
Aquilegia species (columbines)
Campanula rotundifolia (harebell)
Coreopsis cultivars (tickseeds)
Dudleya species (dudleyas)
Eschscholzia californica (California poppy)
Gaillardia hybrids (blanket flowers)
Geum triflorum (prairie smoke)
Gillenia trifoliata (Bowman's root)
Helenium autumnale hybrids (sneezeweeds)
Heliopsis helianthoides cultivars (oxeyes)
Heuchera americana cultivars (alumroots)
Lewisia species (lewisias)
Penstemon digitalis cultivars (beardtongues)
Phlox species (phloxes)
Polemonium reptans 'Stairway to Heaven' (Jacob's ladder)
Ratibida columnifera (Mexican hat)
Rudbeckia cultivars (black-eyed Susans, coneflowers)
Salvia species (sages)
Tradescantia 'Sweet Kate' (spiderwort)

Grasses & Sedges
Carex pensylvanica (Pennsylvania sedge)
Deschampsia species (hair grasses)
Schizachyrium scoparium (little bluestem)

Shrubs, Vines & Small Trees
Clethra alnifolia (dwarf summersweet cultivars)
Cornus species (dwarf dogwood cultivars)
Physocarpus opulifolius (dwarf ninebark cultivars)

Some native plants have strong architectural qualities that allow them to be used as accent plants in unconventional ways. Others work well as groundcovers or austere plantings with only one or two species. While this may not be as beneficial to native fauna as larger mixed plantings, it is still a better option than turning to nonnative plants. Here are some ways to use native plants as design elements in traditional landscapes:

Monoculture Groundcovers with a Contemporary Look

Adiantum pedatum (maidenhair fern)

Bouteloua species (grama grasses)

Carex pensylvanica (Pennsylvania sedge)

Heuchera richardsonii (prairie alumroot)

Mahonia species (Oregon grape, creeping mahonia)

Muhlenbergia capillaris (pink muhly grass)

Opuntia species (prickly pears)

Pachysandra procumbens (Allegheny spurge)

Schizachyrium scoparium (little bluestem)

Sporobolus heterolepis (prairie dropseed)

56

A monoplanting of one prairie grass, such as prairie dropseed, has a highly designed, contemporary look. But try to avoid designing an entire landscape using this approach.

Prairie dock can grow up to 10 feet tall in flower. Use a single plant, with its bold leaves, as a dramatic accent. You will need to deadhead the flowers, however, if you don't want seedlings appearing everywhere.

With a little pruning, American hornbeam becomes a small, sculptural tree that really shows off its smooth, gray bark.

Plants That Are Bold Accents or Focal Points

Baptisia australis (blue false indigo)

Eryngium yuccifolium (rattlesnake master)

Rhus typhina 'Bailtiger' (Tiger Eyes sumac)

Silphium laciniatum (compass plant)

Silphium terebinthinaceum (prairie dock)

Sorghastrum nutans (Indian grass)

Yucca species (Adam's needle, yuccas)

Woody Plants Amenable to Sculptural Pruning

Aesculus pavia (red buckeye)

Amelanchier tree species (serviceberries)

Amorpha canescens (leadplant)

Carpinus caroliniana (American hornbeam)

Cercis canadensis (Eastern redbud)

Chionanthus virginicus (fringetree)

Cornus tree species (dogwoods)

Halesia species (silverbells)

Hamamelis vernalis 'Lombart's Weeping' (witch hazel)

Pinus aristata (bristlecone pine)

Pinus banksiana 'Uncle Fogy' (Jack pine)

Ptelea trifoliata (hop tree)

Rhus typhina cultivars (staghorn sumac)

The woodland gardens at Mt. Cuba Center in Delaware are great examples of how to use drifts and accent plants to create a beautiful yet functional habitat garden.

Plants don't have to have bright, showy flowers to provide interest in your garden. The foliage of starry Solomon's seal (*Maianthemum stellatum*), mayapple (*Podophyllum peltatum*), and wild ginger combine to create a beautiful vignette.

There are no straight lines in nature, so anytime you incorporate them into your landscape, you are sending the signal that this a tended garden.

single plants of similar colors from several different species. For a sense of unity, repeat a few specific plant groupings or color schemes at intervals throughout the landscape. Take a cue from nature and use contrast sparingly to give your garden a natural look.

Include some areas of visual calm where the eye can rest momentarily from stimulation. Small patches of green lawns, a small grouping of green- or silver-foliaged plants, or a simple green deciduous or evergreen shrub all create spots of calm.

Most landscape designers will tell you to incorporate curved lines, especially when designing garden beds. They do this to encourage a natural look and they are right—there are very few perfectly straight lines in nature.

And that is precisely why including some straight lines in your landscape will help give it a tended look. Chances are your landscape already has several straight edges in it in the form of fences, driveway edges, and hedges. If you are installing a patio or deck, consider a square or rectangular form to bring a more-controlled look to your native plants.

Whenever possible, plant the pure species or, better yet, your local genotypes, to ensure that the flowers, bloom times, and plant shapes match the requirements of their respective pollinators. However, in more traditional landscapes in cities and suburbs, cultivars are often better choices. The main reasons for considering cultivars of native flowers and grasses are because they are more compact and therefore less likely to get floppy or require

NATIVE BUZZ

Baltimore Checkerspot Butterfly
Euphydryas phaeton

Females lay large groups of eggs under leaves of host plants, which are primarily white turtlehead. Newly hatched caterpillars move to the tip of the plant and feed together in a web, which is enlarged downward as the caterpillars consume more of the plant. These caterpillars suffer high mortality from falling off the plant and from parasitism by wasps. Fourth-stage caterpillars hibernate in rolled leaves on the ground.

Range: Nova Scotia west across the Great Lakes to southeast Manitoba; south through the eastern US to northern Georgia, Mississippi, and Oklahoma.

Habitat: Wet meadows, bogs, and marshes in the northeast part of the range; dry open or wooded hillsides in the southwest.

Larval Food: Young caterpillars feed primarily on white turtlehead, but older larvae will eat hairy beardtongue (*Penstemon hirsutus*), English plantain (*Plantago lanceolata*), and false foxgloves (*Aureolaria* species). After overwintering, caterpillars may also feed on southern arrowwood (*Viburnum recognitum*), common lousewort (*Pedicularis canadensis*), white ash (*Fraxinus americana*), and other plants.

Adult Food: Nectar from flowers of milkweeds, viburnums, dogbanes, mountain mints (*Pycnanthemum* species), wild blackberries (*Rubus* species), and wild roses.

Larry E. Swanson

Hummingbird Clearwing Moth
Hemaris thysbe

These day-flying moths fly and move just like hummingbirds, remaining suspended in the air in front of a flower while they unfurl their long tongues and insert them in flowers to sip their nectar. They even "hum." Caterpillars pupate in cocoons spun at the soil surface.

Range: Alaska and the Northwest Territories south through British Columbia to Oregon; east through the Great Plains and the Great Lakes to Maine and Newfoundland; south to Florida and Texas.

Habitat: Open areas in gardens and natural areas.

Larval Food: Honeysuckles, snowberries (*Symphoricarpos* species), hawthorns (*Crataegus* species), cherries and plums (*Prunus* species), and dogbanes (*Apocynum* species).

Adult Food: Nectar from monardas, phloxes, snowberries, blueberries, and verbenas.

Larry E. Swanson

staking or they offer greater resistance to diseases. Many are also less aggressive than the species in garden settings, and some are hardier.

When it comes to using shrubs in traditional landscapes, cultivars are often a better choice. Most native shrubs tend to be suckering, spreading plants that can get quite tall in their natural settings. The nursery industry has introduced cultivars of many native shrubs that have more compact growth habits, smaller overall height, better flowering and fruiting, and improved disease resistance.

In addition to design considerations, there are also some maintenance techniques you can employ to help give your landscape a more tended and cared-for look. Where appropriate, consider using "upscale" mulches such as cocoa-bean hulls or shredded bark. Mulching has the added benefits of reducing weeds, which helps the landscape look neater and reduces the need to water.

The true species of *Symphyotrichum novae-angliae* and *Solidago rugosa* can be too aggressive and coarse for traditional garden use. 'Purple Dome' and 'Fireworks' are better-behaved cultivars that make excellent garden plants.

This border of traditional turfgrass separates these taller prairie plants from the driveway and gives the garden a nice finished look.

NATIVE KNOW-HOW
Selections to Consider

Asclepias incarnata (swamp milkweed) selections that are less prolific reseeders and offer different flower colors: 'Cinderella', 'Ice Ballet', 'Soulmate'

Boltonia asteroides (white doll's daisy) selections that don't require cutting back or staking: 'Nana', 'Pink Beauty', 'Snowbank'

Coreopsis (tickseed) selections that are less prolific reseeders and more compact in growth habit: 'Domino', 'Early Sunrise', 'Flying Saucers', 'Sundance', 'Sunray', 'Zagreb'

Gaillardia x *grandiflora* (blanket flower) selections that are less floppy and have showier and longer-blooming flowers: 'Arizona Sun', 'Burgundy', 'Dazzler', 'Goblin', and more

Helenium autumnale (sneezeweed) selections that are more compact and have different flower colors: 'Crimson Beauty', 'Dakota Gold', 'Helena Gold', 'Helena Red Shades', 'Indian Summer', 'Moerheim Beauty', 'Rubinzwerg' [Ruby Dwarf], and others

Heliopsis helianthoides (oxeye) selections that are more compact: 'Ballerina', 'Summer Sun', 'Tuscan Sun'

Monarda didyma (bee balm) selections resistant to powdery mildew, with more flowers, or more compact: 'Gardenview Scarlet', 'Jacob Cline', 'Marshall's Delight', and more

Penstemon digitalis (beardtongue) selections that are longer blooming and have more interesting foliage: 'Dark Towers', 'Husker Red', 'Mystica'

Phlox paniculata (garden phlox) selections that have good powdery mildew resistance: 'Becky Towe', 'Bright Eyes', 'David', 'Frosted Elegance', 'Giltmine', 'Goldmine', 'Lizzie', 'Natural Feelings', 'Peppermint Twist', 'Pleasant Feelings', 'Rainbow', 'Rubymine', 'Shortwood', 'Swirly Burly', 'Wendy House'

Physostegia virginiana (obedient plant) selections that are less aggressive and have alternative flower colors: 'Miss Manners', 'Olympus Bold', 'Variegata', 'Vivid'

Solidago (goldenrod) selections that are less aggressive and longer blooming: 'Baby Sun', 'Fireworks', 'Goldkind', 'Golden Fleece', 'Little Lemon'

Symphyotrichum novae-angliae (New England aster) selections that are more compact, have more abundant bloom, or alternative flower colors: 'Andenken an Alma Potschke', 'Hella Lacy', 'Honeysong Pink', 'Purple Dome', 'Roter Stern' (Red Star), 'Wedding Lace', and more

Keep taller plants away from public areas such as sidewalks and entry areas. People get nervous when they have to walk by herbaceous plants—especially grasses—that are taller than they are. Use a buffer of lawn or mulch between planted areas and sidewalks and streets so plants don't flop over onto the paved areas and make visitors and passersby uncomfortable.

Although it's not something usually advocated because of native plants' benefits to wildlife, consider cutting back at least some of your taller plants in fall. This won't harm the plants, but it may tidy up an area. The truth is, many native plants, especially grasses, turn brown in winter and not everyone finds this attractive.

Hardscapes & Accents

A hardscape is anything in your landscape that isn't living. It includes paths, fences, decks, patios, driveways, and all structures such as arbors, compost bins, and stairways. These structures are important parts of the landscape and should be given as much thought as the plants you choose, perhaps even more, since they are often permanent.

Hardscapes can be made up of many different materials; the most common are brick, wood, stone, and gravel. Keep your overall design in mind when choosing materials. Although no hardscape will look completely natural, certain materials will blend into a native-plant landscape better than others.

Paths and walkways allow access to inner areas of a garden while reducing the chances for delicate plants to be trampled. Some paths are meant to whisper the way to go; others are meant to shout it. Making a path obvious

Be sure to include accent pieces to make your native gardens more fun. Butterflies are a great motif in prairie gardens.

Meandering paths look more natural than straight ones, but a straight path will offer a nice contrast in a naturalistic landscape.

doesn't mean it has to be boring, however. Bend it around a corner so it disappears for a while, and place plants and stones to break up the sight line of the path edges. Avoid edging the path with rigid rows of plants, stones, or logs, and vary the materials that form the path. Plant your smaller, more delicate flowers along paths where they can be seen and enjoyed. Good walkway materials include brick, gravel, and wood chips.

Don't forget to include lots of benches and chairs along your paths and within your gardens so you and your guests have places to sit and enjoy your landscape. If you have a stream or bog garden, you may need to install stepping stones, wooden bridges, or boardwalks.

One of the misconceptions about native-plant landscapes is that they are boring. Unfortunately, sometimes people take native plant design a little too seriously and think they can't use funky garden accents. Not true! There's no reason you can't incorporate any of the accents you'd use in a regular landscape. Native-plant landscapes can include sculpture, sundials, gazing balls, and fountains, as well as feeders, houses, and baths for birds, just like in any other garden. It's your garden, and you should include things that make you happy.

As with all gardens, keep in mind that these items are meant to be accents. They should be used with discretion and carefully placed rather than just plopped down anywhere. Select sculptural pieces that can be nestled into the garden and surrounded by plants, as if they were growing up out of the ground rather than sitting on a concrete pedestal.

If you are trying to recreate a truly natural habitat, limit your accent pieces to well-placed natural materials such as rocks and logs. Take cues from nature and try to place them as if they had been left there. Moss-covered logs should look like they were once part of a tall forest tree that fell to the ground years ago. Rocks should be buried one-half to two-thirds underground, as if a glacier placed them eons ago, rather than set on the surface.

Natives in Traditional Garden Borders

The garden border is the basis of most landscapes. It can be composed of all perennials or a combination of woody and herbaceous plants, including small trees, shrubs, flowers, grasses, and ferns. It is a place to experiment with colors and textures, combining plants that not only grow well together, but also complement each other. A nice early summer-blooming combination comes from spiderwort, prairie phlox, and tickseeds. Orange butterfly milkweed, yellow oxeye daisy, and spiky purple-pink blazing stars make for a showy hot-colored midsummer display.

A well-planned mixed border will have color and interest year-round. Mix heights, shapes, and textures to give depth and dimension; have taller, spikier plants generally located toward the back and shorter, clumpier plants closer to the front of the garden or along paths. For contrast, plant one or two taller, see-through plants toward the front of the border. Fine-textured plants such as blue stars combine nicely with coarser yarrows. Use clumps of native grasses to offer contrast to fuller, rounded plants such as oxeyes and monardas. Delicate maidenhair fern combines nicely with coarser-textured plants such as crested iris in shade borders

Select plants that will work well together, and avoid those that are overly aggressive and may take over their neighbor's spot. A certain amount of plant movement and settling in will result in a more natural-looking border.

However, for the most part, you want plants that will stay where you placed them so you retain the original design.

A mixed border that is made up of all native plants can become a small-scale habitat restoration if you use natives that are indigenous to your area. Such a garden will become a mecca for native pollinating insects, butterflies, birds, and other fauna. If you are not ready to grow all natives or you already have an established landscape with traditional garden beds, rest assured that native plants combine well with nonnatives in mixed-border situations.

NATIVE KNOW-HOW
Neighborly Natives

Homeowners who decide to grow natives are often confronted with an array of laws, regulations, requirements, and sometimes outright hostility. Most of these issues are simply due to ignorance. There are several things you can do to prepare yourself for neighborhood opposition.

Learn your local laws and ordinances. Chances are you will be able to stay well within them by putting some thought into your landscape before you plant. If they don't allow for the use of native plants, go through the proper channels to try to obtain a variance or get an ordinance changed.

Education is key. Take every chance you can get to teach your neighbors about this intricate plant community. Anytime you see a neighbor outside, invite them over to look at a flower or butterfly in your yard. Encourage them to walk through your landscape so they can see some of the important details that may be missed from the outside.

Once your landscape is planted, be attentive and keep up with the necessary maintenance. Let your neighbors know by your presence and activities that your yard is being cared for and not neglected.

Be sensitive to the people around you and approach any conflict calmly and reasonably. Many of your neighbors may have lived in their homes for decades and are used to a certain look and feel in their neighborhood. An attitude of self-righteousness and arrogance will only make things worse.

A mixed border is a place to combine many different types of plants.

This shade garden features yellow lady's slipper (*Cypripedium parviflorum*), foamflower, and wild geraniums, along with traditional non-native shade lovers, hostas and bleeding hearts.

Natives & Shade Gardening

Many gardeners consider shade to be a liability, a spot where they can't grow grass or colorful flowers. However, all landscapes should have a cool, shady retreat from the summer heat, and some of the most interesting plants grow in these areas, protected from the hot sun. With a little effort, you can eliminate the struggle with lawn grasses and fill the area with a beautiful tapestry of colors and textures provided by native plants that thrive in shade. And a shade garden is a joy to tend. It is usually less weedy than sunny gardens and much more comfortable to work in, especially on a hot summer day.

The key to successful shade gardening is in understanding the different degrees of shade, which can range from light to heavy and are different at different times of the growing season. "Light shade" areas receive bright to full sun for all but a few hours each day. Areas with bright light or sun for about half the day are called "partial shade." Most shade plants will do fine in either of these sites, especially if the light comes from morning

Most shade plants do best in filtered shade as opposed to deep, heavy shade. Dappled shade, where patterns of sunlight move across the plants as the day progresses, is ideal.

sun. "Full shade" areas are shaded for most of the day, and "dense shade" is for only the most shade-tolerant plants. Don't be afraid to limb up some taller trees to provide the partial shade that so many woodland natives thrive in.

When it comes to plant selection in shade gardens, simplicity, rather than ostentation, is the key. Textures and shades of green play an important role. If possible, allow flowers and groundcovers to spread, seed themselves, and form natural drifts. You want plants that are adapted, attractive, and long-lived; you also want plants that increase but not so rapidly that they crowd out other desirable plants. Some plants that have many desirable characteristics but tend to spread readily—such as ferns, Canada anemone, violets, and Mayapple—might be too much for smaller gardens.

Most woodland plants require a slightly acidic, fertile soil. Add 2 to 4 inches of organic matter when building the garden or at planting time. Watering is important, especially where large tree roots compete for

Alumroots provide color and Allegheny spurge great texture in this dry shade garden.

available moisture. Mulch with 2 to 4 inches of shredded leaves or bark or pine needles to conserve moisture and replenish nutrients.

If your shade garden is large enough, include curved paths covered with wood chips or shredded bark. Create points of interest along the way—ornaments such as wagon wheels or hollow stumps filled with showier flowers, larger patches of flowers, or trees and shrubs with unique growth patterns or bark that are enhanced by pruning. Allow some branches and logs to remain after falling. To add sound, consider adding a trickling stream lined with marsh marigolds and other moist-soil plants.

Boulevard & Strip Gardens

Boulevard strips are those narrow areas between the sidewalk and the street (sometimes they're called "hell strips"). As prevalent as they are in urban landscapes, boulevard strips are often neglected when it comes to landscaping. This is unfortunate since they are in plain view of anyone who visits or passes by. (Check the laws in your locale; sometimes you cannot plant in city-owned strips.)

There are many reasons to garden on boulevard strips. (Many of these same principles can be applied to other areas in the landscape that are sunny and dry, such as the area between the house and the driveway or a foundation planting on the south or west side of a building.) From a gardening standpoint, they offer extended opportunities for space-starved urban gardeners. From an

Native plants that are great choices for boulevard gardens include prairie alumroot, prairie smoke, and pussytoes (*Antennaria*).

Purple poppy mallow (*Callirhoe involucrate*) is perfect for boulevard gardens. It is low growing, tolerates hot, dry conditions, and is very pretty.

Allium species (wild onions)
Antennaria species (pussytoes)
Aquilegia species (columbines)
Asclepias tuberosa (butterfly milkweed)
Bouteloua species (grama grasses)
Callirhoe species (poppymallows)
Campanula rotundifolia (harebell)
Ceanothus americanus (New Jersey tea)
Coreopsis cultivars (tickseeds)
Dalea purpurea (purple prairie clover)
Gaillardia x *grandiflora* (blanket flower)
Geum triflorum (prairie smoke)
Heuchera richardsonii (prairie alumroot)
Houstonia longifolia (longleaf bluets)
Liatris punctata (dotted blazing star)
Muhlenbergia capillaris (pink muhly grass)
Phlox pilosa (prairie phlox)
Phlox subulata (creeping phlox)
Pulsatilla patens (pasque flower)
Ratibida columnifera (upright prairie coneflower)
Rudbeckia hirta (black-eyed Susan)
Salvia species (sages)
Schizachyrium scoparium (little bluestem)
Silene caroliniana (wild pink)
Silene virginica (fire pink)
Sisyrinchium species (blue-eyed grasses)
Sporobolus heterolepis (prairie dropseed)
Stokesia laevis (Stokes' aster)
Symphyotrichum ericoides (white heath aster)

67

environmental standpoint, they can be very effective at keeping grass clippings out of the street and storm sewers.

But boulevard strips are among the most challenging spots to grow and maintain plants. The soil is usually compacted and low in fertility and often gets bombarded with road salt in winter in cold climates. They are usually hot, dry, and sunny—unpleasant conditions for tending—and often the garden hose doesn't reach that far, creating maintenance issues. Consequently, most boulevards remain covered with weeds or unhealthy turfgrasses. If they are gardened, they are typically filled with high-maintenance annuals that often end up looking worn and tattered by midsummer and can actually be worse from an environmental standpoint than the weeds.

Many native plants, with their ability to withstand hot, dry, and often sunny conditions, are good choices along boulevards. Stick with low-growing, clumping plants. Stay away from prolific self-seeders because even a couple extra plants can make this small-space look weedy. Any plant growing over a foot in height will probably need to be cut back in fall. Plan on cutting back any remaining plants in spring and raking off the debris.

Rain Gardens

In a natural plant community, most rainwater is absorbed into the ground where it is taken up by plants or stored as groundwater. This is not the case in most urban areas, where roofs, roads, and parking lots replace the natural surfaces, preventing rain from being absorbed into the ground. Instead, the rainwater washes pollutants and trash from paved streets and parking lots into storm drains and deposits it, without treatment, into a nearby lake or river. Along with the run-off rainwater goes fertilizers and other lawn chemicals, which can cause real problems in waterways.

A rain garden is a great way to create a useful wetland that helps control runoff from impervious surfaces and filters out pollutants before they reach streams and

Planted with appropriate native species, rainwater gardens become attractive additions to the landscape that reduce pollution, save water, and serve as a haven for butterflies and birds.

Native prairie species, especially those that evolved in seasonally moist prairies, are especially well suited to rain gardens. Most of them have deep root systems that will help them survive summer dry spells. These extensive root systems also create natural channels that help keep the soil loose and improve filtration.

SPECIAL-USE NATIVES
Rain Gardens

Flowers, Ferns & Groundcovers

Actaea racemosa (bugbane)
Adiantum pedatum (maidenhair fern)
Agastache foeniculum (anise hyssop)
Allium species (wild onions)
Amsonia species (blue stars)
Aquilegia species (columbines)
Asarum species (wild gingers)
Asclepias species (milkweeds)
Athyrium filix-femina (lady fern)
Baptisia species (false indigos)
Camassia species (camas)
Campanula rotundifolia (harebell)
Chelone species (turtleheads)
Coreopsis species (tickseeds)
Dalea species (prairie clovers)
Dicentra species (bleeding hearts)
Dodecatheon meadia (shooting star)
Echinacea species (purple coneflower)
Eutrochium species (Joe-pye weeds)
Gaillardia species (blanket flower)
Geranium maculatum (wild geranium)
Geum triflorum (prairie smoke)
Helenium species (sneezeweeds)
Heliopsis helianthoides (oxeye)
Heuchera species (alumroots)
Iris cristata (dwarf crested iris)
Liatris species (blazing stars)
Lobelia species (cardinal flower, lobelia)
Mertensia virginica (Virginia bluebells)
Monarda species (bee balms)
Pachysandra procumbens (Allegheny spurge)
Penstemon species (beardtongue)
Phlox species (phloxes)
Polemonium reptans (spreading Jacob's ladder)
Ratibida pinnata (prairie coneflower)
Rudbeckia species (black-eyed Susans, coneflowers)
Silene regia (royal catchfly)
Solidago species (goldenrods)
Symphyotrichum species (asters)
Thermopsis villosa (false lupine)
Tiarella cordifolia (foamflower)
Tradescantia species (spiderworts)
Verbena hastata (blue vervain)

Grasses & Sedges

Bouteloua species (grama grasses)
Carex species (sedges)
Chasmanthium latifolium (northern sea oats)
Deschampsia cespitosa (tufted hair grass)
Muhlenbergia species (muhly grasses)
Panicum virgatum (switchgrass)
Schizachyrium scoparium (little bluestem)
Sorghastrum nutans (Indiangrass)
Sporobolus heterolepis (prairie dropseed)

Shrubs, Vines & Small Trees

Aesculus species (buckeyes)
Amelanchier species (serviceberries)
Calycanthus floridus (sweetshrub)
Carpinus caroliniana (American hornbeam)
Clethra alnifolia (summersweet)
Cornus species (dogwoods)
Diervilla species (bush honeysuckles)
Fothergilla species (fothergillas)
Hamamelis species (witch hazel)
Hydrangea species (hydrangeas)
Ilex species (hollies, winterberry)
Juniperus virginiana (eastern red cedar)
Kalmia latifolia (mountain laurel)
Lindera benzoin (spicebush)
Photinia species (chokeberries)
Physocarpus opulifolius (ninebark)
Ptelea trifoliata (hop tree)
Rhus species (sumacs)
Thuja species (cedars)
Vaccinium species (blueberries)
Viburnum species (viburnums)

Trees

Acer species (maples)
Betula nigra (river birch)
Celtis species (hackberry, sugarberry)
Cladrastis kentukea (yellowwood)
Gymnocladus dioica (Kentucky coffee tree)
Magnolia virginiana (sweetbay magnolia)
Oxydendrum arboreum (sourwood)
Picea mariana (black spruce)
Quercus bicolor (swamp white oak)
Quercus palustris (pin oak)

SPECIAL-USE NATIVES
Bog Gardens

Bog gardens are areas of permanently moist but not waterlogged, acidic soil. They often occur along the edges of lakes, rivers, or streams. If you have a suitable area, consider installing this specialized habitat garden. Good natives for a bog garden include bog rosemary (*Andromeda polifolia*), pitcher plant (*Sarracenia purpurea*), goldenclub (*Orontium aquaticum*), and meadow beauty (*Rhexia mariana*). Mosses, sedges, and ferns often do well in bog gardens also.

lakes. It is built in a shallow depression, usually about 6 to 8 inches deep, that allows the garden to hold water for a short period of time, usually less than 24 hours, while it is absorbed into the soil. Rain gardens can be as small as the area under your downspout to as large as several city blocks. By slowing down storm-water runoff, rainwater gardens collect moisture and allow it to slowly seep into the soil.

When it comes to deciding what to plant, your main goal is to choose plants appropriate for your site that will take care of the necessary business of managing storm water. Within these requirements, you can also make choices based on wildlife attraction, season-long interest, bloom times, and even your favorite colors. Although most rain gardens are heavy on herbaceous perennial flowers, there are also many grasses and ferns that will thrive in there. And in larger gardens, there are several shrubs and trees to consider. The end result should be a functional garden that manages your rainwater, fits your desired level of maintenance, and still looks good in your yard and neighborhood.

One important thing to keep in mind when selecting plants: You are not looking for wetland or water garden plants nor those that require very dry soil conditions. Rather, you are looking for plants that can tolerate both saturated soil for a period of time as well as drought conditions, especially in the central part of the garden. As you move toward the outsides of the garden, you can incorporate more traditional garden and landscape plants.

A well-designed rain garden will have several different soil moisture zones. Plants in the deepest part of the garden must be able to tolerate periodic or frequent standing or flowing water as well as seasonal dry spells. This is also where you want to place taller plants, keeping in mind that they will appear a foot or so shorter because this area of the garden is usually lower than the edges. Plants along the edges of a rain garden should be those that grow well in average soil moisture. They will need to be able to tolerate some standing water, but not for very long.

Xeriscaping
Xeriscaping is landscaping that promotes water conservation by using drought-tolerant, well-adapted plants within a landscape carefully designed for maximum use of rainfall runoff and minimum care. It is most common in western and southern states where less rain falls and water use is more regulated, but it is good to follow the principles behind water-wise gardening in any landscape.

SPECIAL-USE NATIVES
Drought-Tolerant Species

Flowers, Ferns & Groundcovers

Agastache species (anise hyssops)
Allium species (wild onions)
Asclepias tuberosa (butterfly milkweed)
Baptisia species (false indigos)
Campanula rotundifolia (harebell)
Dalea species (prairie clovers)
Gaillardia species (blanket flowers)
Geum triflorum (prairie smoke)
Liatris punctata (dotted blazing star)
Liatris scariosa (eastern blazing star)
Penstemon species (beardtongues)
Phlox subulata (moss phlox)
Pulsatilla patens (pasque flower)
Ratibida species (prairie coneflower, Mexican hat)
Rudbeckia hirta (black-eyed Susan)
Salvia azurea (azure sage)
Silene virginica (fire pink)
Solidago species (goldenrods)
Stokesia laevis (Stokes' aster)
Thermopsis villosa (false lupine)
Tradescantia species (spiderworts)
Verbena stricta (hoary vervain)
Yucca species (yuccas)

Grasses & Sedges

Bouteloua species (grama grasses)
Muhlenbergia species (muhly grasses)
Panicum virgatum (switchgrass)
Schizachyrium scoparium (little bluestem)
Sorghastrum nutans (Indiangrass)
Sporobolus heterolepis (prairie dropseed)

Shrubs, Vines & Small Trees

Amelanchier alnifolia (western serviceberry)
Amelanchier arborea (downy serviceberry)
Amelanchier laevis (Allegheny serviceberry)
Amorpha canescens (leadplant)
Ceanothus americanus (New Jersey tea)
Clematis virginiana (virgin's bower)
Cornus racemosa (gray dogwood)
Dasiphora fruticosa (potentilla)
Diervilla species (bush honeysuckles)
Gelsemium sempervirens (Carolina jessamine)
Juniperus species (junipers)
Mahonia species (Oregon grape, creeping mahonia)
Photinia melanocarpa (black chokeberry)
Physocarpus opulifolius (ninebark)
Ptelea trifoliata (hop tree)
Quercus ellipsoidalis (northern pin oak)
Quercus macrocarpa (bur oak)
Quercus muehlenbergii (Chinkapin oak)
Rhus species (sumacs)
Viburnum prunifolium (black haw)

Trees

Celtis species (hackberry, sugarberry)
Gymnocladus dioica (Kentucky coffee tree)
Pinus species (pines)

71

Native plants are naturals for xeriscaping since many of them tolerate the hot, dry conditions required for these water-efficient landscapes.

NATIVE PLANTS IN GARDENS & LANDSCAPES

This well-designed xeric front yard shows that practical doesn't mean unattractive. Plants include yuccas, parsnipflower, and sulphur-flowered buckwheats (*Eriogonum heracleoides*, *E. umbellatum*), beardtongues, and goldenbushes (*Ericameria* species).

Mark Turner

There are other things to keep in mind besides plant selection for effective xeriscaping. Before planting, determine whether soil improvement is needed for better water absorption and improved water-holding capacity, and mix compost into soil before planting to help retain water. Reduce water runoff by building terraces and retaining walls.

Use high-maintenance turfgrasses as a planned element in the landscape, not as a default. Avoid impractical turf use, such as in long, narrow areas, and use it only in areas where it provides functional benefits. Raise mower blades to get a higher cut. Taller grass encourages grass roots to grow deeper, making stronger, more drought-resistant plants. In other areas, plant groundcovers and add hard-surface areas such as patios, decks, and walkways, where practical.

Properly timed pruning, weeding, pest control, and irrigation all conserve water. Install drip or trickle irrigation systems in those areas that need watering, and use timers and water-control devices to increase their efficiency even more. Apply organic mulch to reduce water loss from the soil through evaporation and to increase water penetration during irrigation.

Attracting Pollinators

Pollination is a crucial process, both for the insects that collect the pollen and for the plant, which relies on it for reproduction. Pollination is also crucial for the survival of the human species, since without it, many of the food plants the world relies on would not be able to produce.

Some plants rely on wind for pollination, but insects pollinate most plants. They lure these insects by producing flowers that contain nectar and pollen, which the insects use for food. Insects are enticed by flower colors, shapes or forms, and fragrance.

Bees are by far the largest group of pollinators, but wasps, beetles, butterflies, moths, and flies are also pollinators. Encourage a wide variety of these very beneficial

A Virginia ctenucha wasp moth collects nectar from gray dogwood flowers. As a consequence, it will spread the flower's pollen to other flowers.

SPECIAL-USE NATIVES
Attracting Bees

Flowers, Ferns & Groundcovers
Actaea species (bugbane, baneberries)
Agastache species (anise hyssops)
Allium species (wild onions)
Amsonia species (blue stars)
Aquilegia species (columbines)
Asclepias species (milkweeds)
Baptisia species (false indigos)
Camassia species (camas)
Campanula rotundifolia (harebell)
Chelone species (turtleheads)
Coreopsis species (tickseeds)
Dalea species (prairie clovers)
Dicentra species (bleeding hearts)
Dodecatheon meadia (shooting star)
Echinacea species (purple coneflower)
Eutrochium species (Joe-pye weeds)
Gaillardia species (blanket flowers)
Geranium maculatum (wild geranium)
Geum triflorum (prairie smoke)
Gillenia trifoliata (Bowman's root)
Helenium species (sneezeweeds)
Heliopsis helianthoides (oxeye)
Heuchera americana (alumroot)
Iris cristata (dwarf crested iris)
Liatris species (blazing stars)
Lobelia species (cardinal flower, lobelia)
Mertensia virginica (Virginia bluebells)
Mitella diphylla (bishop's cap)
Monarda species (bee balms)
Pachysandra procumbens (Allegheny spurge)
Penstemon species (beardtongues)
Phlox species (phloxes)
Polemonium reptans (spreading Jacob's ladder)
Pulsatilla patens (pasque flower)
Ratibida pinnata (prairie coneflower)
Rudbeckia species (black-eyed Susans, coneflowers)
Salvia species (sages)
Sanguinaria canadensis (bloodroot)
Solidago species (goldenrods)
Stokesia laevis (Stokes' aster)
Symphyotrichum species (asters)
Thermopsis villosa (false lupine)

Tiarella cordifolia (foamflower)
Tradescantia species (spiderworts)
Uvularia species (bellworts)
Verbena species (vervains)

Shrubs, Vines & Small Trees
Amelanchier species (serviceberries)
Amorpha canescens (leadplant)
Ceanothus americanus (New Jersey tea)
Chionanthus virginicus (fringetree)
Clematis virginiana (virgin's bower)
Clethra alnifolia (summersweet)
Cornus species (dogwoods)
Dasiphora fruticosa (potentilla)
Diervilla species (bush honeysuckles)
Fothergilla species (fothergillas)
Gelsemium sempervirens (Carolina jessamine)
Hamamelis species (witch hazels)
Hydrangea species (hydrangeas)
Ilex species (hollies, winterberry)
Kalmia latifolia (mountain laurel)
Lonicera species (honeysuckles)
Mahonia species (Oregon grape, creeping mahonia)
Photinia species (chokeberries)
Physocarpus opulifolius (ninebark)
Ptelea trifoliata (hop tree)
Rhododendron species (azaleas, rhododendrons)
Rhus species (sumacs)
Vaccinium species (blueberries)
Viburnum species (viburnums)
Wisteria species (wisterias)

Trees
Cercis canadensis (Eastern redbud)
Cladrastis kentukea (yellowwood)
Halesia species (silverbells)
Oxydendrum arboreum (sourwood)
Tilia americana (basswood)

Beetles, including this soldier beetle, are responsible for pollinating 88 percent of all the flowering plants. Unfortunately, they can often do damage as they eat their way through petals and other flower parts to get to the pollen. Beetles largely rely on their sense of smell for feeding and egg-laying. They are attracted to flowers that have a strongly fruity fragrance and are open during the day. They visit both large, solitary flowers such as magnolias, as well as clusters of small flowers, such as goldenrods. A side benefit of beetles is that many of them are also bird food.

A Delaware skipper butterfly and a bee visit a purple coneflower to feed on nectar and collect pollen.

insects by planting a diversity of natives with a continuous bloom sequence from early spring through fall. In general, straight native species are better for pollinators than cultivars or hybrids, which often have double blooms or altered flower colors. These hybrid traits can restrict pollinator access and confuse their plant identification skills.

The greatest threats to pollinators come from the use of pesticides (herbicides, fungicides, and especially insecticides) but also from climate change, which alters flowering times and pollinator life cycles, throwing off the delicate plant-insect interactions. Fortunately, the list of native plants that attract pollinators is quite substantial, making it easy for everyone to include these plants in their landscapes and help offset their loss in natural areas.

Attracting Butterflies

Butterflies add a wonderful dimension to the landscape, and they are one of the best side benefits of having a native-plant landscape. Butterfly gardening can be as simple as incorporating a few nectar plants into a flower garden or as elaborate as creating an area entirely devoted to these fascinating creatures. To become a successful butterfly gardener, you should start by learning which butterfly species are found in your area and what plants they like.

Most butterflies are vagabonds on their way somewhere else when you see them in your garden. You can think of your garden as a rest stop along the way, a place where they can linger for a while to enjoy food, water, and shelter. If you want to provide a complete butterfly habitat, you will have to include the proper host plants

Bumblebees are primary pollinators of many plants. This one visits autumn sneezeweed.

Attracting Butterflies

Flowers, Ferns & Groundcovers

Actaea racemosa (bugbane)
Agastache species (anise hyssops)
Allium species (wild onions)
Amsonia species (blue stars)
Aquilegia species (columbines)
Asarum species (wild gingers)
Asclepias species (milkweeds)
Baptisia species (false indigos)
Camassia species (camas)
Chelone species (turtleheads)
Coreopsis species (tickseeds)
Dalea species (prairie clovers)
Dicentra formosa (western bleeding heart)
Echinacea species (purple coneflowers)
Eutrochium species (Joe-pye weeds)
Gaillardia species (blanket flowers)
Geranium maculatum (wild geranium)
Geum triflorum (prairie smoke)
Helenium species (sneezeweeds)
Heliopsis helianthoides (oxeye)
Heuchera americana (alumroot)
Liatris species (blazing stars)
Lobelia species (cardinal flower, lobelia)
Mertensia virginica (Virginia bluebells)
Monarda species (bee balms)
Penstemon species (beardtongues)
Phlox species (phloxes)
Polemonium reptans (spreading Jacob's ladder)
Ratibida pinnata (prairie coneflower)
Rudbeckia species (black-eyed Susans, coneflowers)
Salvia species (sages)
Silene regia (royal catchfly)
Solidago species (goldenrods)
Spigelia marilandica (Indian pink)
Stokesia laevis (Stokes' aster)
Symphyotrichum species (asters)
Thermopsis villosa (false lupine)
Verbena species (vervains)
Yucca species (yuccas)

Grasses & Sedges

Bouteloua species (grama grasses)
Carex pensylvanica (Pennsylvania sedge)
Chasmanthium latifolium (northern sea oats)
Deschampsia species (hair grasses)

Panicum virgatum (switchgrass)
Schizachyrium scoparium (little bluestem)
Sorghastrum nutans (Indiangrass)

Shrubs, Vines & Small Trees

Aesculus species (buckeyes)
Amelanchier species (serviceberries)
Amorpha canescens (leadplant)
Arctostaphylos species (bearberries)
Aristolochia species (pipevines)
Asimina species (pawpaw)
Callicarpa americana (American beautyberry)
Carpinus caroliniana (American hornbeam)
Ceanothus americanus (New Jersey tea)
Cephalanthus occidentalis (buttonbush)
Clematis virginiana (virgin's bower)
Clethra alnifolia (summersweet)
Cornus species (dogwoods)
Dasiphora fruticosa (potentilla)
Diervilla species (bush honeysuckles)
Fothergilla species (fothergillas)
Gelsemium sempervirens (Carolina jessamine)
Itea virginiana (Virginia sweetspire)
Juniperus species (junipers)
Kalmia latifolia (mountain laurel)
Lindera benzoin (spicebush)
Mahonia species (Oregon grape, creeping mahonia)
Photinia species (chokeberries)
Physocarpus opulifolius (ninebark)
Ptelea trifoliata (hop tree)
Rhododendron species (azaleas, rhododendrons)
Rhus species (sumacs)
Ribes species (currants, gooseberries)
Salix species (willows)
Spiraea species (spireas)
Vaccinium species (blueberries)
Viburnum species (viburnums)
Wisteria species (wisterias)

Trees

Acer species (maples)
Betula species (birches)
Carya species (hickories)
Crataegus species (hawthorns)
Celtis species (hackberry, sugarberry)
Cercis canadensis (Eastern redbud)
Fraxinus species (ashes)
Gymnocladus dioicus (Kentucky coffee tree)
Juglans species (walnuts)
Malus species (wild crabapples)
Pinus species (pines)
Populus species (poplars, aspen)
Prunus species (plums, cherries)
Quercus species (oaks)
Ulmus species (elms)

75

for butterflies to lay eggs, keeping in mind that these are not always the showiest plants and that they become even less attractive when they have been eaten by the newly hatched caterpillars. These host plants are important, however, as without them, butterflies will not lay eggs.

When it comes to nectar sources, butterflies are drawn to big, bold splashes of color and concentrations of fragrance. Butterflies like two kinds of flowers: clusters of nectar-filled tubular blossoms that they can probe in sequence and large, rather flat blossoms that provide landing pads. Purple, red, orange, and yellow attract the most butterfly species; blue and white flowers are least popular. However, color preferences can vary from species to species, so you should plant the entire color palette.

Especially valuable for butterflies are early blooming flowers that are open when the first hatches emerge or the first returning migrants arrive, and late-blooming plants that are still in bloom after the first fall frost. Early violets are occasionally weighted down with butterflies, as are late-blooming asters and Joe-pye weeds.

In addition to host plants, butterflies need mud puddles or other wet areas and they need shelter—shrubs, trees, and bushy flowers where they can hide from birds, find shade at midday, and rest at night. They also look for basking stones, where they can build up enough body heat to fly, and windbreaks to temper the wind.

Attracting Birds

Birds and native plants rely on each other for many reasons, and as more and more of their natural habitats are destroyed, native landscaping become crucial for our feathered friends. Birds eat fruits, buds, flowers, and nectar of plants and in return, they help pollinate flowers and disperse their seeds. Unlike rodents, which destroy seeds by gnawing the seed coats, birds eat only the fleshy parts of fruits, allowing seeds to survive and germinate. Birds are also very important in keeping destructive insects under control, as the vast majority of them rely on insects for food.

There are a few things to keep in mind as you plan and plant your landscape if you want to share it with a wide variety of birds. First, try to recreate the layers found in natural habitats, including a high canopy formed by shade trees, an understory layer made up of shrubs and small trees, and lower growing herbaceous plants. Birds use these layers for different purposes such as nesting and protection.

Cedar waxwings love to feast on the fruits of *Amelanchier* species, which are among the first shrubs to set fruit in summer.

Increase the attractiveness of your native plant landscape to birds by adding nesting spots.

76

SPECIAL-USE NATIVES
Attracting Birds

Flowers, Ferns & Groundcovers
Actaea species (bugbane, baneberries)
Adiantum pedatum (maidenhair fern)
Aquilegia species (columbines)
Athyrium filix-femina (lady fern)
Baptisia species (false indigos)
Chelone species (turtleheads)
Coreopsis species (tickseeds)
Dalea species (prairie clovers)
Dicentra species (bleeding hearts)
Echinacea species (purple coneflowers)
Eutrochium species (Joe-pye weeds)
Gaillardia aristata (blanket flower)
Geranium maculatum (wild geranium)
Geum triflorum (prairie smoke)
Helenium species (sneezeweeds)
Heliopsis helianthoides (oxeye)
Liatris species (blazing stars)
Ratibida pinnata (prairie coneflower)
Rudbeckia species (black-eyed Susans, coneflowers)
Salvia species (sages)
Solidago species (goldenrods)
Symphyotrichum species (asters)
Verbena stricta (hoary vervain)

Grasses & Sedges
Bouteloua species (grama grasses)
Carex pensylvanica (Pennsylvania sedge)
Chasmanthium latifolium (northern sea oats)
Muhlenbergia species (muhly grasses)
Panicum virgatum (switchgrass)
Schizachyrium scoparium (little bluestem)
Sporobolus heterolepis (prairie dropseed)
Sorghastrum nutans (Indiangrass)

Shrubs, Vines & Small Trees
Amelanchier species (serviceberries)
Carpinus caroliniana (American hornbeam)
Ceanothus americanus (New Jersey tea)
Celastrus scandens (American bittersweet)
Chionanthus virginicus (fringetree)
Clematis virginiana (virgin's bower)
Clethra alnifolia (summersweet)

Cornus species (dogwoods)
Dasiphora fruticosa (potentilla)
Diervilla species (bush honeysuckles)
Fothergilla species (fothergillas)
Hamamelis species (witch hazels)
Ilex species (winterberry, hollies)
Juniperus species (junipers)
Kalmia latifolia (mountain laurel)
Lindera benzoin (spicebush)
Lonicera species (honeysuckles)
Mahonia species (Oregon grape, creeping mahonia)
Parthenocissus quinquefolia (woodbine)
Photinia species (chokeberries)
Physocarpus opulifolius (ninebark)
Ptelea trifoliata (hop tree)
Rhododendron species (azaleas, rhododendrons)
Rhus species (sumacs)
Ribes species (currants, gooseberries)
Rosa species (wild roses)
Rubus species (raspberries, blackberries)
Sambucus species (elderberries)
Taxus species (yews)
Thuja species (cedars)
Vaccinium species (blueberries)
Viburnum species (viburnums)

Trees
Abies species (firs)
Acer species (maples)
Betula species (birches)
Celtis species (hackberry, sugarberry)
Cercis canadensis (Eastern redbud)
Fagus grandifolia (American beech)
Magnolia species (magnolias)
Malus species (wild crabapples)
Ostrya virginiana (ironwood)
Oxydendrum arboreum (sourwood)
Picea species (spruces)
Pinus species (pines)
Prunus species (plums, cherries)
Pseudotsuga menziesii (Douglas fir)
Quercus species (oaks)
Sorbus species (mountain ashes)
Tilia americana (basswood)
Tsuga species (hemlocks)

Columbines are among hummingbirds' favorite nectar source.

The bright red tubular flowers of Indian pink make it a favorite of hummingbirds.

Select plants that provide a variety of food throughout the year, not just during the growing season. Plants that have fruits that persist through winter are important for early spring migrants. Try to include some evergreen conifers for winter shelter. Allow dead trees to remain, if possible; birds prefer these for perching and some use the cavities for nesting.

In addition to plant selection and planting techniques, you should supply a source of water and consider providing nesting boxes and birdhouses. Leave some litter on your garden beds through the winter to attract earthworms, insects, and other animals that the birds will feed on. Last, but very important: do not use insecticides. Many harm birds directly, while others kill or contaminate insects and other creatures that birds feed on.

Creating a Hummingbird Habitat

Hummingbirds bring movement to a garden, mesmerizing you as they zoom from one plant to the next. There's nothing more enjoyable than a visit from these tiny guests.

Because of its high rate of metabolism, a hummingbird needs to eat more than one-half its weight in food daily. A hummingbird habitat should include several types of flowers, both herbaceous and woody plants of varied heights and bloom dates. Your hummingbird habitat can also include several properly maintained feeders. The most effective habitats also attract and nurture tiny insects and spiders that hummingbirds ingest to meet their protein requirements and to feed to their young.

Since hummingbirds, like most birds, have virtually no sense of smell, the flowers that attract them tend to

Flowers, Ferns & Groundcovers

Agastache species (hyssops)
Allium species (wild onions)
Amsonia species (blue stars)
Aquilegia species (columbines)
Asclepias species (milkweeds)
Baptisia species (false indigos)
Campanula rotundifolia (harebell)
Chelone species (turtleheads)
Dalea species (prairie clovers)
Dicentra species (bleeding hearts)
Echinacea species (purple coneflowers)
Eutrochium species (Joe-pye weeds)
Gaillardia species (blanket flowers)
Heliopsis helianthoides (oxeye)
Heuchera species (alumroots)
Iris cristata (dwarf crested iris)
Liatris species (blazing stars)
Lobelia species (cardinal flower, lobelia)
Mertensia virginica (Virginia bluebells)

Monarda species (bee balms)
Penstemon species (beardtongues)
Phlox species (phloxes)
Pulsatilla patens (pasque flower)
Salvia coccinea (scarlet sage)
Silene species (royal catchfly, fire pink)
Spigelia marilandica (Indian pink)
Symphyotrichum species (asters)
Verbena stricta (hoary vervain)

Shrubs, Vines & Trees

Aesculus pavia (red buckeye)
Bignonia caprealata (cross vine)
Campsis radicans (trumpet vine)
Ceanothus americanus (New Jersey tea)
Clematis virginiana (virgin's bower)
Clethra alnifolia (summersweet)
Diervilla species (bush honeysuckles)
Gelsemium sempervirens (Carolina jessamine)
Gymnocladus dioicus (Kentucky coffee tree)
Kalmia latifolia (mountain laurel)
Lonicera species (honeysuckles)
Mahonia species (Oregon grape, creeping mahonia)
Rhododendron species (azaleas, rhododendrons)
Wisteria species (wisterias)

have little or no fragrance, instead directing resources toward high visibility and nectar production. Most hummingbird-attracting flowers are tubular-shaped, and many are red, though certainly not all. A successful hummingbird garden provides nectar sources from May through the first frost. There is a great temptation to plant acres of wild bergamot or cardinal flower, two of a hummingbird's favorite nectar sources. However, with each of these flowers, nectar is available for just a brief period in a hummingbird's life. Note also that cultivated hybrids often make much less nectar than wild strains.

Your garden should also have space for hummingbirds to nest and locations where they can roost and find shelter from the elements. Have fresh water available for drinking as well as for bathing. Include shady spots where hummingbirds can perch as well as build their nests. Willows provide pliable twigs used for nesting. Hummingbirds also use with bits of leaves, spider webs, moss, and lichens to build their tiny nests.

By giving a little thought to your design before planting, you can have a beautifully designed landscape made up of all or some native plants that not only brings you joy, but which is also good for the environment.

CHAPTER FOUR

Caring for Native Plants

For many, the initial appeal of using natives comes from their desire for "no maintenance." And a long-term goal of creating a native-plant landscape is often to create a sustainable community that requires little or no effort on your part. This is in great contrast to a traditional landscape or garden where human intervention is constant and necessary to keep things looking as planned. However, if you want a "garden," you will still need to perform regular maintenance. Fortunately, most of the required tasks come under the heading of "desirable" for people who enjoy tending plants.

With native plants, the need to water and fertilize is all but eliminated once they are established, and the use of pesticides to kill insects or diseases should never be on the maintenance list. Once you eliminate the nasty tasks of spraying, watering, and fertilizing, you can spend your time tending the plants and improving the overall design of your gardens. If you go one step further and use native plantings to replace areas of traditional lawn, you will reduce your need for weekly mowing and all the other maintenance issues that come with growing turfgrasses.

When developing a maintenance plan for your native landscape, keep in mind the things that make a garden look unattractive and untended. These include an excess of weeds; floppy plants; unhealthy or browned plants; large areas without pathways, ornaments, or other aspects of a hardscape; large areas of nondescript green foliage with little or no color from flowers or foliage; plants with a lot of insect or disease damage; plants that have been eaten back by deer or other herbivores; wilting plants; and bare soil where plants have gone dormant and nothing has filled in. Anything you can do to minimize these things will help your gardens look better and be healthier.

When it comes to maintenance, your goal should be to have a garden or landscape that is pleasing to you, is good for the environment, and is easily maintained at a level that suits your time and interest. This xeric front yard in Boise, Idaho, includes blue spruce, Apache plume (*Fallugia paradoxa*), skunkbush sumac (*Rhus trilobata*), western serviceberry (*Amelanchier alnifolia*), sagebrush (*Artemisia*), evening primrose (*Oenothera*), orange globemallow (*Sphaeralcea*), and a blue grama lawn.

Mark Turner

CARING FOR NATIVE PLANTS

This chapter explains how to make sure your native-plant landscape remains a healthy, vibrant plant community. You'll learn about mulching, watering, and weed control, and how to properly groom, divide, and prune your established plants. It also covers some of the possible problems you may face and offers non-synthetic chemical-free solutions.

Mulching

There are so many good things about mulching, it's hard to know where to start. Organic mulch keeps down weeds, holds water in the soil, and improves fertility. It cools the soil in shade gardens and replenishes the rich soil that woodland plants need. It also sets the plants off nicer than nondescript bare soil.

There are several good organic mulches. Select one based on your plants and garden type. *Shredded leaves* are good in almost any situation, but they are not always available. The same is true of *pine needles*. *Shredded bark* or *wood chips* are good in shrub borders or woodland gardens, but they can be too coarse for flowerbeds. *Chopped straw* is good in flowerbeds but it's not as attractive as

leaves. Mulch prairie and meadow gardens at planting time with a light layer of chopped, weed-free straw 1 to 2 inches deep.

It is a good idea to surround all newly planted woody plants with a ring of organic mulch 2 to 4 inches thick. Keep the mulch a few inches away from the base of trees to discourage gnawing mice from hiding there in winter. Use mulch to protect the thin bark of lawn trees from the lawnmower and to keep the weed whipper away from trunks. Once trees are large enough to have a hard, corky bark, you can eliminate the mulch. However, it is still a good idea to avoid hitting any tree with power equipment.

Replenish mulch as needed throughout the growing season. Once mixed borders and prairie gardens are established, they can be left unmulched, but it is still a good idea to topdress with compost annually.

Avoid using peat moss as mulch. It tends to form a nonpermeable crust that makes it difficult for water to penetrate to the soil. Black plastic should not be used as mulch, and rocks should only be used in gardens in the desert southwest or alpine gardens.

Taking the time to mulch landscape plants will really pay off in terms of weed control but also in reducing the need to water. Mulches also help make a landscape look more tended and cared for.

Ruby-Throated Hummingbird
Archilochus colubris

A single migration can become a nonstop flight of up to 500 miles in one day. Their high energy needs require that abundant supplies of nectar be available throughout the migration corridor.

Range: Migrates from overwintering grounds in Mexico and Central America to the central and eastern United States and southern Canada.

Nectar Sources: Flowers that appeal most to hummingbirds include species with red or orange coloration; long, tubular flower shape; and lots of dilute nectar. Favorites include trumpet honeysuckle, salvias, monardas, and cardinal flower, which relies on hummingbirds for pollination. Spring migrations coincide with flowering periods of red buckeye and columbines.

Other Food: Spiders and tiny insects such as flies, gnats, and aphids as a source of fat and protein.

Larry E. Swanson

Fertilizing

If you've amended the soil with organic matter before planting and you keep plants mulched, most native flowers and groundcovers will not need additional fertilizer. In fact, it may actually be harmful, encouraging growth of exotic weeds at the expense of native plants. If a soil test indicates a need to improve soil fertility, there are several organic products you can use, including compost, rotted manure, peat moss, bone meal, blood meal, fish emulsion, soybean meal, and rock phosphate. After the initial application, yearly addition of finished compost to the surface should be enough to maintain adequate fertility. The best thing you can do for your garden plants is to apply a 1- to 2-inch layer of well-rotted manure or compost around plants in early spring or fall.

Established grasses and ferns rarely need fertilization; too much nitrogen can result in lodging (flopping over). Leaf color and vigor are good guides to nitrogen requirements. If foliage is off color, consider a soil test to see if your soil is lacking in certain elements.

Most woody plants will benefit from a spring application of fertilizer, but especially trees that are three to five years old. Spread a layer of rotted manure or compost around each plant or use Milorganite or fish emulsion. If possible, allow leaves or needles to fall and decay under trees to return nutrients to the soil.

Weed Control

Weeds are *always* a problem for gardeners, even in established landscapes. The best way to keep weeds under control is a good defense. Remove weeds before planting your garden, if possible. It is especially important to remove all grassy weeds before planting, since it is very difficult to remove grass weeds from plantings. If not eliminated, weedy perennial grasses such as quackgrass and canary reed grass will overwhelm desirable plants. Once your garden is prepared, keep the bare soil covered with mulch.

Once your garden is planted and mulched, you'll still need to invest a small amount of time in weed control. Weeds are easiest to pull when they are young and the soil is moist. Try to pull or cut back annual weeds before they go to seed. By taking a weekly walk through your garden after a rain, you should be able to keep weeds under control. Be sure to remove the entire plant root. Use a weeding tool to get leverage if needed.

NATIVE BUZZ

Great Black Wasp
Sphex pensylvanicus

. . . .

These large wasps are important in controlling the grasshopper and katydid populations, as well as pollinating many plants. A single female can capture 16 grasshoppers in one day. Adults build underground nests, where they bring insects to their young. They only sting humans if they are treated maliciously.

Range: Most of North America, except the Northwest.

Habitat: Open and second-growth habitats, gardens, and suburbs.

Larval Food: Living insects that the females paralyze and carry to the underground nest.

Adult Food: Important pollinators of milkweeds and rattlesnake master (*Eryngium yuccifolium*). Also seeks nectar from mountain mints, goldenrods, and buttonbush (*Cephalanthus occidentalis*).

If you have persistent perennial weeds such as thistle or quackgrass in an established garden and hand pulling has not been effective, you may want to consider spot treatments with a nonselective herbicide (containing glysophate). To apply it without harming yourself or nearby desirable plants, choose a calm day; protect yourself with long sleeves, safety glasses, and gloves; and carefully but thoroughly spot-spray individual weeds. If you're concerned about the potential hazards of using chemical herbicides, there are alternative herbicides such as those made from potassium salts of fatty acids. You can also use horticultural vinegar, boiling water, or a butane torch.

In woodland gardens where woody plants such as buckthorn, poison ivy, and raspberries can become weedy, control will require a little more effort. You can pull or dig up smaller specimens by hand, but larger plants may require the use of a nonselective herbicide. Cut the woody trunk low to the ground and use a disposable foam paintbrush to immediately apply a triclopyr-based herbicide labeled for woody plants such as poison ivy or buckthorn on the fresh cut. The herbicide will work its way into the trunk, destroying the plants and any plants that grow from the same root system. If you are careful and selective about using these herbicides and do not use them near water, they can effectively control weeds in the garden while causing little harm to the environment.

Not all weeds come in on their own. Many "weeds" are actually good garden plants that are a little too prolific

Weeds come in from many sources, including neighbors' yards, surrounding fields, visiting birds, and even the wind. Most weeds have their origins in Europe or Asia, but not all. Certain species of native plants such as goldenrods (Canada goldenrod, *Solidago canadensis*, pictured) can become weedy in landscape situations.

when it comes to seed production. It is hard for plant lovers to get rid of any plant, but it is crucial that you thin out and/or divide garden plants regularly. Be ruthless in pulling out extra plants, and don't put the added stress on yourself of feeling like you need to find a new home for everything you pull out or divide. This adds to the task and makes it likely you will put it off until it's too late. A good time to do this is in spring when you are doing your initial weeding of your gardens.

Some native plants that can spread aggressively and take over large areas include bulblet fern (*Cystopteris bulbifera*), ostrich fern (*Matteuccia struthiopteris*), and other ferns monarda obedient plant mountain mint (*Pycnanthemum tenuifolium*) and goldenrods. If you want to use these plants in formal garden situations, you should plan on spending some time each spring pulling out some of the plants to keep them from overwhelming their neighbors. Usually one good pulling session in spring is enough to keep these plants from taking over.

To reduce the height of late-summer blooming perennials such as sneezeweed, cut plants back in spring.

If you are incorporating new plants into an established bed, use a stake or some other type of marker to remind yourself to give them extra water.

Watering

One of the main perks of using native plants is reducing or even eliminating the need for supplemental watering. If you've chosen plants correctly, improved the water-holding capacity of sandy soils by adding organic matter, and have covered the soil with organic mulch, then established native plants rarely need supplemental watering.

However, almost all plants—drought-tolerant natives included—need supplemental water while becoming established. Keep soil adequately moist until new plants have a full year of growth on them. All trees, shrubs, and vines need to be watered regularly at least the first full year after planting. In hot weather they may need supplemental water once or twice a week. If the autumn is dry, continue watering until the first hard frost. Once fully established—after three to four years—most native woody plants should be self-sufficient as far as watering.

Encourage deep rooting by watering less often and more deeply. The most efficient way to water is to apply water to the soil, not the plants. Avoid overhead sprinklers. Not only are they inefficient, but also the wet foliage can lead to disease problems on plants.

Controlling Plant Height

One of the major complaints about native plantings is that they look messy. A big part of this comes from taller plants that flop over, either in the garden or along paths,

86

Use stakes and twine to support taller plants that aren't supported by nearby plants.

sidewalks, and driveways. There are several things you can do to avoid this. You can simply avoid using these taller plants, but that's no fun! All gardens need varying heights and textures. Staking is a popular solution, but it takes a lot of time and needs to be done within a specific window of time.

One technique to reduce the height of late summer and fall-blooming perennials is to cut them back in mid-spring. To do this, prune back plants to 6 to 10 inches, or about half their original height. This may seem ruthless at the time, but the plants will soon bounce back and you won't even be able to tell the cuts were made. And your reward will be a compact, often heavier blooming plant that won't require staking. Blooming may also be delayed a few days or a week, but this can also be used to your advantage: by pruning back only the plants in the front of a grouping, you will get an extended bloom time.

Some plants shouldn't be cut back in spring. These include blanket flowers, gentians (*Gentiana* species),

Michigan lily (*Lilium michiganense*), false indigos, blazing stars, royal catchfly, and vervains. Sprawling plants look messy, so you should plan to provide some type of support for these plants. In a closely planted informal garden, grasses and nearby plants can provide natural support. For the flower border, many systems using hoops and sticks of wood or metal are available from nurseries. Use small tomato cages for bushy plants. Long-stemmed plants will need a stake for every blooming stem. Get stakes in the ground as early as possible to avoid root damage, and loosely tie plants to the stake with inconspicuous green or brown twine.

Managing Natives

Almost every gardener wants more flowers. And a common complaint against using native plants is that they don't bloom as long as many exotics. The best solution for this is to plant a wider variety of plants with an extended range of bloom times. You can also plan to do some deadheading, or removing of spent flowers, before they go to seed. Cut back to the next set of leaves to encourage new buds to open. Many native perennials will have an extended bloom time if you deadhead them regularly. These include tickseeds, blanket flowers, oxeye, hairy false goldenaster (*Heterotheca villosa*), bluets (*Houstonia longifolia*), wild sweet William, obedient plant, prairie coneflower, black-eyed Susans, and spiderworts.

Many native plants are heavy reseeders. They needed this adaptation to make sure they were able to reproduce in the highly competitive native plant communities in which they evolved. Only a small percentage of seeds would survive to germinate and grow into mature plants. But in gardens, where competition is less, the soil is richer, and the water is usually more plentiful, a high percentage of seeds germinate and grow into plants. These extra plants turn into weeds in your garden.

It is important that you learn what plants are heavy seeders and then plan to deadhead them or weed out unwanted seedlings each spring. This list includes tickseeds, rattlesnake master (*Eryngium yuccifolium*), prairie coneflower, sneezeweeds, hairy false goldenaster, bee balm, spiderworts, black-eyed Susans, wild petunia, and goldenrods.

Along these same lines, learn which plants are short lived: bluets (*Houstonia* species), golden alexanders (*Zizia aurea*), and cardinal flower, to name a few. Make sure you allow some seedlings to remain to fill in as older plants fade away. With time, you will come to recognize the seedling stage of the plants in your garden and know whether to pull them or allow them to grow on.

Many plants have flowers that turn into showy seedheads that offer winter interest or seeds for birds. It is nice to allow these flowers to remain whenever possible. But some plants have flowers that turn brown after flowering and detract from the more attractive foliage. By removing spent flowers, you will get a nicer looking plant for the remainder of the gardening season. Consider removing spent flowers from yarrows (*Achillea* species), queen of the prairie (*Filipendula rubra*), alumroots, obedient plant, wild petunia, blue-eyed grasses (*Sisyrinchium* species), spiderworts, and hoary vervain.

Some plants don't really have showy seedheads and can be gently cut back after flowering to improve their shape and overall appearance in the late-summer garden. These include blue stars, purple poppy mallows (*Callirhoe* species), harebell, large-flowered tickseed, obedient plant, spiderworts, and hoary vervain.

Dividing Perennials

If you are growing perennials, ferns, and grasses in mixed borders or foundation plantings, they will benefit

Bumblebees
Bombus species

• •

There are about 40 species of bumblebees in North America. Bumblebees are able to fly in cooler temperatures and lower light levels than many other bees. Many plants depend on them to achieve pollination, and the decline of bumblebees can have far-ranging ecological and economic impacts.

Range: Throughout northern temperate regions.

Habitat: Nests in rodent holes, leaf piles, and other premade cavities in the ground, flying about 1 mile.

Nectar Source: Bumblebees are important pollinators of many native as well as nonnative plants, especially in cooler climates. They are generalists, not dependent on any one flower type.

Spiderwort (*Tradescantia ohiensis*) and large-flowered tickseed are beautiful additions to gardens. But they both reseed prolifically. If you want to use them in a small garden, deadhead them regularly and pull unwanted seedlings as soon as they are spotted.

not only encourages healthier plants, it also helps native plants, which often have a more irregular growth habit, look neater and tidier in the landscape.

Many native shrubs and small trees have a suckering growth habit, meaning they send up shoots at the base. This is a survival trait that allows them to survive when eaten back by animals. However, this trait is often undesirable in the garden. Plan to get rid of suckers on hazelnuts (*Corylus* species), chokeberries, dogwoods, plums and cherries (*Prunus* species), and serviceberries if you want them to remain as specimen plants and not turn into thickets.

Some native shrubs are best treated like herbaceous perennials in the garden. Cutting them back to ground in spring helps invigorate them and produce bushier, more compact plants. These include leadplant, New Jersey tea, virgin's bower, and summersweet.

from being divided every three or four years. Dividing prevents overcrowding and keeps the plants healthy, vigorous, and more prone to flower production. *Iris* species, monardas, obedient plant (*Physostegia virginiana*), wild onions, blue-eyed grasses (*Sisyrinchium* species), and Culver's root (*Veronicastrum virginicum*) tend to turn into large expanses of nondescript foliage if they are not divided regularly.

The best time to divide most plants is early spring so they have a full growing season to recover. However, very early spring-flowering plants are best divided in fall when they are dormant so as not to interfere with flower and seed production.

To divide herbaceous plants, simply unearth the plant with a spade or trowel, shake excess soil from roots, pull or cut apart rooted sections, and replant. With grasses, dig up a whole clump, cutting it up like a pie, removing any dead parts in the center of the clump, and then replanting what is needed. Dividing mature grass clumps can be difficult and may require the use of an ax or saw to separate the large clumps into useable transplants.

Pruning Woody Plants

Almost every tree, shrub, and vine in your landscape will need pruning at one time or another, and the better job you do, the healthier your plants will be. Proper pruning

NATIVE KNOW-HOW
Cutting Back Grasses

On established grass plants, leave the foliage so you and the birds can enjoy the flowers in winter. Cut back plants in late winter before new growth begins. If you only have a few plants, use a hand pruners or hedge shears. A string trimmer can be used if you have a large number of grasses to cut back. If practical, burning is also effective.

The keys to successful pruning are appropriate timing and the right tools. Most native trees and shrubs are best pruned in their dormant period, reducing the chance of infection from insects and diseases. You can also see a deciduous plant's silhouette when the leaves are off. Remove any dead, damaged, or diseased parts anytime, cutting back to just above a healthy, outfacing bud.

Evergreen conifers should be pruned in late spring and early summer just after you see new growth. Spring-blooming shrubs begin setting their flower buds soon after flowering and should be pruned as soon as possible after flowering. If you prune them in winter or spring, you will be cutting off their flower buds; this won't kill them, it will just mean you won't have flowers for one season. Summer-flowering shrubs are best pruned in early spring. Don't wait too long, however, or you may cut off flower buds, which start to form in spring. Shrubs that have become overgrown will benefit from renewal pruning; cut the plants back to 4 to 6 inches from the ground in early spring. Surround them with a layer of compost or rotted manure and water them well to help them recover.

Pruning tools must be sharp and clean. The basic pruning tool is a hand-held bypass pruner. Larger shrubs and small trees require loppers and a pruning saw. If you have large trees in need of major pruning, you should have it done by a professional tree trimmer.

Pruning is somewhat of a subjective activity, but there are some basic rules to follow. Always remove dead wood and branches that rub against one another. It is usually best to try to maintain the natural shape of a tree, especially with evergreens. On trees, remove branches that have narrow-angled crotches as these branches are weaker than wide branches and are likely to split as the tree gets older. Remove lower branches only if they interfere with the use of the areas under the tree.

Pruning large trees is a way to alter available light. Don't be afraid to limb up large shade trees by removing some of the lower branches. This change will allow more light to penetrate the garden underneath and allow you to grow a wider variety of plants. In general, do not remove more than one-third of the branches in one pruning.

Pest Management

No plant looks nice when it's suffering from insect or disease damage or has been eaten back by deer or rabbits. Fortunately, most native plants are low on the list of plants seriously affected by pests.

NATIVE KNOW-HOW
Training and Pruning Vines

Star Showers® Virginia creeper (*Parthenocissus quinquefolia* 'Monham') being trained to cover a trellis.

Begin training and anchoring vines when they are young. You can tie them with soft twine or gently wrap the young stems around or through supports. Vines require pruning throughout their lives to look good and function properly. They may also need to be pruned to prevent property damage or blockage of windows or doors. You should also plan to remove dead and damaged stems whenever you see them. And most flowering vines need to be pruned regularly so that the flowers form all along the vine rather than just at the ends. The timing of pruning is similar to shrubs, right after blooming for early-flowering species and early spring for later-flowering species.

A good pruning cut done during the dormant season will not require any paint or wound covering.

insecticides. They kill too many beneficial insects, including bees and butterflies.

Keep in mind that many problems are due to cultural conditions, not pests. Yellowing or browning foliage, stunted growth, and buds that rot before opening could be signs that you have poor soil drainage or your plants are overcrowded. Once again, making sure you have the right plant for the site and the appropriate soil conditions are the best ways to avoid such problems.

Some insects and diseases do regularly plague natives. These include mildews, aster yellows, rusts, leaf spots and feeding from aphids, leaf miners, and plant bugs. These problems are usually not fatal, but they can make plants quite unsightly. Pesticides are not the answer. Better solutions include avoiding these plants in small gardens where they will really stand out. Or, plant them in the middle or back of the garden where the damage will not be out front and center. There are also some cultivars available that are less susceptible to diseases.

Diseases

Because native plants are adapted to a particular region, diseases and viruses are rare. If they do occur, they are rarely serious and can usually be prevented the next year by altering cultural practices, such as changing watering habits or thinning out branches. Prevention in the form of good site selection and proper planting distance is the best way to avoid disease problems. If problems become severe, you'll need to pull up the infected plants and choose another plant for that site. Here are some diseases you may find in your native-plants landscape.

Aster Yellows Possible hosts: asters, black-eyed Susans, blanket flowers, coneflowers, sneezeweeds, tickseeds

Symptoms: Discoloration and irregular, stunted growth. Flowers often do not open.

What to do: Get rid of infected plants; they will not recover. Keep weeds in check since they can harbor the virus.

Leaf and Twig Blights Possible hosts: American hornbeam, flowering dogwood, hydrangeas, junipers, sourwood

Symptoms: Dark green, water-soaked spots appear in tissue, and leaves and twigs become blackened and shriveled. Tender growth often develops a shepherd's crook and wilts and dies. Cankers develop on the stems.

The key to pest management is to really get to know your gardens and the plants in them. Keep your eyes open on daily walks. The earlier you spot problems, the easier they are to control. If you spot a problem, identify it correctly (get help from a local expert, if needed), find out what is causing it, and decide if it is serious enough to warrant attention. Most pest problems are purely cosmetic and won't do any lasting damage to your plants.

You have to decide what your level of tolerance is and determine whether you want to take action or live with the problem. If you want to welcome butterflies and birds to your garden, you'll have to learn to live with the few holes in leaves that come from caterpillars feeding. If you find a heavily damaged plant, put in a few more plants to compensate for what you'll be sharing with the caterpillars. Whatever insect problems you face, don't resort to

What to do: Provide good air circulation. Clean up plant debris. Remove infested plant parts. Cover soil with mulch. Avoid overhead watering. Select resistant cultivars.

Leaf Spots POSSIBLE HOSTS: Allegheny spurge, American hornbeam, asters, beardtongues, black-eyed Susans, flowering dogwoods, goldenrods, hollies, mahonias, mountain laurel, New Jersey tea, serviceberries, sneezeweeds, sourwood, viburnums

SYMPTOMS: Spots vary in size and color and can be small, distinct areas or coalesce to form large, irregular shapes. Spots often have concentric rings or dark margins. Leaves may turn yellow and drop.

WHAT TO DO: Provide good air circulation. Clean up plant debris. Remove infested plant parts. Cover soil with mulch. Avoid overhead watering. Select resistant cultivars.

Powdery Mildew POSSIBLE HOSTS: asters, blanket flowers, bush honeysuckle, flowering dogwoods, fringetree, hackberries, hollies, hydrangeas, Joe-pye weeds, monardas, New Jersey tea, ninebarks, oxeyes, phloxes, scarlet sage, serviceberries, sneezeweeds, viburnums

SYMPTOMS: Whitish powdery patches on leaf surfaces. As the disease progresses, black spots may appear in the powder. Leaves, flowers, and fruits may be misshapen.

WHAT TO DO: Provide good air circulation by pruning out inside branches and removing some nearby plants. Clean up plant debris. Remove infested plant parts. Cover soil with mulch. Avoid overhead watering. Select resistant cultivars. Cornell University has developed a baking-soda-based spray for fighting powdery mildew. Mix 1 tablespoon baking soda and 1 tablespoon horticultural oil with 1 gallon of water. Spray each plant completely about once a week, starting before infections appear.

Root Rots POSSIBLE HOSTS: anise hyssop, bloodroot, dwarf fothergilla, phloxes, prairie smoke, tickseeds

SYMPTOMS: Leaves appear drought-stressed and may turn color. They eventually die and fall off. Perennial plants may survive several years before the disease becomes fatal.

WHAT TO DO: Improve soil drainage. Remove diseased plants. Dig out and replace soil to a depth of 8 inches around plants.

Rusts POSSIBLE HOSTS: asters, goldenrods, hawthorns, mahonias, pines, serviceberries, sneezeweeds

SYMPTOMS: Yellow, orange, or brown spots usually appear first on the undersides of leaves and stems. Plants are usually weak and stunted and have yellow leaves that wither and drop early; severely infected plants may die. Some rusts, such as cedar-hawthorn rust, alternate between two plant hosts, and you need both plants present within a certain distance for the disease to occur.

WHAT TO DO: Clean up plant debris. Remove alternate hosts, if possible. Remove diseased plant parts. Plant resistant cultivars.

Leaf spot on black-eyed Susan.

Powdery mildew on monarda.

Stem and Trunk Cankers Possible hosts: American hornbeam, flowering dogwoods, redbuds

Symptoms: Areas on a stem, trunk, or branch that are sunken or raised and are usually dry and dead and often discolored. Cankers may ooze or bleed. Infected branches will die back and trunk cankers may girdle and kill entire trees.

What to do: Avoid injury to bark and stems. Prune out infected branches. Improve plant health with watering, mulching, and fertilizing.

Rust on dotted hawthorn.

Insect Pests

After emphasizing the importance of welcoming insects to your garden throughout the rest of this book, it seems inappropriate to talk about insect "pests." But there are some insects such as Japanese beetles that can really wreak havoc on gardens. By including a wide range of native plants in your landscape, you will encourage natural predators and birds, which help keep things in check.

Never resort to using insecticides. Not only are they toxic to you and your garden guests, they destroy too many beneficial insects and are harmful to birds. It's cruel to lure wildlife to your landscape and then use insecticides and other pesticides that can poison and destroy them. If an insect problem becomes so bad that the health of your plant is questionable, you should consider replacing the plant with something better suited to the conditions.

Keep in mind that insects may chew and tatter leaves by the season's end, but this is usually not a serious problem for most plants. If any of your trees or shrubs has severely infested branches, prune the branches off well beyond the problem and dispose of them off site. Here are some insects that may cause problems in your native-plant landscape.

Aphids Possible hosts: Allegheny spurge, basswood, honeysuckles, junipers, mahonias, milkweeds, oxeyes, tickseeds

Symptoms: Aphids are small (up to ¼ inch), somewhat pear-shaped, soft-bodied insects. They can be orange, green, black, or white. Foliage turns pale or has yellow spots. Whole leaves may turn yellow or brown, or may be curled, puckered, or stunted. Flower buds may be seriously damaged and the blossoms distorted. A sticky honeydew residue is another sign of aphid feeding.

What to do: Dislodge them by spraying the foliage daily with a hard spray from the garden hose. Wipe aphids off the leaves with a cloth, if practical. Discourage lush, new growth by reducing the amount of nitrogen added to the garden and avoiding heavy pruning in early spring.

Bagworms Possible hosts: cedars, junipers

Symptoms: Plants usually are partially defoliated and weakened, but complete defoliation can occur. Protective 1- to 2-inch long bags formed by the larvae can be seen attached to a branch.

Aphids on Joe-pye weed.

What to do: Handpick the bags and destroy them. Encourage birds, which feed on sawflies.

Borers Possible hosts: flowering dogwoods, fringetree, mountain laurel, serviceberries

Symptoms: The larvae of various insects, mainly beetles, tunnel and feed under the bark, causing branch dieback, structural weakness, overall decline, and often death. Damage often appears in the upper branches of tree crowns first and progresses downward as the tree weakens. Common symptoms include sudden wilting and discoloration of foliage in the treetops and branch dieback. Infested trees will probably also exhibit D-shaped emergence holes and sinuous or zigzag patterns in their bark.

What to do: Most borers are secondary invaders on stressed plants, so select the proper planting site and keep plants healthy to prevent them. Avoid injury to trunks. Prune properly, and at the right time. Remove and destroy infested plant parts. Once infected, water, mulch, and fertilize to help plants fight off the damage.

Leaf Miners Possible hosts: basswood, birches, cedars, columbines, Joe-pye weeds, serviceberries

Symptoms: Affected leaves have light green to brown serpentine mines or tunnels; dark specks of excrement or tiny maggots may also be visible. Affected leaves may turn completely brown or yellow, look blistered or curled, or collapse.

What to do: Keep gardens weed-free. Cultivate soil in fall to expose insects to birds and other predators. Destroy

Leaf miner damage on columbine.

infested plant parts. Crush the small eggs or tunneling insects when seen in the leaves.

Plant Bugs Possible hosts: Most plants are potential hosts for some type of plant bug.

Symptoms: Both the nymphs and adults damage plants by sucking juices. Small, discolored areas appear on leaves and, after several weeks, the dead tissue may drop out leaving small holes. Foliage and flower buds can be distorted. Leaves may wilt, curl, and turn brown.

What to do: Tolerate the damage, since it is usually only cosmetic. Remove leaf litter to get rid of overwintering sites. Learn to identify egg masses and prune them out in winter, when practical.

Four-lined plant bug damage on vervain.

Sawflies Possible hosts: pines, serviceberries

Symptoms: Plants have sparse, patchy foliage or may become completely defoliated. Needles appear brown, wilted, or strawlike. You may see clusters of larvae feeding on needles or leaves.

What to do: Maintain plant vigor, watering during dry weather. Encourage birds, which feed on sawflies. Clip off heavily infested branches and place in plastic bag to destroy

Scales Possible hosts: Allegheny spurge, basswood, fringetree, magnolias, mahonias, pines, serviceberries

Symptoms: Scales are sucking insects with hard or soft scale coverings. After hatching, the young scales wander over the plant searching for a spot in which to settle and

Katydids are a favorite food of insect-feeding birds.

begin producing their distinctive shell coverings. Adults are sedentary. The most common symptom is yellow or dropping leaves. Plants may also be stunted and covered with sticky honeydew that attracts ants. You will need a hand lens to detect the tiny young scales; they will resemble minute, animated pancakes.

WHAT TO DO: Early infestations can be scraped off plants or dabbed with a cotton swab dipped in rubbing alcohol. Heavily infested plants can be cut back to the ground in spring, if possible.

Slugs POSSIBLE HOSTS: Allegheny spurge, dwarf crested iris, ferns, wild gingers

SYMPTOMS: Slugs are not true insects, but rather soft-bodied, soil-dwelling gastropod related to snails. They are ½ to 3 inches long and can be gray, black, or brown. Slugs have rasping mouth parts and produce holes in leaves, stems, flowers, and fruits. The succulent tissue of young seedlings and bulbs are especially susceptible to slug damage. Sometimes slugs may shear off whole leaves.

WHAT TO DO: Install physical barriers, such as plastic-bottle cloches, or sprinkle lime, eggshells, or sawdust around plants. Slugs are attracted to saucers or plastic pots of milk or beer. Lay rolled-up newspaper or boards on the soil. Slugs will seek out these protected areas and can be easily removed. Drop them in a bucket of a 5 percent alcohol-water solution or soapy water, or spray the slugs with an ammonia-water solution. Toads, frogs,

and beetles eat slugs, and they are worth encouraging in your garden.

Spider Mites POSSIBLE HOSTS: Allegheny spurge, basswood, beardtongues, cedars, hollies, phloxes, potentilla, summersweet

SYMPTOMS: Spider mites suck juices from plants, causing them to look stippled, dull, and unhealthy. Leaves become bronzed, curled, and completely enveloped in webbing when infestations are severe. Leaves may drop and plants may suffer from overall reduction in vitality.

WHAT TO DO: Dislodge mites by spraying plants, including the undersides of leaves, with a strong stream of water. Remove severely infested plants or plant parts.

Other Problems of Trees

While some insect and disease problems, such as oak wilt, ash borer, and Dutch elm disease, can be fatal, most problems are purely cosmetic and don't really threaten the tree's life. On large trees, control measures are rarely practical.

Bigger problems on trees often come in the form of mechanical damage. Once a tree's bark is girdled by animal feeding or lawn mower or weed-whipper damage, it loses its ability to take up water and it will die. Prevent animal damage by wrapping young trees with cylinders or hardware cloth that is placed several inches into the soil and extends up to the lowest branch. This hardware

Salt placed on roads and sidewalks in winter can be a problem for some trees, especially evergreens. Avoid planting sensitive trees such as pines near roadways.

cloth can be removed once the tree's bark is hard and corky. An organic mulch around the base of the trunk will keep lawn mowers and weed whippers away.

Some thin-barked trees such as maples and mountain ashes need to be protected from winter sunscald while they are young. Trees are susceptible to sunscald until they have developed a thick corky trunk. Wrapping trees with a tree wrap made of weather-resistant paper in fall minimizes sunscald.

Some cultural-caused problems to watch for on young trees are iron chlorosis (acidify soil to lower pH) and leaf scorch (water trees well during dry periods and mulch soil). The best defense against insect and disease problems is a vigorously growing tree. By choosing a tree appropriate for your site conditions and providing it with the necessary nutrients and ample water, most pest problems will not become serious.

Deer & Rabbits

Insects aren't the only pests you'll find in your garden. Deer and rabbits are often more serious and difficult to control. There are many repellents available. However, all of them are temporary solutions, and they require a lot of time and effort to be effective, especially against deer.

Rabbits are repelled by blood meal or hot-pepper spray, which needs to be applied after every rain. To revive eaten plants, fertilize with a mixture of 1 tablespoon fish emulsion in 1 gallon of water.

Owning a large dog can be effective in deterring deer. But the best long-term solution for a serious deer problem is to install some type of fencing, which must be at least 8 feet tall to be effective.

You can also make plant choices based on deer feeding. For starters, plant a wide variety of plants so an entire section of your landscape won't be eliminated in one

SPECIAL-USE NATIVES
Deer-Resistant Plants

Flowers, Ferns & Groundcovers
Actaea species (bugbane, baneberries)
Agastache species (hyssops)
Allium species (wild onions)
Amsonia species (blue stars)
Aquilegia species (columbines)
Asarum species (wild gingers)
Asclepias species (milkweeds)
Baptisia species (false indigos)
Campanula rotundifolia (harebell)
Chelone species (turtleheads)
Dicentra species (bleeding hearts)
Dodecatheon species (shooting stars)
Echinacea species (purple coneflowers)
Eutrochium species (Joe-pye weeds)
Gaillardia species (blanket flowers)
Geranium maculatum (wild geranium)
Geum triflorum (prairie smoke)
Gillenia trifoliata (Bowman's root)
Helenium species (sneezeweeds)
Heuchera americana (alumroot)
Iris cristata (dwarf crested iris)
Lobelia species (cardinal flower, lobelia)
Mertensia virginica (Virginia bluebells)
Monarda species (bee balms)
Pachysandra procumbens (Allegheny spurge)
Penstemon species (beardtongues)
Polemonium reptans (spreading Jacob's ladder)
Pulsatilla patens (pasque flower)
Ratibida pinnata (prairie coneflower)
Rudbeckia species (black-eyed Susans, coneflowers)
Salvia species (sages)
Sanguinaria canadensis (bloodroot)
Silene species (royal catchfly, fire pink)
Solidago species (goldenrods)
Spigelia marilandica (Indian-pink)
Stokesia laevis (Stokes' aster)
Symphyotrichum species (asters)
Thermopsis villosa (false lupine)
Tiarella cordifolia (foamflower)
Verbena species (vervains)
Yucca species (yuccas)

Grasses & Sedges
Bouteloua species (grama grasses)
Carex pensylvanica (Pennsylvania sedge)
Chasmanthium latifolium (northern sea oats)
Deschampsia species (hair grasses)
Muhlenbergia species (muhly grasses)
Panicum virgatum (switchgrass)
Schizachyrium scoparium (little bluestem)
Sporobolus heterolepis (prairie dropseed)
Sorghastrum nutans (indiangrass)

Shrubs, Vines & Small Trees
Calycanthus floridus (sweetshrub)
Ceanothus americanus (New Jersey tea)
Clematis virginiana (virgin's bower)
Dasiphora fruticosa (potentilla)
Gelsemium sempervirens (Carolina jessamine)
Hamamelis species (witch hazels)
Ilex species (winterberry, hollies)
Juniperus species (junipers)
Lindera benzoin (spicebush)
Lonicera sempervirens (trumpet honeysuckle)
Mahonia species (Oregon grape, creeping mahonia)
Ptelea trifoliata (hop tree)
Wisteria species (wisterias)

Trees
Acer species (maples)
Betula species (birches)
Cercis canadensis (Eastern redbud)
Gymnocladus dioicus (Kentucky coffee tree)
Halesia species (silverbells)
Magnolia species (magnolias)
Picea species (spruces)
Quercus species (oaks)

Rabbit damage on a shrub.

meal. Although no plant can really be considered "deer proof" under all conditions, deer generally avoid thorny and aromatic leaves, as well as plants with leathery, fuzzy, or hairy foliage.

Planting patterns can deter deer as well. Deer do not like to cross hedges or solid fences where they can't see what's on the other side. They do not like to force their way through dense shrubs or shrubs with thorns and firm branches. By massing plants, you will discourage deer from feeding in the center of the planting, where you can plant especially susceptible plants.

Once deciduous trees reach about 6 feet in height and their bark has become corky, they are out of reach of deer browsing. Young trees can be protected with a wire cage.

Consider this: Nonnative tropical annuals often require weekly watering, fertilizing, and deadheading to keep them going all summer, and nonnative perennials are often plagued by insects, diseases, and deer feeding, things that are rarely serious problems on natives. While native plants are certainly not maintenance-free, once established they usually require much less in the way of watering, fertilizing, and grooming than traditional landscape plants. This gives you more time to enjoy your garden and the native pollinators and birds it attracts and to concentrate on the tasks that make it more of an enjoyable hobby and less of a burden. It's your choice.

Deer damage on white cedar.

CHAPTER FIVE

Native Plants for Landscape Use

This chapter highlights some of the many North American native plants to consider. Featured plants were chosen based on their suitability for garden use; their availability in the nursery trade; their value to native insects, birds, and other wildlife; and their lower maintenance needs. Most are resistant to insect and disease problems and deer feeding and are adapted to natural rainfall amounts.

In each individual plant listing, you will find the information you need to help you decide if it is a good choice for your landscape. Each entry starts with the botanical name followed by the most recognized common names. Keep in mind that *many* plants will have more than one common name, so to verify that you are getting the correct plant, be sure to cross-check it with its botanical name.

The *Hardiness Zones* are the USDA Plant Hardiness Zones. See the map on page 36. *Size* refers to the mature size of the plant. Some plants take several years to reach their full height and width. The descriptive paragraph describes the plant's growth habit as well as the characteristics of the foliage, flowers, fruits, and bark, if

applicable. *Pollinator and Wildlife Value* provides information about the beneficial insects, butterflies, birds, and other wildlife that the plant attracts. *How to Use* offers suggestions for how the plant can be used in landscapes and gardens. *How to Grow and Maintain* covers information on soil, sunlight, maintenance, and the plant's susceptibility to pests, including insects, diseases, deer, and rabbits. *Beyond the Species* highlights related species and cultivars that are also worth considering for garden use. Cultivars are listed when they offer something to the landscape that the species doesn't, such as foliage color, compact growth habit, or disease resistance. Try to avoid choosing cultivars with very different flower colors or shapes, as this can make it difficult for native pollinators to recognize the plants.

In the US, if you want to know if a certain species is native in your state or even your county, go to www.plants.usda.gov. You can search by individual plant species or pull up a checklist for your state.

This well-designed landscape includes native flowers, trees, shrubs, and grasses.

NATIVE PLANTS FOR LANDSCAPE USE

Flowers, Ferns & Groundcovers

Growing ornamental plants—flowers, grasses, and groundcovers—is where you can really let your creativity shine. In most cases, these plants will all be chosen for their beauty, but they can also serve important practical roles in gardens, such as providing a haven for butterflies and pollinating insects rather than an oasis of lawn, as would be typical in this driveway turnaround garden.

100

NATIVE BUZZ

Leafcutter Bee
Megachile species

These native bees are usually seen midseason, June to mid-July. They cut the leaves of plants and use the fragments to form nest cells within the cavity. They sting only when handled, and their sting is very mild. They are solitary and don't produce colonies.

Range: Most of North America.

Habitat: Nest in pre-existing cavities found in wood and hollow stems of large, pithy plants such as roses.

Nectar Source: Especially fond of beardtongues, but visit many other native plants, and are important pollinators of many crop plants.

Larry E. Swanson

Actaea rubra
Red Baneberry

Zones: 2 to 8
Size: 20 to 30 inches tall

Baneberries are herbaceous perennials with a strong enough presence that they can serve as a shrub if needed. They have showy, dense clusters of fluffy white flowers that first appear in early to mid-spring and continue well into late spring. The flowers have small white petals, showy stamens, and a slight fragrance. The shiny red berries follow the flowers in mid- to late summer. Both the flowers and the berries rise well above attractive, deeply cut compound leaves. While the flowers and fruits are showy, it is this plant's structure and beautiful compound foliage that carries it through the growing season.

NOTE: All parts of red and white baneberry are poisonous to humans, with the greatest concentration of oil in the roots and berries.

Pollinator & Wildlife Value: Sweat bees visit the flowers looking for nectar and end up collecting pollen. Though poisonous to people, the berries are enjoyed by birds such as yellow-bellied sapsucker, gray-cheeked thrush, robin, brown thrasher, gray catbird, and grouse. Some mammals eat the fruits.

How to Use: Baneberries are well suited to woodland or shade gardens, where they will be an attractive addition throughout the growing season. Mature plants have a shrublike appearance, so they are good in foundation plantings and mixed borders. Place them where the showy fruits will be enjoyed in late summer; zigzag goldenrod and woodland asters are good companions then. Flowering plants combine nicely with other taller woodland plants such as ferns, columbines, and wild geranium.

How to Grow & Maintain: Prefers moist, humus-rich, slightly acidic soil in partial to full shade. Once established, baneberries require little care and have no serious pest problems. They spread slowly to form showy clumps that seldom need division. Self-sown seedlings may appear. Deer and rabbits find the foliage unpalatable.

Beyond the Species: White baneberry (*A. pachypoda*) is similar to red baneberry except for fruit color, which is white with a single black dot. It is also called doll's eyes because the berries resemble the china eyes once used in dolls. Zones 3 to 8. 'Misty Blue' is a selection with very nice bluish-green foliage.

101

Actaea pachypoda

Adiantum pedatum
Maidenhair Fern

Zones: 2 to 8
Size: 12 to 24 inches tall

Adiantum pedatum

Of all the native ferns, maidenhair fern is probably the most popular and the best adapted for garden use. It is easy to grow and it has a lot to offer in terms of color, texture, hardiness, and tolerance of tough conditions. This elegant fern is attractive from spring through fall, with its horizontal, fan-shaped fronds—a unique arrangement among native ferns. The delicate, arching branches and wiry, shiny, black stems give it a fine texture. The lacy fronds are green throughout summer, turning golden yellow in fall.

Pollinator & Wildlife Value: Provides cover for toads, lizards, and other small animals and birds.

How to Use: This delicate fern adds a certain softness to the landscape and can be used in almost any shady or partial shade situation. It's great for taking the edginess off stone walls or brickwork. Like most ferns, it does well and looks good when planted alongside water features. Since the fronds do not fully mature until late spring, maidenhair fern is a good companion for spring ephemerals and bulbs, which die back in early summer.

Its fine texture is especially effective with coarse-textured plants; however, there really isn't a shade or woodland plant that maidenhair fern doesn't combine well with. Use it as a groundcover, under large shrubs and small trees, in the dry shade under large trees, in rain gardens, or in a shady rock garden. It also makes a nice edging plant along woodland paths.

How to Grow & Maintain: Prefers a rich, organic, slightly acidic soil in partial to full shade but tolerates alkaline soils, low fertility, and all but very dry soils. The only time this tough fern needs careful handling is during planting or transplanting, when you need to avoid damaging the thin stems. Plant it in groups, spaced about 18 inches apart, or tucked here and there in a shade garden. With time, 2-foot-wide clumps will cover the ground. It requires adequate water during establishment, but is quite drought tolerant once established; fronds may turn brown in late summer during dry years. It does not have any serious insect or disease problems. Deer usually avoid it.

Agastache foeniculum
Anise Hyssop, Blue Giant Hyssop

Zones: 3 to 9
Size: 2 to 4 feet tall

Agastache foeniculum

Anise hyssop has small, blue-purple flowers tightly packed into a 4- to 5-inch terminal spike starting in midsummer and continuing well into fall. The fragrant, anise-scented leaves are 2 to 3 inches long, lance-shaped, pointed with serrated margins, and whitish underneath. Plant growth habit is upright: it grows taller than it does wide, with several strong central stems and many side branches.

Pollinator & Wildlife Value: Flowers are attractive to many types of bees, including native, digger, leaf-cutting, bumble-, and honeybees, as well as butterflies and hummingbirds.

How to Use: Anise hyssop adapts well to perennial gardens, cottage gardens, or mixed borders, where it offers great color and an upright form. Contrast the blue-purple color with other sun-loving perennials such as black-eyed Susan, oxeye, goldenrods, and coneflowers. It is well suited to rain gardens and prairie gardens and looks especially nice with little bluestem grass. Grow it in herb gardens and harvest the anise-scented, edible leaves for salads, teas, and other drinks. It is a good fresh-cut or dried flower.

How to Grow & Maintain: Prefers full sun to light shade in well-drained soil. Does well in low-fertility soils and is very drought tolerant once established. Plants self-sow, but seedlings are easily weeded out. You can remove the spent flower heads before they drop their seeds, but this means losing some of the purple color since seeds start dropping before the flower has turned completely brown. Staking may be required. Or plants may be cut back to about a foot tall in late spring to keep them more compact. Deadhead to promote more blooms. No serious pest problems. Crown rot may occur in poorly drained soils. Plants may also get rust, powdery mildew, and leaf spots. The anise scent of the foliage repels deer, rabbits, and leaf-chewing insects.

Beyond the Species: Thread-leaf giant hyssop (*A. rupestris*) is a good choice for southwestern gardens in Zones 5 to 9. It grows 2 to 5 feet tall and thrives in hot, sunny, well-drained soil. Hummingbirds love the rosy orange flowers, which are set off nicely by the silver foliage. 'Apache Sunset' is a selection with orange-pink flowers and smoky gray leaves. It typically stays under 2 feet in height.

Allium cernuum
Nodding Onion

Zones: 3 to 9
Size: 12 to 24 inches tall

Nodding onion grows from bulbs that look like miniature versions of cultivated onions. The grasslike, flattened leaves grow about 12 inches long in neat clumps that resemble chives. Its nodding flower clusters are held nicely above the foliage on slightly bent stems. They can be white to pink to lavender and bloom for about a month starting midsummer, followed by papery seedheads. All parts of the plant have a mild oniony scent when crushed.

Pollinator & Wildlife Value: Flowers attract hummingbirds, hairstreak butterflies, and several types of bees and beetles, which visit for nectar and leave with pollen.

How to Use: Nodding onion adds a touch of lavender to the garden in midsummer. Plant it with goldenrods, Stokes aster, butterfly milkweed, and hoary vervain. The foliage is attractive all season, and the seedheads are decorative in autumn. Use it in rock gardens, in the front of perennial borders, along paths and the edges of rain gardens, and in containers. It can be grown under black walnut trees.

How to Grow & Maintain: Prefers average to rich, well-drained soil in full sun to very light shade. Soil can be neutral to slightly alkaline. Plants naturalize by self-seeding and expand outward by bulb offsets in optimum growing conditions but rarely become pesky. Divide plants every third year or so in early spring or as they go dormant in fall to promote better flowering. Deadhead flowers before seeds set to control unwanted seedlings. No serious pest problems. Deer usually avoid this plant but may feed on young shoots in spring. Ground squirrels may feed on bulbs.

Beyond the Species: Prairie onion (*A. stellatum*) has smaller, rose to pink flowers that are more upward facing when open and bloom a little later. Plants grow 6 to 12 inches tall. It does well in cultivation when grown on a sunny exposure in a limy, rocky soil. Zones 3 to 8.

Allium cernuum

104

Amsonia tabernaemontana
Blue Star

Zones: 3 to 9
Size: 2 to 3 feet tall

Amsonia tabernaemontana

Blue star is among the best native perennials for garden use. This erect, clumping plant has clusters of very showy light blue, starlike flowers in late spring continuing well into early summer. The narrow, willow-shaped foliage is neat and tidy and turns an attractive golden yellow in fall.

Pollinator & Wildlife Value: Nectar source for butterflies, especially mourning cloaks, as well as hummingbirds, bees, and hummingbird moths.

How to Use: The long season of interest makes this plant a valuable addition to perennial gardens and mixed borders, where the dense, shrublike clumps add structure and mass. It can be grown as a single specimen or a massed planting, which is stunning in fall. Plant it with columbines and prairie phlox for a spring show, and Joe-pye weeds and asters for a striking fall display. It can be used in rain gardens.

How to Grow & Maintain: Prefers evenly moist soil in full sun or light shade. Tolerates heavy soil and some drought. Plants may require staking, especially if they are in shade, to keep them more upright. Plants can be cut back by one-third to one-half after flowering for a neater appearance going into fall and to reduce unwanted seedlings. Divide in fall as needed. Plants are long-lived and older plants can become woody and difficult to divide, so choose a site carefully. No serious pest problems, and deer avoid it.

Beyond the Species: Var. *salicifolia* has narrower leaves. 'Montana' is a compact-growing selection and has deeper blue flowers. It grows 18 to 24 inches tall. 'Short Stack' is a selection that only grows 10 to 18 inches tall. 'Blue Ice' is a popular hybrid (the other parent is unknown) that has deeper blue flowers and a longer bloom time.

Aquilegia canadensis
Wild Columbine, Canada Columbine

Zones: 2 to 9
Size: 12 to 24 inches tall

Wild columbine is an open, airy plant with unique flowers that dance above lush mounds of foliage. The nodding, upside-down, red and yellow flowers dangle from the tips of branching stems. The grayish leaves are compound, divided into lobed leaflets grouped in threes. It blooms midspring to early summer, and the attractive foliage usually dies back by late summer.

Pollinator & Wildlife Value: In some areas, the flowers bloom about the same time as returning hummingbirds, and they are an important nectar source for the exhausted migrators. Bees climb into the flowers to feed on nectar, which is also enjoyed by butterflies and hawk moths. Finches and buntings eat the seeds. Larvae of columbine duskywing butterfly, borer moth, columbine sawfly, and several leaf miner flies feed on the foliage.

How to Use: Grow this charming plant anywhere, from perennial gardens to cottage gardens to woodland borders. Include it in rock gardens or scatter it around a garden pool. Allow it to self-sow and form natural drifts in wild gardens. Plant it with ferns, prairie smoke, wild geranium, and Virginia bluebells for a showy spring display. In mixed borders, it looks nice with late tulips, hostas, iris, pulmonarias, peonies, and perennial geraniums. These other plants fill in when most of the columbine foliage dies back later in summer.

How to Grow & Maintain: Does well in a wide variety of conditions, including moist to dry, well-drained soil in full sun to almost full shade. Seedlings need moisture to establish, but mature plants survive dry spells. Garden plants are rather short-lived, usually about three years. They reseed, but not to the point of becoming a pest. Deadhead if you don't want plants to self-sow. Leaf miner feeding can cause tan tunnels or blotches. Cutting back upper foliage after flowering keeps plants looking neater. Deer and rabbits avoid the foliage.

Beyond the Species: 'Corbett' is a pale yellow selection that combines beautifully with blue forget-me-nots or blue phlox in partial shade. 'Little Lanterns' is a diminutive selection growing only 8 to 10 inches tall. Colorado columbine (*A. caerulea*) has beautiful upward-facing, white and purple-blue flowers on 18- to 30- inch plants. It does best in western gardens and at high elevations. 'Blue Star' is heat- and drought-tolerant. Zones 3 to 8. Yellow columbine (*A. chrysantha*) needs well-drained summer soil. It has yellow flowers on 18- to 24-inch plants. It does best in southwestern gardens and at high elevations. Zones 3 to 8.

Aquilegia canadensis

Asarum canadense

Wild Ginger, Canada Wild Ginger

Zones: 2 to 8
Size: 6 to 8 inches

Asarum canadense

Wild ginger has so many attributes it's difficult to know where to start. It tolerates light to heavy shade and, once established, even the dry shade found under large-canopied trees and along foundations. It spreads quickly via creeping rhizomes but rarely becomes invasive or overtakes neighboring plants and is very easy to keep in bounds by pulling if needed. The elegant, heart-shaped, textured leaves can get up to 8 inches in diameter and remain green and disease-free all season long. The elusive purplish flowers are a delight, but only seen by those gardeners willing to get down on their hands and knees.

Pollinator & Wildlife Value: Larval host of pipeline swallowtail butterfly. Ants, attracted to the smell of the fruit, take part in seed dispersal. Quail use plantings for nesting.

How to Use: Wild ginger is an excellent groundcover in shady areas. It forms an extensive carpet that is good for hiding empty spots left by spring ephemerals. Combine it with foamflower in dappled shade to get a solid groundcover with widely differing leaf shapes and sizes.

How to Grow & Maintain: Prefers consistently moist, humus-rich soil in partial to full shade but tolerates drier soils. Wild ginger is quite drought tolerant once established, but make sure new plants receive adequate water. Divide in spring or as plants go dormant in fall if you want to increase your numbers. Plants may wilt during dry spells but quickly recover with watering. No serious pest problems. Snails and slugs may feed on leaves. Deer usually avoid it.

Beyond the Species: Western wild ginger (*A. caudatum*) is slightly smaller and has shinier, evergreen leaves. It is better for western gardens in Zones 5 to 8.

107

Asclepias tuberosa
Butterfly Milkweed

Zones: 3 to 9
Size: 2 to 3 feet tall

Asclepias tuberosa

Butterfly milkweed has dense clumps of leafy stems topped with broad, flat clusters of fiery orange, red, or sometimes yellow flowers late spring to late summer. Older plants have larger, and more, flowers. Plants may send up additional stems from the crown as they get older, giving mature plants an almost shrublike appearance. Unlike other milkweeds, it has clear sap. Long, slender, 4- to 5-inch fruits are filled with seeds waiting to fly away on their silky "parachutes."

Pollinator & Wildlife Value: As the name implies, it attracts butterflies and their larvae. It is a nectar source for hummingbirds, many bees, wasps, flies, and beetles. *Asclepias* species are the sole food source for the larval stage of monarch and queen butterflies.

How to Use: Butterfly milkweed is a wonderful garden and landscape plant, adding a bright splash of color to summer gardens. It is particularly striking when planted with complementary-colored blue and purple flowers. Good native companions include blazing stars, silky aster, leadplant, purple prairie clover, spiderworts, and monarda. Plant it in perennial gardens, mixed borders, or butterfly gardens. It makes a nice cut flower, and the seedpods look nice in dried arrangements.

How to Grow & Maintain: Tolerates moist or dry soils in full sun or light shade. Mature plants can take full sun and dry soil and can withstand drought. Set out young plants in their permanent locations, as the deep taproot makes plants difficult to move. Good drainage is essential; plants may rot in overly rich or damp soil. Plants don't like competition during establishment. No major insect or disease problems, but plants may die over winter from root rot if the soil is too heavy. Plants are slow to emerge in spring, so cultivate carefully until new growth appears; you may want to mark the site each fall. Apply winter mulch in cold areas to prevent frost heaving until young plants are established. Plants can get a little top heavy and may require gentle staking. Plants rarely need dividing, and they are not prolific seed producers. Aphids can be a problem on milkweeds in hot, dry weather. Be ready to spray plants with a garden hose. Plants tend to be avoided by deer.

Beyond the Species: It's hard to improve on the species, but if you are looking for different flower colors,

108

'Gay Butterflies' is a seed-grown strain of mixed yellow, red, pink, and orange flowers, and 'Hello Yellow' is golden yellow. Swamp milkweed (*A. incarnata*) has flat, terminal clusters of pale rose to rose-purple flowers on 3- to 4-foot sturdy plants in summer. It grows best in constantly wet soils in full sun, such as in bog and rain gardens, but it adapts well to the conditions in sunny perennial borders if it receives supplemental water. It is a food source for several butterflies and their larvae. It does self-seed prolifically. 'Ice Ballet' has creamy white flowers. 'Cinderella' and 'Soulmate' have fragrant, long-lasting, rose-pink flowers. These cultivars do not produce as many seedlings as the species and tolerate drier soils, so they are better choices for traditional gardens. Zones 3 to 9. Purple milkweed (*A. purpurascens*) is 1 to 3 feet tall in flower with very showy rose-purple blooms starting in late spring. It is less invasive than common milkweed (*A. syriaca*) but still may be too aggressive for formal gardens and is best used in naturalized areas and butterfly gardens. It prefers full sun and well-drained soil but is tolerant of a wide range of soils and light levels. Zones 3 to 9. Prairie milkweed (*A. sullivantii*) is among the better behaved milkweeds that can be considered for garden use. Plants grow 2 to 3 feet tall, and the short-stalked umbels of pink, starlike flowers emerge from the axils of the upper leaves at the apex of the plant. The blooming period is early to midsummer and lasts about a month. A rich loamy soil in full sun is best. Use it in borders, butterfly gardens, rain gardens, and naturalized areas as a nectar source for hummingbirds. Zones 3 to 7.

Asclepias incarnata 'Ice Ballet'

Athyrium filix-femina
Lady Fern

Zones: 2 to 8
Size: 1 to 3 feet tall

Athyrium filix-femina

Lady fern forms a cool green carpet of lacy, deeply cut fronds that arch from the crown and spread slowly from rhizomes. The bright green to light yellow, 1- to 2-foot fronds are produced continually during the growing season, which keeps plants looking fresh.

Pollinator & Wildlife Value: Provides seasonal cover and hiding places for amphibians and birds such as robins, wrens, and thrushes.

How to Use: Lady fern is among the best native ferns for heavy shade. Use it to brighten a spot in a garden or under shrubs. Its light color sets it off nicely from other ferns, and it is a good backdrop for bloodroot, merry bells, and other smaller native flowers. Lady fern is an excellent groundcover in moist woodland gardens. It can naturalize along stream banks or shady water gardens or be used in rain gardens. It is large enough to be used with shrubs in foundation plantings.

How to Grow & Maintain: Lady fern is easy to grow provided plants receive consistent moisture. It prefers a slightly acidic, moist to wet soil in partial to full shade, but tolerates a wide variety of soils. Plants can take some sun if the soil is kept moist. Mulch plants and water during dry periods. The fronds are somewhat brittle, and older fronds may become tattered by late summer if they are grown in high-traffic areas or windy sites. Cut back old fronds before new growth begins in spring. No serious insect or disease problems. Deer and rabbits avoid it.

Beyond the Species: 'Lady in Red' has attractive deep red stems. Zones 3 to 9.

Baptisia australis
Blue False Indigo, Blue Wild Indigo

Zones: 4 to 9
Size: 3 to 4 feet tall

Blue false indigo has attractive bluish-green, compound leaves on nicely shaped, almost shrublike, plants. Deep blue, pealike flowers occur on spikes up to 1 foot long from late spring into summer and are very showy. They open and mature from the bottom up. Individual flowers last three to four days. They turn into ornamental charcoal-gray seedpods that persist into winter. Plants are tough and long-lived.

Pollinator & Wildlife Value: Larval food source for wild indigo duskywing, hoary edge skipper, frosted elm, marine blue, clouded sulphur, and orange sulphur butterflies. Queen and worker bumblebees are the primary pollinators. Hummingbirds seek nectar, and chickadees eat the seeds in winter.

How to Use: This very nice garden plant can be used in formal borders, cottage gardens, or natural areas. It is best as a specimen, or in groups of three on large sites. It does well in rain gardens. The dried seedpods are often used in floral arrangements. Blue false indigo doesn't really need any companions when in bloom. The blue-green foliage makes a nice backdrop for lower-growing, later-blooming plants such as butterfly milkweed, black-eyed Susans, wild geranium, and blanket flowers, which hide the bare lower stalks.

How to Grow & Maintain: Prefers slightly acidic, well-drained soil in full sun or very light shade. Tolerates drought and poor soils but not high pH. This long-lived perennial starts out slowly but eventually forms huge clumps that are difficult to transplant, so choose a site carefully. Plants rarely need dividing and resent disturbance. Trimming or shearing foliage to shape after bloom helps maintain the rounded appearance but eliminates the attractive seedpods. Peony hoops placed over plants in early spring will support larger plants or those grown in shadier spots. All *Baptisia* species are nitrogen-fixing legumes. No serious pest problems. Deer will occasionally eat the flowers and nibble back the leaves, but rabbits avoid the slightly toxic foliage.

Beyond the Species: Var. *minor* is smaller than the species, staying about 2 feet in height, with very showy flowers.

Baptisia australis

White false indigo (*B. alba*) grows 3 to 4 feet tall and has white flowers mid- to late spring. Zones 4 to 8. 'Purple Smoke' is a hybrid between *B. alba* and *B. australis*. It grows a little over 4 feet tall and has smoky purple blooms with darker purple centers. It rarely produces seedpods. Zones 4 to 9.

Camassia leichtlinii
Camas

Zones: 5 to 8
Size: 24 to 36 inches tall

This neat, clump-forming plant grows from a tuliplike bulb. The long, narrow, basal, somewhat floppy leaves form a tight clump. Beautiful blue-violet to white flowers appear in loose racemes in late spring. Sweet-scented flowers have six petal-like segments and protruding yellow stamens and last for two to three weeks. The basal leaves turn yellow and wither away by midsummer.

Pollinator & Wildlife Value: The flower nectar attracts bees, butterflies, flies, wasps, and beetles. Bees are the primary pollinators.

How to Use: Camas is a very nice landscape plant. Use it in traditional perennial borders, in gardens, or as an accent near water. It is beautiful when allowed to naturalize in moist-soil areas. Keep in mind that plants go dormant in summer and leaves must be allowed to remain until dormancy so plants can store food for the next year. Surround it with plants, such as Joe-pye weeds, obedient plant, and cardinal flower that will fill in once the plants go dormant.

How to Grow & Maintain: A soil that is humusy and moist to wet is ideal, but plants do fine with drier conditions once they go dormant in midsummer. Best bloom is in full sun to very light shade. Plants can be slow to develop but are fairly long-lived. Vegetative growth and development occurs during the cool weather of spring when adequate moisture is essential. Purchase dormant bulbs in fall and plant immediately so roots can establish before winter. Plant four times as deep as bulbs are tall in groups of five to seven or more. The strong stems usually do not require staking. No serious insect or disease problems. The bulbs are usually safe from rodent feeding.

Beyond the Species: Ssp. *suksdorfii* has larger, darker blue flowers. Prairie camas (*C. angusta*) grows up to 2½ feet tall, and the leaves are larger. Flowers are similar but usually smaller and lighter in color. The blooming period is a little later, from late spring to early summer. Zones 5 to 9. Common camas (*C. quamash*) is smaller, growing 12 to 18 inches in flower, and has narrower leaves. Flowers are pale to dark violet-blue. The variety *utahensis* is larger and has blue anthers; var. *maxima* has large dark blue flowers. Zones 4 to 8. Wild hyacinth (*C. scilloides*) only grows 12 to 16 inches tall in flower. The pale blue flowers are held in loose racemes. It is the hardiest of the species and looks best when naturalized in a large mass. Zones 3 to 9.

Camassia leichtlinni

Campanula rotundifolia
Harebell, Bluebell Bellflower

Zones: 2 to 8
Size: 6 to 18 inches tall

Campanula rotundifolia

Harebell has charming, violet-blue, bell-shaped, nodding flowers on wiry stems that arise from an overwintering rosette of small, roundish leaves. Once flowering begins, the basal leaves start to wither away so you are left with a wispy plant with nodding, bell-shaped flowers borne in loose clusters on slender stalks at the ends of branched stems. Plants begin blooming in late spring and continue sporadically into fall.

Pollinator & Wildlife Value: Small bees, orange mint moths, and hummingbirds visit the flowers for nectar.

How to Use: Plant harebell where the delicate flowers won't be overpowered by nearby plants. Other diminutive, dry-soil plants include alliums, columbines, prairie smoke, and beardtongues. It does well in rock walls, in rock gardens, and between pavers on a terrace. It can be grown in containers.

How to Grow & Maintain: Despite its delicate appearance harebell is surprisingly easy to grow and requires very little care if properly sited. It needs a well-drained soil in full sun. Avoid overly rich soils, which can encourage vigorous growth on nearby plants that can overtake harebell. It tolerates alkaline soil. In the right setting, the underground stems will spread and plants do reseed, but not too prolifically. The seedlings help ensure the future of this often short-lived perennial. Plants may flop over from the weight of the flowers. There are no serious insect or disease pests. Deer usually leave it alone.

Coreopsis verticillata
Threadleaf Tickseed, Whorled Tickseed

Zones: 3 to 9
Size: 1 to 2 feet tall

There are many native species of tickseeds that can be considered for garden use. Most have cheery yellow flowers that bloom for a long time. Threadleaf coreopsis has golden yellow, daisylike flowers with ragged petals and yellow centers late spring to late summer. The fine-textured leaves are attractive throughout the growing season and into winter. Plants have thick clumps of mostly basal leaves and smaller stem leaves.

Pollinator & Wildlife Value: Most species attract a wide range of insects, including bees, butterflies, wasps, moths, flies, and beetles. Birds eat the seeds.

How to Use: Tickseeds tend to be tough, vigorous plants that are good choices for naturalizing, dune restoration, and prairie and meadow gardens. The sunny yellow flowers look especially nice with other hot-colored summer-blooming plants such as butterfly weed, wild bergamot, flowering spurge, purple prairie clover, spiderworts, purple coneflower, and prairie phlox. The cultivars are better choices for traditional garden use, since they tend not to reseed and spread as rampantly and can be used in perennial borders and containers. Most make good cut flowers.

How to Grow & Maintain: Most species like well-drained soil in full sun and are very drought tolerant; they do not like poorly drained soils. Plants reseed, often prolifically. Deadheading reduces unwanted seedlings and helps prolong bloom. Divide plants when the centers begin to die out and blooms are fewer. Plants often spread by rhizomes and older dense clumps are difficult to weed out. No serious pest problems, but aphids may be a problem and plants may develop root or crown rot if drainage is poor. Rabbits, groundhogs, and deer occasionally consume the foliage.

Beyond the Species: Several selections will be better behaved in the garden. 'Zagreb' has golden yellow flowers on 18-inch plants. 'Moonbeam' has soft yellow single flowers and blooms for a long time but is not as hardy. It does not require division as frequently as other types. Lobed tickseed (*C. auriculata*) grows anywhere from 3 to 18 inches tall and has golden orange flowers in late spring. It spreads slowly by stolons. 'Nana' is a commonly available compact form that grows into low-spreading clumps 6 to 9 inches tall. Zones 4 to 9. Large-flowered tickseed (*C. grandiflora*) is a short-lived perennial that has showy flowers and attractive foliage on 1- to 2-foot-tall plants. It blooms for a long time beginning in early summer. The single composite flower is 2 inches or more across and has yellow ray florets surrounding golden yellow disk flowers. Each ray floret has four to five notches along the outer edge, giving the flowers an attractive pinked edge. It is not usually long lived in gardens and should be replanted every year or two or allowed to reseed just a bit. Several cultivars are available that are much better behaved in the garden. 'Early Sunrise' has double gold-yellow flowers on 18-inch plants. 'Sunfire' has a deep burgundy center. 'Domino' stays 18 inches tall and has a burgundy flower center. 'Flying Saucers' is compact with 2-inch sterile flowers that bloom a long time and don't require deadheading. 'Sundancer' is a prolific bloomer with semi-double flowers on 10-inch plants. Zones 3 to 9. Lanceleaf tickseed (*C. lanceolata*) is similar to *C. grandiflora* in appearance and is native in much of the country. It is a prolific reseeder and has a fairly short bloom time. 'Sterntaler' is a 16-inch selection with a frilly center surrounded by a brown ring and a double row of yellow petals. Zones 3 to 9. Stiff tickseed (*C. palmata*) grows 2 to 3 feet tall

Coreopsis verticillata 'Zagreb'

and flowers earlier than other *Coreopsis* species. The 1½- to 2-inch composite flowers are pale to bright yellow. Plants spread by rhizomes and can form large colonies, which can be quite impressive when in flower. Zones 3 to 8. Pink tickseed (*C. rosea*) is a rare species that is threatened in the wild but has been responsibly propagated and is quite widely available for garden use. It grows 1 to 2 feet tall and has soft pink flowers and fine-textured, needlelike leaves. 'American Dream' grows up to 18 inches tall and has longer bloom. 'Sweet Dream' is similar with raspberry-white bicolor flowers. Both are nice garden plants. Zones 4 to 8. Golden tickseed (*C. tinctoria*) is an annual species growing 2 to 4 feet tall with daisylike flowers with yellow rays with reddish brown centers. It blooms all season and reseeds prolifically. Many selections have been made. Tall tickseed (*C. tripteris*) grows 3 to 6 feet tall. It blooms later, midsummer through early fall. The slightly smaller flowers have yellow petals surrounding a brown disk and appear singly on the upper stems. Plants often form loose colonies and this is another prolific seeder, so tall tickseed's landscape use is restricted to the back of large borders and rainwater gardens, where it provides a soft cloud of airy flowers. Plants will be a bit less aggressive in drier soils and deadheading will help reduce seedlings. It may need staking. 'Sterntaler' is a long-flowering selection with red-brown bicolor flowers. Zone 3 to 8.

Coreopsis grandiflora 'Sunfire'

Coreopsis Palmata

Dalea purpurea
Purple Prairie Clover

Zones: 3 to 9
Size: 2 to 3 feet tall

Purple prairie clover is a delicate-looking plant with unique rose-purple to crimson flowers. Densely packed, ½- to 2-inch flowers bloom in a ring around the flower head, starting at the bottom and working to the top. It starts blooming in early summer and continues for a month or more. The foliage is pinnate and fine-textured and seedheads are attractive in winter. Older plants may tiller at the base and send up multiple stems, creating vase-shaped clumps.

Dalea purpurea and D. candida

Pollinator & Wildlife Value: The flower nectar attracts many bees, including honeybees and bumblebees, which collect pollen. Wasps, flies, small butterflies, hummingbirds, beetles, and plant bugs also visit. The larvae of dogface sulphur and riker blue butterflies feed on the plants. Songbirds enjoy the seeds.

How to Use: Purple prairie clover doesn't look like much in spring (including in the nursery container), but it will reward you in midsummer with its showy flowers. A mature plant is quite attractive in full bloom. Plant it in groups of three to five in perennial borders or butterfly gardens or use a single plant as an accent in rock gardens. The fine-textured foliage remains attractive throughout the growing season and the seedheads offer winter interest. Plant it with other summer-blooming flowers such as monarda, leadplant, butterfly milkweed, prairie onions, and smaller grasses such as little bluestem and prairie dropseed. Allow seedheads to remain for winter interest.

How to Grow & Maintain: Purple prairie clover is slow to develop, but once it settles in it is a tough, low-maintenance garden plant. Mature plants tolerate summer drought, and clumps seldom need dividing. It grows best in moist to dry soils in full sun. The soil can be quite poor, since *Dalea* species are nitrogen-fixers. Be careful not to weed it out in spring. You may need to use an inoculant to help plants become established in some soils. It may self-seed in optimum growing conditions but rarely becomes a pest. Mulch the first winter to prevent frost heaving. It is a favorite food of herbivores, especially rabbits.

Beyond the Species: White prairie clover (*D. candida*) is taller, growing 3 to 4 feet, and has white flowers and sparser, lighter foliage. The white color is good for balancing the hot colors of other summer prairie plants. Zones 3 to 9.

Dicentra eximia
Fringed Bleeding Heart, Turkey Corn

Zones: 4 to 8
Size: 12 to 18 inches tall

Dicentra eximia

This charming shade plant has beautiful fernlike, grayish green foliage that persists throughout the growing season. The pink to purplish red, nodding, heart-shaped flowers are carried above the foliage on long, leafless, leaning stems. In cooler areas, plants may bloom throughout the summer. Plants grow from slow-creeping rhizomes and will form small colonies with time.

Pollinator & Wildlife Value: Early nectar source for native bumblebees and migrating hummingbirds. Birds eat the seeds. Ants collect seeds as food, so you may see seedlings appear in other areas of your garden. Small animals use plants as cover.

How to Use: This plant should be in every shade and woodland garden. It is one of those great plants that has foliage that is just as attractive as the long-blooming flowers. It looks very nice with Jacob's ladder and bloodroot.

How to Grow & Maintain: This plant does very well in gardens. It likes a moist, humusy soil in partial shade, but does well in average, well-drained soil in full shade also. Avoid wet winter soil and very dry summer soil. It reseeds when it is happy in its spot. No serious insect or disease problems. Deer and rabbits avoid it.

Beyond the Species: 'Alba' and 'Snowdrift' have white flowers. Most plants you will find for sale at traditional nurseries will be hybrids with western bleeding heart. Popular selections include 'Bacchanal', 'Luxuriant', and 'Adrian Bloom'. These cultivars may not provide the same benefits to wildlife as the species. Western bleeding heart (*D. formosa*) is similar, but the plants tend to spread faster and can form larger clumps. It is native in the Pacific Northwest and is a better choice for gardens there. It is the larval host of the Parnassius clodius butterfly. Zones 4 to 8. Dutchman's breeches (*D. cucullaria*) and squirrel corn (*D. canadensis*) are two ephemeral species growing 6 to 12 inches tall. They have interesting white flowers that bloom very early in spring, then plants go dormant mid- to late spring. They do well in woodland and shade gardens in spring sun and moist soil. Plant them with other spring ephemerals as well as plants that will fill in, such as Allegheny spurge, ferns, and wild ginger. Zones 3 to 8.

Dodecatheon meadia
Shooting Star, Pride of Ohio

Zones: 4 to 8
Size: 10 to 20 inches tall

These fascinating flowers have five delicate, white to pink, strongly reflexed petals surrounding a yellow and red conelike center, giving them the appearance of shooting stars. Plants bloom for a long time starting mid- to late spring. The lush green basal foliage has reddish tints at the base. The entire plant dies down when summer heat arrives, but the dried flower stalks persist somewhat longer.

Pollinator & Wildlife Value: Bumblebees are the most typical visitors of the oddly shaped flowers, but other types of bees visit as well, all coming to collect pollen.

How to Use: Shooting star is an adaptable plant at home in rock gardens and perennial borders as well as partial shade areas of woodland gardens. Plant it in groups of at least three and do not crowd it. A large grouping makes a stunning show when in flower. Surround it with persistent foliage plants that will fill in once plants go dormant in midsummer. Good choices are golden alexanders, prairie smoke, prairie phlox, wild geranium, Jacob's ladder, and maidenhair fern.

How to Grow & Maintain: Any good soil, in sun or light shade, will do, but it does best in rich garden soil. Requires direct sun in spring but shade is okay in summer. It likes adequate soil moisture when actively growing. Avoid poorly drained, wet soils, particularly in winter. Plants need moisture while blooming but are drought tolerant after that. Plants develop slowly and take several years to bloom from seed. Fall transplanting is recommended, but planting in early spring is also fine. You may want to mark the spot so you don't disturb dormant plants in late summer and fall. The ideal soil pH is 6 to 7; add limestone before planting if necessary. No serious insect or disease problems. Deer avoid it.

Beyond the Species: Jeweled shooting star (*D. amethystinum*) is similar but with very showy light to dark pink flowers. It is rare in the wild, but makes a nice garden plant when purchased from responsible propagators. Zones 4 to 8. *D. clevelandii, D. dentatum, D. hendersonii, D. poeticum,* and *D. pulchellum* are all West Coast species that make good garden plants (if you can find them). Flower color ranges from white to magenta, and mature heights are from 6 to 20 inches. They range in hardiness from Zones 4 to 8, depending on the species.

Dodecatheon meadia

Echinacea purpurea
Eastern Purple Coneflower

Zones: 3 to 8
Size: 3 to 4 feet tall

This popular garden plant has showy flowers with 3- to 4-inch, purple-pink petals and bristly orange center cones. It begins blooming early to midsummer and often continues into fall. Plants are shrubby and branching with dark green leaves and fibrous root systems. The seedheads are attractive well into winter.

Pollinator & Wildlife Value: All *Echinacea* species attract many species of bees, birds, and butterflies, including monarchs, red admirals, fritillaries, painted ladies, swallowtails, skippers, sulfurs, and whites. Caterpillars feed on the foliage as well. Hummingbirds look for the insects that visit these plants. Goldfinches eat the ripened seeds.

How to Use: The beautiful, well-behaved purple coneflower can be used almost anywhere in the landscape, including natural areas, the perennial border, cottage and cutting gardens, and partial shade areas of woodland gardens. The plant itself isn't that attractive, so use lower-growing plants in front as a distraction. It look nice with other summer-blooming prairie flowers such as black-eyed Susan, leadplant, monarda, blazing stars, butterfly milkweed, and prairie coneflower as well as native grasses.

How to Grow & Maintain: Growth is best in fertile loam, but the soil can contain some gravel or clay, in full or partial sun. It has some drought tolerance, but plants wilt if the soil becomes too dry, particularly in strong sun. Deadheading doesn't really give more flowers and takes food from the goldfinches. Divide only when you have to, since divisions usually don't produce as many flowers. A better way to get more plants is to dig up seedlings in spring, which can be prolific when plants are happy. It is not a favorite of herbivores such as deer and rabbits. Aster yellows can be a serious problem.

Beyond the Species: The breeding of purple coneflower has gotten a bit out of hand, and there are many cultivars available—some just a bit too far out ('Razzmatazz'). The species itself is so beautiful it's hard to see the need for anything else. And the increase in cultivars has put stress on native populations, which are suffering from genetic homogenization because of their cross pollination with the species. If you are interested in a white-flowered selection, 'Alba', 'White Lustre', and 'White Swan' have white ray petals and coppery centers. Most cultivars are only reliably hardy in Zones 4 to 8.

Echinacea purpurea

Eutrochium maculatum
Joe-pye Weed

Zones: 3 to 8
Size: 3 to 7 feet tall

Eutrochium maculatum

Joe-pye weeds are tall, unbranched perennials with whorls of four or five yellowish green leaves up to 8 inches long with serrated margins and conspicuous veins. The flat-topped, 4- to 5-inch clusters of feathery rose-purple to mauve flower heads appear on top of purple or purplish stems mid- to late summer into fall. The flowers are often fragrant. Seedheads are ornamental in winter. Until recently, Joe-pye weeds were in the same genus as the bonesets, *Eupatorium*.

Pollinator & Wildlife Value: The numerous tiny flowers in the large flower heads of Joe-pye weeds are excellent sources of late-season nectar for bees, wasps, flies, moths, and hummingbirds. It is a butterfly magnet, especially swallowtails. The seeds are a source of food for swamp sparrows and wild turkeys. Ducks and grouse eat the leaves.

How to Use: Despite their affinity for moist soil, Joe-pye weed adapt very well to typical garden settings and can be used in cottage, butterfly, and cutting gardens, where its architectural form will make a statement. They can be used in perennials borders, especially if plants are pinched or cut back in spring to form a more compact mound. They do very well in rain gardens and naturalized plantings, especially in low areas along lakes and streams or in bog gardens. The smoky purple color is a nice complement to yellow flowers such as prairie coneflower, black-eyed Susans, sneezeweed, and goldenrods.

How to Grow & Maintain: Preference is full or partial sun and wet to moist soil, but they do well in all but extremely dry soils. Plants can tolerate occasional flooding. Plants are late to emerge in spring so don't forget where they are planted. Joe-pye weeds are generally strong of stem and don't require staking. Plants can be cut back when they are 2 to 3 feet tall to produce smaller but fuller flowers. Cut plants back to about 6 inches in spring if shorter plants are desired; bloom will be delayed about a week. Plants reseed but usually not too prolifically in typical drier garden soils. No serious insect or disease issues. Leafminers may feed on leaves. Plants that are too close together may suffer from powdery mildew. Leaves may scorch if the soil is too dry. The foliage is not a preferred food of herbivores but it may be eaten by deer and rabbits on occasion.

Beyond the Species: *E. dubium, E. fistulosum,* and *E. purpureum* are similar species with native ranges in the eastern US. They are good garden plants as well. 'Little Joe' is a dwarf selection of *E. dubium* that stays 2 to 3 feet tall. 'Atropurpureum' and 'Gateway' are popular cultivars selected for sturdier, richly colored stems and reduced height, but they still often get 6 feet tall and are not really a better choice than the true species. Zones 3 to 7.

Gaillardia aristata
Blanket Flower

Zones: 3 to 9
Size: 2 to 3 feet tall

Blanket flowers are among the showiest of native prairie flowers, the reason behind their increased popularity in recent years. The descriptive common names, which also include firewheel and Indian blanket, come from the flowers' resemblance to brightly colored blankets made by Native Americans. The perennial *Gaillardia aristata* has 2- to 4-inch, golden yellow, daisylike ray petals with a narrow band of burgundy at the base where they join the dark red disk flowers. It starts blooming midsummer and continues into early fall. The gray-green leaves are hairy and lobed or egg-shaped and appear in leafy clumps that will continue to increase in size but never become aggressive.

Pollinator & Wildlife Value: Flowers are pollinated by soft-winged flower beetles, honeybees, and leaf-cutting bees. Hummingbirds and butterflies seek nectar. Butterfly visitors include Edwards' fritillary and Dakota skipper. Goldfinches and other songbirds eat the seeds.

How to Use: Blanket flower is a good addition to sunny perennial borders, cottage gardens, butterfly gardens, and xeriscaped yards. It can be used as a cut flower, and the compact-growing hybrids adapt well to container use. Set off the showy bicolor blooms by planting blanket flower with single-colored summer bloomers such as Mexican hat, butterfly milkweed, harebell, and monarda.

How to Grow & Maintain: It needs well-drained soil and full sun. It is drought, salt, and heat tolerant. Deadheading is not necessary but will tidy up plants and may encourage additional bloom; stop in late summer so you'll have some of its attractive seedheads going into winter. Plants may need support of some sort. Plants can be cut back midsummer to encourage a fall bloom. There are no serious pest problems. Plants may get powdery mildew if conditions are right, and aster yellows can be a problem. Deer and rabbits avoid it.

Beyond the Species: Indian blanket (*G. pulchella*) is an attractive annual species native in more southerly and westerly prairies. Flower color is highly variable in any population, ranging from shades of yellows to reds to purples with some bicolor. Plants grow about 2 feet tall. It grows in dry, lean soils and will reseed and naturalize. Hybrid blanket flower (*G.* x *grandiflora*) is a showy cross between *G. aristata* and *G. pulchella*. The resulting floriferous hybrids have orange and yellow flowers, often with dark red bands or eyes. Plants are showy but often short-lived perennials that are good choices for containers and any type of garden. 'Arizona Sun' only grows about a foot tall and has large orange-red blossoms edged in yellow. There are an abundance of cultivars available, with more being added each year. 'Burgundy' has large wine-red flowers. 'Dazzler' has golden yellow flowers with maroon centers. 'Goblin' is a 12-inch plant with red-centered flowers with yellow edges. Zones 4 to 9.

***Gaillardia* x *grandiflora* 'Arizona Sun'**

Geranium maculatum
Wild Geranium, Spotted Geranium

Zones: 3 to 8
Size: 12 to 24 inches tall

Geranium maculatum

Wild geranium has loose clusters of five-petalled flowers rising above pairs of grayish-green leaves, each with three to five distinct palmate lobes and coarse teeth. Flowers appear early midspring into summer, ranging from pale to deep magenta-pink to light purple. The fruits that appear after flowering resemble a crane's bill. Foliage turns a lovely red color in fall.

Pollinator & Wildlife Value: Several types of bees looking for nectar carry pollen to and from the flowers. Butterflies, moths, skippers, syrphid flies, and fruit worm beetles feed on nectar. Chipmunks, bobwhite quail, and mourning doves may eat the seeds.

How to Use: This hardy perennial is easy to grow and easy to use. Plant it in drifts in woodland gardens, where it will interweave among other plants without crowding them out. Plant it with other woodland denizens such as baneberries, golden alexanders, blue phlox, Canada columbine, and ferns. In perennial borders, it can grow in part sun, as long as it has good soil moisture in spring. It works in rain gardens.

How to Grow & Maintain: Prefers moist, rich soils in partial sun to light shade, but tolerates drier conditions in summer. Wild geranium is easy to grow and transplant. Divide the slow-creeping rhizomes in early spring or early fall. Shelter plants from strong winds. It doesn't pay to deadhead, since plants don't usually rebloom. Flowering stalks can be cut back in midsummer to get neater-looking plants. Deer and rabbits usually leave it alone, but will occasionally browse on the leaves.

Beyond the Species: 'Espresso' has a nice compact growth habit, light pink flowers, and dark purple foliage. 'Album' and 'Hazel Gallagher' are white-flowered cultivars. Zones 4 to 8. Sticky purple geranium (*G. viscosissimum*) is a similar species native in the western US. Zones 4 to 9.

Geum triflorum
Prairie Smoke, Old Man's Whiskers

Zones: 2 to 7
Size: 6 to 16 inches tall

Prairie smoke brings something to the landscape almost year-round. The evergreen leaves stand out nicely against mostly brown foliage in gardens as soon as the snow recedes. Prairie smoke has pink- or rose-colored, nodding flowers that look like they never completely open. They begin blooming in early spring and continue well into summer. This plant's greatest show actually comes from the mauve-colored seedheads that follow the flowers. Resembling plumes of smoke, the seedheads catch the summer sunlight, making it look like there is a layer of pink-tinged silvery smoke hanging over plants. Ferny, blue-green leaves are covered with soft hairs and grow in rosettes.

Pollinator & Wildlife Value: The early flowers are an important food source for insects emerging from hibernation. Bumblebees are strong enough to pry open the flowers and pollinate the plants. Butterflies visit the flowers for nectar, and goldfinches and other songbirds eat the seeds.

How to Use: Use prairie smoke in boulevard gardens, perennial borders, rock gardens, and for xeriscaping. It eventually forms a dense groundcover. The seedheads can be dried for flower arrangements. Combine it with Canada columbine and prairie phlox as well as later-blooming plants that will set off the showy plumes such as blue-eyed grasses (*Sisyrinchium* species), golden alexanders, and harebell. In perennial borders or rock gardens, it combines nicely with spring bulbs and low-growing perennials such as creeping phlox.

How to Grow & Maintain: Prairie smoke is a tough plant that withstands bitter cold, high heat, and drought. It does best in dry, well-drained soil in full sun but tolerates light shade, especially afternoon shade in hot summers. It will die out if subjected to wet soil in winter. Rhizomes should be divided every third or fourth year to alleviate overcrowding. It has no serious insect or disease problems, but root rot can be a problem in wet soils, particularly in winter. Deer and rabbits usually avoid it.

Geum triflorum

Gillenia trifoliata
Bowman's Root

Zones: 4 to 8
Size: 2 to 3 feet tall

This upright, clumping perennial blooms late spring into summer with masses of five-petalled, starlike, white (sometimes pale pink) flowers. They are held loosely in branching, red stems above the clean, green foliage, giving the plants an ethereal appearance. The attractive red stems and orange-yellow leaves provide fall color, and the seedheads persist into winter. It is also known as *Porteranthus trifoliatus*.

Pollinator & Wildlife Value: Small carpenter bees, mason bees, and sweat bees visit the flowers for pollen.

How to Use: This is a nice plant for formal borders as well as in more natural woodland and shade gardens. A mass planting has an airy effect while in bloom and is a nice filler, but a single plant looks nice also. The white flowers bloom for a long time, brightening a shady spot.

It can be used in containers and as a cut flower. Good companions are wild geranium, columbine, woodland phlox, ferns, and fringed bleeding heart.

How to Grow & Maintain: This plant thrives in fertile, evenly moist soil in partial shade or full sun, but some shade in the heat of the day is beneficial. Plants grown in sun should be mulched to help keep the soil evenly moist. Mature plants are quite drought tolerant and rarely need dividing. Flower stems may require gentle support to keep them upright. There are no serious insect or disease issues. Deer avoid it.

Beyond the Species: *G. stipulata* is a similar species native a little farther west. It is a bit more drought and heat tolerant. Zones 4 to 9.

Gillenia trifoliata

Helenium autumnale
Sneezeweed, Helen's Flower, Dogtooth Daisy

Zones: 3 to 8
Size: 3 to 5 feet tall

Sneezeweed's abundant daisylike flowers really brighten up the garden in late summer and fall. The 1- to 2-inch-wide flowers have wedge-shaped, bright yellow rays and prominent domelike, duller yellow center disks. It flowers for a long time beginning in late summer and continuing through fall. The bright green leaves are lance-shaped with toothed edges. Plants are erect, clump-forming perennials. Insect-pollinated sneezeweed does not derive its common name from the effects of its pollen, but rather from its past use as a snuff that promoted sneezing. Pollen is distributed by insects, not by wind.

Pollinator & Wildlife Value: Several types of bees act as pollinators. Other visitors include wasps, butterflies, and beetles looking for nectar. Seeds are eaten by songbirds and upland game birds.

How to Use: Autumn sneezeweed provides nice late-summer color in perennial borders, cottage gardens, rain gardens, and naturalized areas. It does best in a low, moist area such as bogs or near streams, but it can be grown in many landscape situations. In borders, use it with Joe-pye weed, tall phloxes, and asters. Its fibrous root system is good for stabilizing stream banks and shorelines. The flowers can be used for cutting and in dried arrangements.

How to Grow & Maintain: Although native to moist soils, sneezeweed adapts readily to most garden soils. Plants in moist, rich soil are quite robust, while those grown in drier soils are shorter and less vigorous. Taller plants may need some sort of support to keep from flopping over. Prune back plants to about 12 inches in late spring to keep them smaller and more compact and encourage more blooms. Deadheading will also encourage more blooms. Plants will bloom better if they are divided every three or four years. Mulch garden plants and give them extra water during dry times, especially in midsummer, to encourage good flowering. No serious insect or disease problems, but foliage may get powdery mildew, rust, and leaf spot. Deer and rabbits avoid it because of toxins in the leaves.

Beyond the Species: Many hybrid cultivars have been bred for a more compact growth habit, different colored flowers, and double flowers. They may not have as much value for insects seeking nectar and pollen. 'Dakota Gold' stays under 2 feet tall. 'Moerheim Beauty' has bronze-red blossoms. 'Rubinzwerg' (Ruby Dwarf) has ruby red flowers on 2½-foot plants. H. flexuosum (*purplehead sneezeweed*) grows 2 to 3 feet tall with clusters of flowers that have dropping yellow petals and much darker brown-purple centers. It is more adaptable to dry soil and is a good landscape plant. Zones 5 to 9.

Helenium autumnale

Helenium autumnale 'Rubinzwerg'

Heliopsis helianthoides
Oxeye, False Sunflower

Zones: 3 to 8
Size: 3 to 6 feet tall

Heliopsis helianthoides

Oxeye is a rather coarse plant with large, rough, medium green foliage. It's redeemed by its abundance of sunny yellow flowers that appear from early summer continuing well into fall. The daisylike composite flowers are 2 to 3½ inches across and held erect at the ends of the stiff stems. The root system is fibrous. Do not confuse it with oxeye daisy *(Leucanthemum vulgare)*, a weedy plant from Europe that should *not* be grown in North American landscapes.

Pollinator & Wildlife Value: The nectar and pollen of flowers attract several insects, including a wide variety of bees, butterflies, and soldier beetles. Hummingbirds visit the flowers for nectar, and goldfinches and other birds look for the seeds.

How to Use: Oxeye is an excellent landscape plant, providing summer-long color in perennial borders and cutting gardens. It is also great for naturalized plantings and in butterfly gardens. It can also be used in rain gardens. It does well at higher elevations. Plant oxeye with other summer-bloomers such as blazing stars, butterfly weed, prairie phlox, monarda, wild indigo, asters, and grasses.

How to Grow & Maintain: Oxeye adapts readily to garden use and does well in moist or dry, average to rich soil in full sun to light shade. It is easy to grow from seed, often flowering the first summer if started indoors in winter. It tolerates drought, but plants require watering during dry periods to prevent wilting. Plants may get floppy, especially if grown in partial shade; pinch them back in midspring to reduce height. The named cultivars are less floppy. Oxeye will self-seed but the shallow-rooted seedlings are easily weeded out. Deadheading will extend the bloom period and prevent seeding, but leave some seedheads for the goldfinches. And plants tend to be short lived, so you'll want some seedlings. Occasionally aphids and powdery mildew attack, but neither do permanent damage.

Beyond the Species: Several cultivars are available; 'Summer Sun' is the most popular and easiest to locate. It is more compact than the species, growing to about 3 feet with large flowers. 'Prairie Sunset' has bright yellow flowers with contrasting orange-red centers. Plants grow to 6 feet with attractive purplish stems and purple-veined leaves. 'Summer Nights' has deep golden yellow flowers with mahogany centers and stems and foliage tinged with red. 'Ballerina' stays 2 to 3 feet tall with semi-double flowers. 'Tuscan Sun' is a dwarf typically staying under 20 inches tall.

Heuchera americana
Alumroot, Heuchera, Coralbells

Zones: 3 to 9
Size: 1 to 2 feet tall in flower

Heuchera americana

Alumroot has mottled, silvery green, 3- to 4-inch, heart-shaped leaves with scalloped edges. Long slender stalks rise above the mounds and end in airy sprays of tiny, cream-colored flowers, but it is mainly grown for the showy foliage. Plants grow from neat mounds that slowly increase in size. Leaves turn red to purple in fall.

Pollinator & Wildlife Value: Small bees visit the flowers for nectar and pollen. Butterflies and hummingbirds visit the flowers for nectar.

How to Use: This well-behaved plant does well in a wide variety of landscape situations. The attractive foliage and airy flower panicles provide color and contrast in rock gardens, perennial borders, and woodland gardens. It is a good plant for edging a sidewalk or driveway as it tolerates drier soil conditions than most shade plants. It will fill in to make a nice groundcover.

How to Grow & Maintain: It does best in moist, rich, well-drained soil in partial sun, but it tolerates full sun and dry soil in more northern locations. Leaves may bleach out in too much sun, and foliage color is paler in shade. Remove the spent flower stalks to better show off the foliage. Plants benefit from dividing every three to five years; discard the central woody part.

Plants can heave out of the soil in winter and may need to be replanted in spring. It has no serious insect or disease problems. Deer and rabbits usually avoid the bitter-tasting leaves.

Beyond the Species: 'Bartram' has dark green leaves with dark red veins and silver blotches. 'Dale's Strain' has leaves that emerge chartreuse with olive green markings and mature to silvery gray with dark green veins. 'Ring of Fire' has large silvery leaves. A plethora of hybrids are available, most selected for dramatic, colorful foliage. 'Green Spice' has green-purple leaves with silver accents. 'Caramel' has unique apricot foliage and light pink flowers. 'Plum Pudding' has plum-colored, ruffled foliage with darker purple veins. 'Chocolate Ruffles' has deeply cut, ruffled leaves that emerge coppery pink and mature to a deep purple. 'Electra' has gold foliage with red veins. Prairie alumroot (*H. richardsonii*) grows 1 to 2 feet tall. It is a tough, cold-hardy plant with a neat basal clump of heart-shaped, shallow-lobed leaves. Tiny, greenish, bell-shaped flowers in open, airy panicles are borne on slender, wiry stems that extend well above the mound of leaves in spring to early summer. Zones 3 to 9.

Heuchera 'Green Spice'

Iris cristata
Dwarf Crested Iris

Zones: 3 to 9
Size: 3 to 6 inches tall

Iris cristata

This dwarf woodland iris has charming pale blue, lilac, or lavender flowers with showy gold crests on the falls. The flowers float above the mats of low-growing sword-shaped leaves in early to midspring. It forms dense colonies in optimum growing conditions.

Pollinator & Wildlife Value: Flowers attract hummingbirds and bees. A large mat of foliage provides shelter and cover for small animals.

How to Use: A large bed of crested iris in full flower is quite stunning in a shade garden. Use it to edge a shady path or perennial garden or in a shady rock garden. It is slower-moving in drier, less fertile soils and will spread more rapidly in richer soils. It will grow in the dry shade under hardwood trees. It does well on slopes, where it helps in erosion control. It can be used along the edges of rain gardens.

How to Grow & Maintain: It grows best in rich, medium moisture, well-drained soil in partial shade. Once established, it can tolerate drier, shadier soils, but in sunnier spots it needs good soil moisture. It has no serious disease problems; snails and slugs may chew on plants. Deer avoid it.

Beyond the Species: 'Alba' has white flowers with gold centers. 'Powder Blue Giant' has larger flowers with pale blue petals with yellow centers and darker blue accents.

Liatris spicata
Dense Blazing Star, Kansas Gayfeather

Zones: 3 to 8
Size: 2 to 4 feet tall

Dense blazing star has very showy red-violet to mauve terminal flower spikes midsummer through early fall. The alternate, grasslike leaves increase in size from top to bottom. The root system consists of corms, which occasionally form offsets near the mother plant. The flowers of all *Liatris* species open from the top down and can be one of two general forms—spike or button. All species have strong stems with thin, closely set leaves whorled on the stem.

Pollinator & Wildlife Value: Several types of bees, hummingbirds, monarchs, and other butterflies, including fritillary, painted lady, swallowtail, and sulphur, gather on the flowers all summer looking for nectar. Birds eat the seeds on all *Liatris* species.

How to Use: Blazing stars are great for perennial borders, cutting gardens, rain gardens, and cottage gardens. Plant them with other summer prairie plants such as coneflowers, monarda, oxeye, goldenrods, and milkweeds. They are good cut flowers and hold their color well when dried.

How to Grow & Maintain: It needs well-drained soil in full sun and likes an even moisture. Lower leaves may turn yellow and wither if conditions become too dry.

Liatris aspera

Plants reseed but never become weedy and seldom need dividing. Cut back plants in spring rather than fall so birds can feast on the seedheads. Young *Liatris* species may need a little pampering, but once established they are easy to maintain. Taller types need staking. Rabbits and groundhogs may eat younger plants, while mature plants are likely targets of deer. Pocket gophers, mice, and voles may eat the corms, and an abundance of these animals can make it difficult to get plants established.

Beyond the Species: 'Kobold' is a popular compact cultivar that is less likely to need staking than the species, usually staying under 2 feet. 'Floristan Violet' grows 2 feet tall with violet flowers. 'Floristan White' has creamy white flowers. Rough blazing star (*L. aspera*) is a button form with clusters of 1-inch, pale purple or pink flowers on short stalks on top of 3- to 5-foot stems. It is a good garden plant but needs staking or support from nearby plants (Zones 3 to 9). Rocky Mountain blazing star (*L. ligulistylis*) is a button type with dark violet flowers. It grows 3 to 5 feet tall (Zones 3 to 8). Prairie blazing star (*L. pycnostachya*) is very similar to dense blazing star but grows up to 5 feet tall (Zones 3 to 9). Dotted blazing star (*L. punctata*) grows 8 to 14 inches tall with pink-purple wands of dense flowers and silvery gray leaves. It is tolerant of hot, dry conditions (Zones 3 to 9). Eastern blazing star (*L. scariosa*) is a button type growing 1 to 4 feet tall. 'White Spire', 'Alba', and 'Gracious' have white flowers (Zones 3 to 8).

Liatris spicata

Lobelia cardinalis
Cardinal Flower

Zones: 3 to 9
Size: 2 to 4 feet tall

Lobelia cardinalis

Pollinator & Wildlife Value: Cardinal flower depends on hummingbirds, which feed on the nectar, for pollination. Bees may also visit. Butterflies, especially swallowtails, like it.

How to Use: Cardinal flower is one of the few natives with true red flowers, and they are a welcome addition to late-summer landscapes. Plant it in groups of five to seven in a moist area of perennial borders or semi-shaded areas. It thrives in rain gardens, at the edges of water gardens, and in bogs, and will naturalize when conditions are right. It definitely takes a bit of coddling, but the cardinal red color in late summer and the hummingbirds it attracts make it worth a little extra effort. Good companions are sneezeweed, goldenrods, and white turtlehead. A backdrop of ferns helps set off the red flowers.

How to Grow & Maintain: It requires moist to wet, average soil in partial sun. It tolerates full sun as long as the soil is always at least slightly damp. Plants have shallow root systems and will not survive drought. Amend the soil with lots of organic matter before planting and mulch plants. It transplants easily but is short-lived, so add seedlings every couple of years or plan to nurse along the offsets that appear in fall. Winter mulch is helpful in colder areas. It self-seeds prolifically in optimum growing conditions. It has no insect or disease issues. Deer and rabbits usually avoid it.

Beyond the Species: Great blue lobelia (*L. siphilitica*) has electric blue flowers arising from the upper leaf axils mid- to late summer. The leafy stalks typically grow 2 to 3 feet tall. It is easily grown in rich, humusy, medium to wet soils in full sun to part shade. It will self-seed prolifically in optimum growing conditions and form large colonies, so it is best used in naturalized areas or garden areas with drier soil. The shallow-rooted seedlings are easy to weed out. Zones 3 to 9.

Cardinal flower gets its name from the brilliant red flowers that grow in an elongated cluster atop its stems midsummer through early fall. The tubular flowers are two-lipped; the three lobes of the lower lip appear more prominent than the two lobes of the upper lip. White- and rose-colored forms can be found. The finely toothed, dark green to purple, lance-shaped leaves get about 4 inches long. It is a somewhat short-lived, clump-forming perennial.

Mertensia virginica
Virginia Bluebells

Zones: 3 to 9
Size: 12 to 24 inches tall

Mertensia virginica

Virginia bluebells can hardly wait to get up out of the ground in spring, their deep purple, lettuce-like leaves poking up while most of their garden companions are still slumbering. The charming flowers have a bloom pattern similar to *Pulmonaria* species, starting as soft pink buds opening to clusters of violet-blue, trumpet-shaped flowers; an occasional white- or pink-flowered rebel may appear. Buds and open flowers appear on the same plant, creating a mosaic of pinks and purples that later turn to a sea of sky blue. Then, as if exhausted by this dazzling spring display, Virginia bluebells usually plunge into dormancy by midsummer.

Pollinator & Wildlife Value: Plants are an early nectar source for bees, including honeybees, bumblebees, and mason bees, as well as butterflies, skippers, and sphinx moths. Ruby-throated hummingbirds visit the flowers. Large colonies offer protective cover for wildlife in spring.

How to Use: Virginia bluebells is easily grown in woodland or shade gardens, where its flowers provide a soothing sea of blue for many weeks. It can also be used as a "weaver" in semi-shady perennial gardens, where it will grow among the other plants, tying the garden together. It does well in rain gardens and can be grown under black walnut trees. Plant this early bloomer with yellow- or orange-flowered spring bulbs in perennial borders for a striking spring display. In woodland gardens, combine it with large-flowered bellwort, shooting star, and columbines. In sunnier sites, it looks nice with prairie phlox, daffodils, and dwarf iris. Use wild ginger and ferns to fill in after Virginia bluebells go dormant. Gently pull mulch away from emerging plants so you can enjoy the striking deep purple color of the new foliage.

How to Grow & Maintain: It prefers moist, rich soil in part sun or shade. Bloom is best where plants will receive nearly full spring sun with some protection from summer sun. A site under late-leafing deciduous trees such as green ash, Kentucky coffee tree, or hackberry is ideal. Add humus to the soil when planting, mulch well, and water during dry springs. Space plants 15 to 18 inches apart, and strive for a drift effect rather than massing. Plants may die back after flowering in June, so interplant them with ferns or wild ginger. Do not plant directly over the clumps; allow a one-foot area around each clump so the bluebells can grow unimpeded. You may need to mark plants so you do not accidentally dig into the dormant clumps. Plants self-sow readily on bare soil, but not to the point of becoming a nuisance. It has no insect or disease problems. Deer and rabbits usually avoid it.

Monarda didyma
Bee Balm, Oswego Tea

Zones: 3 to 9
Size: 2 to 4 feet tall

Monarda didyma **'Gardenview Scarlet'**

Monarda fistulosa

Bee balm has showy tubular flowers in dense, round, terminal clusters in shades of red, purple, pink, and white. It blooms midsummer through early fall. The foliage is rather coarse and the stems are square, a mint-family characteristic, branching frequently in the upper half. The root system consists of deep, strongly branched roots and shallow rhizomes that typically send up multiple leafy stems in a tight cluster, giving plants a bushy appearance.

Pollinator & Wildlife Value: The flowers attract bees and butterflies, especially fritillaries, as well as the ruby-throated hummingbird. The caterpillars of some moths feed on the foliage.

How to Use: Bee balm is a great plant for the perennial border, prairie garden, cottage garden, or rain garden. It is best placed toward the back where its lackluster foliage and stems will be hidden by lower-growing plants. The uniquely shaped flowers, good for cutting, pair nicely with black-eyed Susan, blazing stars, goldenrods, and butterfly flower. It can be grown under black walnut trees.

How to Grow & Maintain: It's quite adaptable but does best in well-drained but evenly moist soil in full sun to very light shade. Plantings have a tendency to die out in the middle. Dividing every three to four years helps keep plants vigorous and reduces their spread. Plants self-sow; cut back after flowering to reduce self-sown seedlings. Deadheading prolongs bloom and improves a plant's appearance. Cut back some plants in late spring to encourage compact growth. It has no insect problems, but it is very susceptible to powdery mildew. Give plants good air circulation and avoid overhead watering to reduce your chances of disease. Newer cultivars are quite disease resistant. Deer and rabbits ignore the minty leaves.

Beyond the Species: Many cultivars and hybrids are available, selected for their various flower colors, more compact growth, and resistance to powdery mildew. 'Gardenview Scarlet', a hybrid with *M. fistulosa*, has bright red flowers on 3-foot plants and good mildew resistance. 'Jacob Cline' has deep red flowers on 4-foot plants and shows good mildew resistance. 'Marshall's Delight' has bright pink flowers and good mildew resistance. Wild bergamot (*M. fistulosa*) has soft lavender to pale pink flowers and grows 3 to 4 feet tall. It can be used in the middle to back of large perennial borders, in rain gardens, in prairie gardens, and in butterfly gardens but should be kept out of small beds as it spreads and reseeds readily. Zones 3 to 9.

Pachysandra procumbens
Allegheny Spurge

Zones: 5 to 10
Size: 6 to 12 inches tall

This shrublike groundcover has matte blue-green, strongly toothed leaves mottled with purple and white. Tiny, greenish-white to white fragrant flowers bloom in early spring before new leaves are up. Plants are evergreen in Zones 7 and warmer, but by spring plants look pretty tattered. Do not confuse it with nonnative Japanese spurge (*Pachysandra terminalis*), which spreads rapidly and is a problem in some natural areas. It is a good substitute for English ivy (*Hedera helix*), another invasive exotic.

Pollinator & Wildlife Value: Bees visit the flowers for nectar and remove pollen.

How to Use: Plants spread slowly from rhizomes to form a beautiful groundcover for use in shady areas under trees, in foundations, and around shrubs. It is a great addition to the woodland garden, where it mingles with rather than overtakes neighboring plants.

How to Grow & Maintain: It does best in acidic, organically rich soil with medium moisture in partial to full shade. Plants are drought tolerant once established. It does very well under large shade trees. Avoid cutting back the tattered-looking leaves in spring: you may cut off flower buds, and the new foliage will quickly distract from the older leaves. It has no serious insect or disease problems. Leaf blight can be a problem, especially if overhead sprinklers are used regularly. Watch for aphids, slugs, scale, and mites. Deer avoid it.

Pachysandra procumbens

Penstemon digitalis
Beardtongue, Smooth White Penstemon

Zones: 3 to 8
Size: 2 to 4 feet tall

This clump-forming perennial has white, two-lipped, tubular flowers from midspring to midsummer. The flowers appear in panicles atop rigid stems that rise above rosettes of semi-evergreen basal leaves. Leaves are medium green, sometimes with reddish tints. The rhizomatous root often produces new plantlets around the base.

Pollinator & Wildlife Value: Hummingbirds, bees, butterflies, and sphinx moths visit the flowers. Caterpillars of moths and butterflies feed on beardtongue's foliage.

How to Use: Beardtongues adapt well to cultivation and can be used in most typical garden settings. They are especially nice massed in sunny borders, in cottage gardens, and in rain gardens. The white flowers combine well with almost all prairie forbs, including butterfly milkweed, spiderworts, black-eyed Susans, and prairie phlox. Their tolerance of dry soil makes them well suited to rock gardens. Keep in mind the rather uninteresting foliage, however, and plant later-blooming plants nearby to distract from nonblooming plants.

How to Grow & Maintain: It prefers well-drained soil in full sun to very light shade. It's very drought tolerant, but does not do well in heavy, poorly drained soils. Divide as needed; plants may reseed, but not too prolifically. Plants spread slowly to form dense clumps. Taller plants may need staking. For a neat appearance, cut bloom stalks once they've turned brown. It has no serious pest problems. Root rot may occur in poorly drained soils. Leaf spot may also show up some years. Under severe drought conditions, the leaves may turn yellow and the plant will wilt. Plants are not favorites of deer or rabbits.

Beyond the Species: 'Husker Red', 'Dark Towers' (a hybrid), and 'Mystica' are burgundy-leaved selections that greatly extend the season of interest for this species. Showy beardtongue (*P. cobaea*) grows 1 to 2½ feet tall and has loose panicles of flowers ranging from white to pink to deep purple midspring through early summer. The flowers are somewhat larger than most penstemons, almost 2 inches long, and quite showy. Plants are short lived but self-sow readily. Zones 5 to 9. Large beardtongue (*P. grandiflorus*) has beautiful flowers and foliage, though it only blooms two or three weeks in late spring. Its large flowers (up to 2 inches) are lavender or pink with bluish tints. It grows anywhere from 2 to 4 feet tall. Both basal and stem leaves are blue-gray or blue-green and smooth, and have a rather succulent appearance. Zones 3 to 9.

Penstemon digitalis

Penstemon 'Dark Towers'

Phlox divaricata
Woodland Phlox, Blue Phlox

Zones: 3 to 8
Size: 10 to 20 inches tall

This shade-tolerant phlox has clusters of fragrant, pretty, pale blue to dark purple-violet flowers mid- to late spring. The glossy, semi-evergreen foliage spreads at a moderate rate by creeping rhizomes that form loose mats.

Pollinator & Wildlife Value: Butterflies love phlox flowers, which are tailor-made for easy landing. The flowers also attract bees and hummingbirds. Some moth caterpillars eat the flowers and leaves.

How to Use: Woodland phlox is one of the best groundcovers for woodland gardens. It is ideal for planting beneath deciduous trees and large shrubs, where it will receive early spring sun and summer shade. Use it to hide dying spring bulb foliage. It forms natural drifts and is good for covering hillsides. Plant woodland phlox with spring bulbs and wildflowers such as columbines, Virginia bluebells, foamflower, and bleeding hearts.

How to Grow & Maintain: Woodland phlox thrives in partial to full shade in cool, well-drained soil that is rich in organic matter. Flowering will diminish and foliage will brown if conditions are too sunny or too dry. Cut back flower stalks after flowering to keep plants neat. Plants seldom need dividing. Woodland phlox has a shallow root system and benefits from a summer mulch to conserve soil moisture. Phloxes are favorite foods of deer and rabbits.

Beyond the Species: Var. *laphamii* is a naturally occurring variety with deeper blue flowers. 'Fuller's White' is a good white-flowered cultivar. 'Dirgo Ice' has pale blue to white flowers. 'Clouds of Perfume' has very fragrant ice-blue flowers. 'Chattahoochee' is a hybrid of *P. divaricata* var. *laphamii* and *P. pilosa* and has lavender-blue flowers with dark purple centers. Creeping phlox (*P. stolonifera*) is another shade-tolerant species with white to lavender flowers. Plants thrive in cool, moist soils, where they will spread by stolons to form large mats of 6- to 10-inch-tall plants. 'Sherwood Purple' is a popular selection with mauve-purple flowers. Zones 4 to 9. Moss phlox (*P. subulata*) grows about 6 inches tall and is covered with pink, lavender, or white blooms in spring. Plants spread to form large mats of evergreen, needlelike leaves. It makes an attractive groundcover and is very popular in traditional gardens. It needs well-drained soil and sun to thrive. Many cultivars have been selected. Zones 3 to 9.

Phlox divaricata

Phlox subulata 'White Delight'

Phlox paniculata
Garden Phlox, Summer Phlox

Zones: 3 to 9
Size: 2 to 4 feet tall

Phlox glaberrima 'Morris Berd'

This staple of the perennial border has fragrant, five-petalled, tubular flowers densely arranged in large clusters atop stiff, upright stems with narrow leaves. Plants form stiff clumps.

Pollinator & Wildlife Value: Butterflies love garden phlox, and the flowers attract bees and hummingbirds. Some moth caterpillars eat the flowers and leaves.

How to Use: Garden phlox can be used in rain gardens. Taller types make good cut flowers.

How to Grow & Maintain: Garden phlox likes well-drained soil in full sun to light shade. It is intolerant of drought, so water during dry spells but avoid overhead watering. Remove faded flowers to prolong bloom and to prevent unwanted self-seeding. Taller types may need staking or cutting back in spring. Powdery mildew and root rot can be serious problems on some species. Spider mites and plant bugs can also be a problem, particularly in

hot, dry conditions. All *Phlox* species tend to be favorites of rabbits, deer, and groundhogs, and it may be difficult to establish plants where these animals are prevalent.

Beyond the Species: There are many cultivars of garden phlox available, most chosen for different flower colors and resistance to powdery mildew. 'Bright Eyes' has soft pink flowers with red centers. 'David' has white flowers and good resistance to mildew. 'Franz Shubert' has lilac flowers with white centers. 'Katherine' has lavender flowers with white centers. 'Red Riding Hood' has cherry red flowers. Smooth phlox (*P. glaberrima*) grows up to 2½ feet tall with similar flowers. It is a good garden plant, growing best in fertile, moist soil in full sun to partial shade. It tolerates more soil moisture than other phloxes and does well in rain gardens. It has good resistance to powdery mildew. Young plants can be killed by summer heat and drought, particularly in locations that lack adequate moisture. Plants may need support to keep them from flopping over. 'Morris Berd' has hot pink flowers with a white center. Zones 4 to 8. Wild sweet William (*P. maculata*) grows 2 to 3 feet tall with large, conical clusters of fragrant, pink, lavender, or white flowers in summer. The lance-shaped green leaves look nice all season. Plant it in average to rich, moist but well-drained soil in full sun or light shade in perennial borders or prairie gardens. Divide the multi-stemmed clumps every three to four years to keep plants vigorous. It is a good alternative for the more mildew-susceptible garden phlox in areas where powdery mildew thrives. Spider mites can also be a problem in hot, dry conditions. Deadheading prolongs the bloom. 'Alpha' has rose-pink flowers with darker eyes. 'Rosalinde' has deep pink flowers and grows 3 to 4 feet tall. Zones 3 to 8. Prairie phlox (*P. pilosa*) grows 10 to 30 inches tall with clusters of lavender, pink, or sometimes whitish fragrant flowers atop downy stems and leaves. It blooms late spring and early summer. The leaves are sparsely distributed along the stem giving plants a fine texture. Grow it in sandy, well-drained, slightly to moderately acidic soil in full sun or light shade in prairie gardens or perennial borders. It is not bothered by powdery mildew like garden phlox but the lower leaves tend to turn yellow and drop off when the plant becomes stressed. It reseeds but not obnoxiously. Zones 3 to 9.

Polemonium reptans
Spreading Jacob's Ladder, Greek Valerian

Zones: 3 to 8
Size: 8 to 16 inches tall

Polemonium reptans

Jacob's ladder is distinctive with its interesting foliage and baby blue, bell-shaped flowers. It is long-blooming and well-behaved—ideal traits for use in woodland or shade gardens and under shrubs or flowering trees. This low-branching, clumping plant is technically rhizomatous, but plants do not spread as the common name somewhat erroneously suggests. They tend to sprawl a bit, however. Attractive, dark green, pinnately divided leaves consist of five to fifteen leaflets and are up to a foot long. The plants are covered with small, sky-blue flowers in terminal clusters held slightly above the leaves, starting in midspring and often continuing well into June.

Pollinator & Wildlife Value: The nectar and pollen of the flowers attract several types of bees. Syrphid flies and beetles feed on pollen. Butterflies and moths visit flowers for nectar.

How to Use: This plant works well in woodland or shade gardens and under shrubs or flowering trees. Combine Jacob's ladder with Virginia bluebells to provide blue color after the latter goes dormant. It looks nice under flowering trees such as serviceberry or fothergilla. It can be grown along the edges of rain gardens. In shade gardens, combine it with bloodroot, wild geranium, foamflower, wild ginger, and ferns. Jacob's ladder combined with daffodils or white tulips is a striking spring show.

How to Grow & Maintain: Prefers a fertile, damp soil with a pH of 6 to 7 in part shade, but can be grown in almost full sun with adequate soil moisture. Despite the common name, plants do not creep and they seldom need division, but they do reseed. The brittle flower stems are easily broken, so be careful when cultivating around flowering plants. Cut bloom stalks to the ground after flowering for a neater appearance, to reduce reseeding, and to encourage a possible rebloom; foliage will remain attractive all season. Plants seldom need division. No serious insect or disease problems. Deer avoid it.

Beyond the Species: 'Blue Pearl' stays at 10 inches tall and has abundant rich blue flowers. 'Stairway to Heaven' has variegated foliage.

Pulsatilla patens
Pasque Flower

Zones: 2 to 8
Size: 6 to 12 inches tall

Pulsatilla patens

Starting in early sring, pasque flower has solitary, lavender, blue, or white crocus-like flowers that bloom for several weeks. Flowers are about 2 inches across with a ring of gold stamens and a central tuft of grayish pistils inside the sepals. Each plant has many flower stalks. Occasionally plants send up a flower stalk or two in early autumn. Showy, silvery, long-tailed seedheads resembling those of clematis follow the flowers, extending the ornamental value. The entire plant is covered with silky hairs that give it a silvery sheen that begs to be touched. These hairs protect plants from late-season frosts. The basal foliage persists through summer and eventually covers about a square foot. It blooms early enough that flowers often appear in matted remains of the previous year's foliage. This plant's nomenclature is confusing: you'll find it also listed as *Anemone patens, Pulsatilla nuttalliana,* or *P. hirsutissima.* Avoid planting the commonly available European species *P. vulgaris,* which is no more ornamental and less beneficial to native insects.

Pollinator & Wildlife Value: Pasque flower is an early pollen source for several types of bees, which cross-pollinate plants and collect pollen for their larvae. Hummingbirds use the soft foliage for nest building, and they may visit the flowers for nectar. The seedheads attract goldfinches.

How to Use: Pasque flower is the earliest of the prairie wildflowers, making it a must for prairie gardens that are looking a bit tired in early spring. Select a spot where it won't be overwhelmed by taller plants. It does well in perennial borders and rock gardens. Combine it with other small spring bloomers such as minor bulbs, prairie smoke, and columbines. Pick the seedheads before they are fully ripe for use in dried bouquets.

How to Grow & Maintain: Pasque flower prefers a dry, well-drained soil in full sun to very light shade. A gritty soil containing gravel or rocky material is fine. This plant is much tougher than it looks. The early flowers can handle late-spring snows and cold snaps. It needs moisture while flowering, but otherwise is quite drought tolerant. Root rot can be a problem if the soil becomes waterlogged from poor drainage. If soil is heavy, add sand and organic matter before planting. It grows best where there is little or no competition from grasses or tall plants. Plants may go dormant in summer. The woody taproot may send out new flower stalks but plants never become invasive. There are no serious insect or disease issues. Deer and rabbits are repelled by the foliage, which contains a blistering agent.

Ratibida pinnata
Prairie Coneflower, Gray-Headed Coneflower

Zones: 3 to 9
Size: 3 to 5 feet tall

Prairie coneflower is a stiff, erect plant with rough-feeling, coarse leaves. It is redeemed by its showy 2½-inch flowers that appear throughout summer and well into fall. They have drooping, soft-yellow rays and elevated, conelike green centers that change to dark purple or brown and offer interest after the petals fall. The root system is rhizomatous, often forming a dense clump.

Pollinator & Wildlife Value: Many insects, including bees and beneficial predators, visit the flowers. Other insects include wasps, flies, small butterflies, and beetles. Some butterfly and moth caterpillars feed on the foliage. Goldfinches eat the seeds.

How to Use: The soft yellow color of prairie coneflower is a welcome and relaxing contrast to other hot-colored summer flowers. It adapts well to perennial borders and weaves nicely through prairie gardens. The flowers bloom a long time and are good for cutting. Once established, it is drought tolerant and can be used in xeriscapes. It also does well in rain gardens. Plant coneflowers with other summer-blooming plants such as blazing stars, blanket flower, butterfly weed, purple prairie clover, monarda, anise hyssop, and prairie grasses. Individual plants are narrow and somewhat sparsely leafed so they should be surrounded by other plants, which will also offer support. Blooms are so abundant and plants bloom for a long time, so one plant is often all you'll need. The delicate flowers sway with each passing breeze, giving a real sense of prairie to a landscape.

How to Grow & Maintain: Requires average to rich, well-drained soil in full sun or light shade. Plants cannot tolerate heavy, wet soils. It tolerates poor, dry soils but it will wilt in summer's heat. Prairie coneflower seldom needs division. Seedlings can be replanted while they are still small to refresh the supply of plants. There is a tendency for the flowering stems to flop around if this plant is spoiled by too much water or fertile soil. Garden plants may need staking. Plants reseed abundantly, so you'll need to pull as needed. Once plants get large, the dense root system is hard to pull. It has no serious insect or disease problems. Deer avoid it.

Beyond the Species: Mexican hat (*R. columnifera*) is smaller, growing 1 to 3 feet tall. It has the same lemon-yellow ray petals but the center disk is twice as tall, up

Ratibida pinnata

to 2 inches. It stays under 2 feet tall and has nice stiff flower stems. The finely cut grayish-green foliage is attractive even when the plant is not in flower. It must have well-drained soil, however; wet feet will be its death. It is not nearly as prolific of a seeder as its taller cousin, and since it tends to be short-lived, you'll want to find a few seedlings. If you're lucky, you'll find a few seedlings with showy splotches of red on the ray petals, a common occurrence in wild populations. Mexican hat is a better choice in smaller landscape situations but is best grown in small groupings rather than individual plants. It is a nice companion for other medium-sized, summer-blooming prairie plants such as butterfly milkweed, purple prairie clover, and prairie phlox. Its small size and long bloom also make it suitable for container use. The rays of the less common but very showy var. *pulcherrima* are brownish purple. 'Red Midget' grows 15 to 18 inches tall and has very showy mahogany-red ray petals that have a narrow edging of golden yellow. Zones 3 to 9.

Rudbeckia hirta
Black-Eyed Susan, Yellow Coneflower

Zones: 2 to 9
Size: 1 to 3 feet tall

Rudbeckia fulgida var. sullivantii 'Goldsturm'

Black-eyed Susan may well be the most recognizable native flower. It is a short-lived perennial with golden yellow rays surrounding a conical cluster of rich brown disc florets. Its long bloom period starts midsummer and continues well into fall. The lance-shaped leaves are grayish green and covered with small stiff hairs which give them a rough texture. It blooms the first year from seed planted in early spring and is often grown as an annual. The root system consists of a central taproot and is without rhizomes.

Pollinator & Wildlife Value: The composite flowers appeal to a wide range of insects, particularly bees and flies, as well as some wasps, butterflies, and beetles. Caterpillars of silvery checkerspot feed on the leaves. The seeds are occasionally eaten by goldfinches and other birds, and some birds use the plants for cover.

How to Use: Black-eyed Susans and coneflowers bring long-lasting color to prairie gardens and mixed borders. All types do well in rain gardens. The flower heads provide winter interest. It is one of the few natives that adapt well to container culture; especially cultivars. Almost anything looks nice with black-eyed Susans, but especially blazing stars, asters, butterfly milkweed, flowering spurge, monarda, little bluestem, and prairie dropseed.

How to Grow & Maintain: It prefers moist, average, well-drained soil in full sun but tolerates light shade and a wide range of soil conditions. Sow seeds two years in a row for yearly blooming. Once a planting is established, plants self-seed to keep the color coming year after year. Rich soils tend to produce weak-stemmed plants. Plants are easy to propagate from seeds or by transplanted seedlings. The foliage of *Rudbeckia* species is susceptible to several diseases, including botrytis and powdery mildew. Proper plant spacing and avoiding overhead watering helps keep them in check. Deadhead spent flowers to encourage additional bloom and/or to prevent any unwanted seedlings. Plants reproduce entirely by seed so they never become aggressive vegetatively. Deer and rabbits usually avoid the coarse leaves, but slugs and snails (remember, they are bird food!) may eat seedlings.

Beyond the Species: Many cultivars are available, with more introduced every year. 'Becky' is a dwarf selection staying about 8 inches tall. 'Indian Summer' is a popular form with larger flowers on compact plants. 'Prairie Sun' has flowers with golden petals tipped in primrose yellow surrounding a light green cone. 'Cherokee Sunset' is a mix of fully double flowers in shades of yellow, orange, bronze, and russet. Most are

Rudbeckia hirta

grown as annuals, and they make good container plants. Showy hybrids called gloriosa daisies are derived from *R. hirta*. They are annuals or short-lived perennials with 5- to 6-inch, yellow, orange, red, or multicolored flowers on 2- to 3-foot plants. They bloom all summer and are good for cutting and containers. Orange coneflower (*R. fulgida*) is similar in appearance but usually blooms later and is rhizomatous. It typically grows 3 feet tall and will form colonies. It's rare to find the species offered by nurseries; they mainly sell the very popular 'Goldsturm', which is a selection of var. *sullivantii*, a more compact form. This cultivar appears to be more susceptible to bacterial angular leaf spot, which causes brown or black angular spots on the leaves that can expand to blacken the whole leaf. It self-sows and produces abundant offsets. Zones 3 to 9. Cutleaf coneflower (*R. laciniata*) grows 3 to 6 feet tall and has leaves with cut, irregular lobes. The abundant clusters of yellow flowers have light green central disks. It requires moister soil conditions and is great for soggy stream banks. Use it in informal gardens and wet prairies. Plants can take light shade, but with fewer flowers. 'Herbstonne' ('Autumn Sun') is a 5- to 7-foot-tall hybrid with *R. nitida* that makes a dramatic statement in perennial borders. Zones 3 to 9. Sweet coneflower (*R. subtomentosa*) is native to mesic to wet prairies in most of the tallgrass region. It grows taller than most species, 3 to 5 feet, and is a little more sunflower-like in appearance with dark brown-purple center disks and yellow rays. The gray-green, sweet-scented leaves form large bushy clumps, but it is not rhizomatous. It likes full sun but consistent moisture. Pinch plants back lightly in spring to reduce their lankiness. 'Henry Eilers' has yellow rays that are rolled instead of flat, giving the flowers a quilled effect. Zones 3 to 9.

141

Rudbeckia hirta 'Prairie Sun'

Sanguinaria canadensis
Bloodroot

Zones: 3 to 8
Size: 4 to 10 inches tall

Sanguinaria canadensis

Bloodroot is an excellent example of how rewarding it is to include natives in your garden. This exquisite early-blooming flower is something everyone should have a chance to see, but its fleeting nature and the constant degradation of habitats make it a challenge to view this native plant in bloom. Bloodroot's appearance can change greatly in a matter of hours, and it's a real treat to witness the unfolding of its pure white flowers. Bloodroot's first blooms appear in early spring on sunny, south-facing slopes, with the main bloom beginning in midspring. Each flower stalk typically emerges wrapped by one palmate, deeply scalloped, grayish-green basal leaf, giving the plant the look of tulips. As the flower blooms, the leaf unfurls, and the plants become more daisylike. The elegant, 1½- to 2-inch flower has eight to ten (occasionally twelve or sixteen) oblong petals and numerous golden yellow stamens. The flower is initially taller than the leaf, but as it turns to fruit, the leaf unfolds and flattens to shade the fruit. Leaves continue to grow in size after bloom (sometimes to as much as 9 inches across), turning darker green with heavier veining and remaining attractive until mid- to late summer when the plants often go dormant.

Pollinator & Wildlife Value: Bees are the primary pollinators. Ants gather the seeds for food and, in the process, help disperse plants. Small animals use the leaves for cover.

How to Use: The short-lived but showy pure white flowers really say spring has arrived. It makes a great groundcover in shade or woodland gardens because the leaves remain through most of summer and are ornamental. Tuck groups of threes, fives, or sevens here and there in shady borders, allowing them to naturalize and imitate bloodroot's natural growth habit. Plant bloodroot with other early spring bloomers such as bellworts, spreading Jacob's ladder, and Virginia bluebells. It combines nicely with lady fern, spring bulbs, primroses, and pulmonarias. The long-lasting foliage fills bare spots when spring ephemerals go dormant.

How to Grow & Maintain: It prefers moist, humus-rich soil with direct sunlight in early spring and summer shade but will tolerate drier soils if well mulched. Improve poor or sandy soil by adding generous amounts of peat moss and compost. Mulch plants with a thin layer of pine needles or shredded leaves. Heavy mulch can lead to stem rot at the soil surface. Plants may go dormant during dry spells. The thickened, elongated rhizome exudes red sap when broken. Self-sown seedlings will appear when conditions are favorable and are usually a welcome sight. It has no pest problems. Deer and rabbits usually avoid it.

Beyond the Species: 'Flore Pleno', also sold as 'Multiplex', is an exquisite double-flowered cultivar but it doesn't offer any value to pollinators.

Silene regia
Royal Catchfly

Zones: 4 to 9
Size: 2 to 4 feet tall

This unbranched, upright perennial has clusters of showy red or scarlet flowers at the top of the plants. The star-shaped flowers can be up to an inch across and have five petals. They start blooming midsummer and are showy for about a month. The blue-green leaves are up to 4 inches long and 2 inches wide. The root system consists of a central taproot and short rhizomes, which enable this plant to spread vegetatively to form small colonies. Most sources list it as hardy to Zone 4 but it may not survive every winter in colder regions.

Pollinator & Wildlife Value: Since many insects are insensitive to the color red, it is an uncommon color among prairie plants. Some butterflies, including black swallowtails, perceive red, and royal catchfly flowers are tailor-made for them. The long narrow tube formed by the calyx is ideal for their proboscis and the flared petals provide a colorful landing platform. All *Silene* species are hummingbird favorites.

How to Use: This is one of only a few natives to give red color to the summer garden. So even though it isn't all that attractive when not in flower, it's worth making a place for it in the perennial border or cottage garden. It's a must for butterfly and hummingbird gardens. Its red color provides a great contrast to the numerous yellow and gold flowers blooming at same time. Plant it near smooth oxeye, black-eyed Susan, and prairie coneflower for a striking show.

How to Grow & Maintain: Royal catchfly will do well in full or partial sun in moist to slightly dry soil. It prefers a sandy or gravelly soil but will grow on heavier clay soils as long as drainage is good. Royal catchfly is fairly easy to grow but is somewhat slower to develop than other plants and resents excessive shading. During drought, the lower leaves may turn yellow and fall off. Plant lower-growing plants around it to help hide lower foliage. Plants begin to bloom while small in size but it takes several years to reach their full potential. Taller plants may need some support. It has no serious insect or disease problems. Deer and rabbits usually avoid it.

Beyond the Species: 'Prairie Fire' is a prolific bloomer that grows 4 feet tall. Wild pink (*S. caroliniana*) is a low-growing, mounding plant that reaches 4 to 8 inches in height. It has spikes of light to dark pink flowers atop dark green leaves. It likes well-drained soil in full to part sun. Zones 4 to 9. Fire pink (*S. virginica*) is similar to royal catchfly but much shorter, only 12 to 18 inches tall. It needs well-drained soil and does very well in rock gardens. Plants self-sow readily, which can be a good thing since they tend to be short-lived. Zones 4 to 9.

Silene regia

Solidago speciosa
Showy Goldenrod

Zones: 4 to 9
Size: 2 to 5 feet tall

Solidago speciosa

As the common name implies, showy goldenrod is indeed very showy while in bloom from late summer through fall. Its inflorescences are up to 1 foot long, consisting of erect panicles of small, bright yellow, compound flowers. The flowering stems are held erect or curve upward, unlike most goldenrod flowers that flop down. The plant is rather coarse when not in bloom with alternate leaves up to 6 inches long and 1½ inches

wide. The root system is fibrous and rhizomatous, occasionally forming vegetative offsets. Insect-pollinated goldenrods have been wrongly accused of causing hay fever, which is actually an allergic reaction to wind-borne pollen from other plants such as ragweed.

Pollinator & Wildlife Value: This is the area where goldenrods really shine. The flowers attract honeybees, bumblebees, ants, beetles, and an occasional moth or butterfly. Caterpillars of many moths feed on various parts of plants. Other insect feeders include various leafhoppers, lace bugs, plant bugs, and beetles. Eastern goldfinch, juncos, sparrows, grouse, and the greater prairie chicken eat the seeds. Grouse eat the leaves.

How to Use: While goldenrods are a staple of prairie gardens, most are too aggressive for traditional garden settings. This is one species that adapts well to sunny perennial borders, providing good color and contrast in late summer. Several goldenrods can be used in rain gardens. Their flowers work well in fresh and dried arrangements. Plant goldenrods with asters, Joe-pye weed, blazing stars, and grasses. Breeders have introduced hybrids that are less aggressive and have compact growth habits, making them more suitable for garden use. Hopefully the flowers on these introductions will retain their benefits to wildlife.

How to Grow & Maintain: Goldenrods tolerate a wide range of conditions, from full to partial sun and slightly moist to dry soil. The soil can contain significant amounts of loam, sand, or rocky material. Cut plants back hard after flowering if reseeding is a problem. Plan to divide plants every two to three years to control growth. Plants may topple over if they are given excessive moisture or fertilizer. Rust and other foliar diseases can be a problem, but are not usually serious if plants are in full sun. Deer and rabbits occasionally eat the leaves, stems, and flowers.

Beyond the Species: 'Fireworks' is a cultivar of *S. rugosa*, a weedy species that is too aggressive for landscape use. However, this selection is a very nice garden plant, with long, drooping flower stalks on 2½- to 3-foot, compact plants. Zones 3 to 9. Zigzag goldenrod (*S. flexicaulis*) grows 2 to 4 feet tall with erect, somewhat zigzagged stems and flowers in small clusters. It prefers richer soil and light shade and is a

Solidago nemoralis

good candidate for woodland gardens, where fall color is hard to come by. It will spread. Zones 3 to 8. Gray goldenrod (*S. nemoralis*) is more compact, growing only 1 to 2 feet tall, and has attractive gray-green foliage. The narrow, wandlike inflorescence has a tendency to nod. It blooms a little later than showy goldenrod and lasts about a month. It is somewhat shade and drought tolerant and does well in poor soils where little else does well. The rhizomatous root system will eventually form colonies. Zones 3 to 9. Stiff goldenrod (*S. rigida*, now classified as *Oligoneuron rigidum*) grows from 2 to 5 feet tall. The attractive flattened flower panicles grow in contrast to most goldenrod flowers. It has nice gray-green, downy leaves that turn dusty rose in fall. It can be used in large perennial gardens, rain gardens, and cottage gardens. It self-sows and can become weedy in small gardens. Plants grow from clumping or spreading rhizomes that will spread but can easily be controlled if needed. Zones 3 to 9. Autumn goldenrod (*S. sphacelata*) grows 2 to 3 feet tall and has a spreading growth habit. 'Golden Fleece' is more compact, growing about 15 inches tall and only spreading about 2 feet, making it better for garden use. Zones 4 to 9.

Spigelia marilandica
Indian Pink, Woodland Pinkroot, Worm Grass

Zones: 5 to 9
Size: 12 to 18 inches tall

Spigelia marilandica

This tropical-looking plant grows into bushy clumps of upright stems with glossy green leaves and gorgeous red tubular flowers with yellow throats. Primary bloom is early to midsummer, but you may see sporadic bloom throughout summer and a flush of bloom again in fall.
Caution: Plants are poisonous.
Pollinator & Wildlife Value: Its bright red, tubular flowers are tailor-made to attract hummingbirds, its primary pollinator. Butterflies also visit the flowers.
How to Use: Indian pink looks best planted in drifts in woodland, perennial, or shade gardens. It brings much-needed summer color to shady areas of the landscape. Plants will fill in to form a groundcover when conditions are right. It does well in rain gardens.

How to Grow & Maintain: It prefers moist, rich soil in partial shade but will tolerate quite a bit of sun if the soil is moist. Plants do take a bit of time and effort to get established. They rarely need division and resent transplanting. Once established, it is relatively carefree and doesn't have any serious pest problems. Deer and rabbits avoid it.

Stokesia laevis
Stokes' Aster

Zones: 5 to 9
Size: 1 to 2 feet tall

This upright perennial has fluffy, cornflower-like, soft blue flowers up to 4 inches across. The ray florets are fringed and blue, lavender, pink, or white in two concentric rows, and the disc florets are darker shades of the same colors. Plants bloom for several weeks from late spring to midsummer. Erect, leafy stems grow from a rosette of evergreen leaves.

Pollinator & Wildlife Value: Skippers and butterflies, especially American painted lady and pipe vine swallowtail, flock to the flowers. Bees and wasps are pollinators.

How to Use: Use Stokes' aster at the front of perennial borders in small groups where its deep green basal leaves provide color and texture all winter. It does well in rock gardens, cottage gardens, and butterfly gardens and as a groundcover. It makes a nice cut flower.

How to Grow & Maintain: It blooms best in full sun and needs slightly acidic soil. Stokes' aster likes plenty of moisture, but soil should be light and well drained. It is imperative that the soil be dry during winter. Promptly deadhead to encourage more bloom. Plants are quite drought tolerant once established. The flower stems tend to be weak, and plants may be flattened by thunderstorms or high winds. It has no pest problems. Deer and rabbits tend to avoid it.

Beyond the Species: A plethora of cultivars is available. 'Blue Danube' has large lavender flowers with white centers. 'Peachie's Pick' is a compact, late-blooming selection with cornflower blue flowers. 'Blue Moon' has deep blue flowers. 'Bluestone' is smaller, to 10 inches. 'Wyoming' has the darkest blue flowers of all. 'Rosea' has rosy pink flowers. 'Alba' has white flowers. 'Silver Moon' has larger, silvery white flowers. 'Omega Skyrocket' is vigorous, growing 3 to 4 feet tall with long-stemmed, white to pale blue flowers.

Stokesia laevis **'Peachie's Pick'**

Symphyotrichum novae-angliae (Aster novae-angliae)
New England Aster

Zones: 3 to 8
Size: 3 to 6 feet tall

***Symphyotrichum novae-angliae* 'Purple Dome'**

New England aster flowers have violet or lavender petals surrounding yellow centers on heads 1 to 2 inches wide. Daisylike flowers are clustered at the ends of branches from late summer through fall. This is a tall plant with leaves clasping hairy stems. Mature plants have woody, fibrous root systems and form thick clumps after a few years. The showy flowers have petals ranging from violet to pink to white surrounding yellow centers and can be up to 2 inches wide. *Aster* species have been reclassified and most North American species are now in *Symphyotrichum.*

Pollinator & Wildlife Value: All asters are important late-season nectar sources for migrating butterflies and hummingbirds. The flowers are heavy with pollen, a great food source for many types of bees. Several butterfly and moth larvae, including crescent and checkerspot butterflies, feed on plants. Birds eat the seeds, and some species provide cover for waterfowl.

How to Use: This fall bloomer brings purple shades to fall gardens. The species can be a bit coarse for formal settings but the many cultivars are excellent garden plants. Use them in mixed borders, cottage gardens, and even large rock gardens. Several species do well in rain gardens. Plant asters with other late-season plants such as goldenrods, grasses, and smooth oxeye for an outstanding fall show. Lower-growing plants, especially grasses, help hide browned leaves and stems on lower parts of the plant.

How to Grow & Maintain: New England aster likes consistent soil moisture; an ideal location is moist, average soil in full sun to partial shade. Avoid soils that dry out completely. The tall stems of the species can become top-heavy when in bloom and usually need some type of support. Cut plants back to about a foot in spring to promote bushier plants. Divide plants in spring every third year to promote vigorous growth. Avoid too much nitrogen, which can result in abundant foliage and floppy plants. Plants are susceptible to leaf spot, rust, and mildew, which can leave lower leaves in bad shape by flowering time but usually do no permanent harm. Plants can be cut to ground after flowering if they look too unsightly. Deer usually avoid asters.

Beyond the Species: There are dozens of cultivars of New England aster, mainly selected for more compact growth habit, better lower leaf retention, and earlier and longer bloom time than the species. 'Andenken an Alma Potschke' is covered in bright rose-pink flowers on 3- to 4-foot plants. 'Harrington's Pink' has unique light salmon-pink flowers and grows up to 5 feet tall. 'Hella Lacy' grows 3 to 4 feet tall with violet-blue flowers. 'Honeysong Pink' grows about 3½ feet tall and has pink petals with bright yellow disks. 'Purple Dome' is a naturally dense dwarf cultivar (18 to 24 inches) with semi-double, deep purple flowers. 'Roter Stern'

148

Symphyotrichum laeve

(Red Star) stays about 15 inches tall and has red flowers. 'Wedding Lace' grows 4 feet tall with whitish flowers. Heath aster (*S. ericoides*) has hundreds of white or pale blue flowers on 1- to 3-foot stiffly branched plants. Plant it in average to rich, dry to moist, slightly acidic soil in full sun. 'Blue Star' has sky blue flowers. 'Esther' has pale pink flowers. 'Pink Star' has light pink flowers. 'Snow Flurry' ('Prostrata') only grows 6 to 8 inches tall (good for rock gardens) and has white flowers. Zones 3 to 8. Smooth blue aster (*S. laeve*) has loose panicles of light blue flowers on 2- to 4-foot plants that have lovely waxy, blue-gray leaves. It starts blooming in late summer and is one of the last asters to bloom in autumn. It is a very nice landscape plant. Plant it in average to rich, moist but well-drained soil in full sun or light shade. It is not as floppy as New England aster but it may need staking in shadier spots. Seedlings will appear but this beautiful plant is worth a little effort. 'Blue Bird' is a compact selection with deep sky blue flowers. Zones 3 to 8. Calico aster (*S. lateriflorum*) grows 2 to 4 feet tall. This bushy plant has especially attractive foliage in addition to bearing hundreds of small white flowers. It forms clumps but is never invasive. Grow it in average to rich, well-drained soil in full sun or light shade. 'Prince' and 'Lady in Black' were selected for their deep plum-purple foliage that really sets off the white flowers. Zones 3 to 7. New York aster (*S. novi-belgii*) grows best in moist soil. It grows 2 to 6 feet tall with violet to purple or rose flowers. There are many cultivars available, and they are usually better choices for garden use. 'Alert' is a dwarf (12 to 15 inches tall) cultivar with crimson-red flowers. 'Professor Anton Kippenberg' is a popular selection growing 10 to 14 inches with blue flowers. Aromatic aster (*S. oblongifolium*) has sky blue flowers on stiff 1- to 3-foot stems. Its smaller size makes it a good garden plant. 'October Skies' and 'Raydon's Favorite' are two compact selections especially good for garden use. Zones 3 to 8.

Tiarella cordifolia
Foamflower

Zones: 3 to 8
Size: 6 to 12 inches tall

Tiarella cordifolia

Tiarella 'Spring Symphony'

Foamflower gets its name from the frothy conical clusters of white flowers that are sometimes flushed with pink. They appear in midspring. The handsome, bright green, maple-leaf foliage is attractive all summer, turning a beautiful red in autumn and remaining semi-evergreen in winter. Plants spread by trailing stolons (horizontal stems), eventually forming a weed-smothering mat of foliage.

Pollinator & Wildlife Value: The tiny flowers are pollinated by small bees and syrphid flies. Plants provide cover for toads and other small animals.

How to Use: Foamflower is an attractive groundcover that will eventually form a mat of foliage in shade and woodland gardens. Use it under trees or shrubs alone or with other groundcovers. It can be used along the edge of rain gardens and does well along stream banks. The less-aggressive and often mound-forming cultivars are great additions to perennial gardens.

How to Grow & Maintain: It will do best in an evenly moist, rich, slightly acidic soil in partial to full shade. Remove unwanted rooted runners anytime to keep plants from spreading too far. Foamflower is not drought tolerant and may need supplemental water during dry periods. It has no serious insect or disease problems and is deer and rabbit resistant.

Beyond the Species: 'Oakleaf' has large deeply lobed, oaklike leaves that take on reddish tints in fall. Many hybrid selections have been made, mainly for their interestingly shaped and colorful foliage and more mounding growth habit. 'Cygnet' has deeply cut, dark green leaves with dark centers and dense spires of pink flowers that can rise as high as 18 inches. 'Iron Butterfly' forms a mound of deeply cut, dark green leaves with black center blotches and black striping along the midveins. 'Pink Skyrocket' has deeply cut leaves with attractive red veins and abundant pink flowers. 'Spring Symphony' has deeply lobed leaves with a black star pattern in the middle and soft pink flowers on mounded plants.

Uvularia grandiflora

Large-Flowered Bellwort, Merrybells

Zones: 3 to 8
Size: 12 to 16 inches tall

Looking for an easy-to-grow yet stunning accent plant for your woodland garden? Large-flowered bellwort is just the ticket. This spring bloomer has 1- to 2-inch, lemon-yellow flowers that dangle bell-like from downturned stems. It blooms mid- to late spring, bringing a sort of daffodil look to the woodland garden. The alternate, long, sea green leaves have smooth margins and downy white undersides, and they clasp the stem at their bases. The flowers expand first, while the petiole-less leaves are still soft and furled. The foliage expands after flowering to create a soothing, soft green groundcover that remains attractive all summer. Flowers have a subtle but sweet fragrance.

Pollinator & Wildlife Value: The showy flowers attract several types of bees and flies for nectar, which, in turn, perform pollination. Ants disperse the seeds.

How to Use: The bright yellow color is a real attention-getter in early spring woodland gardens. Place clumps here and there for interest or mass several for greater impact. The long-lasting, attractive foliage is a bonus. Plants compete well with tree roots, and established plantings survive the dry shade conditions under large shade trees. Large-flowered bellwort grows well with almost any early-flowering woodland plant, but it is especially attractive with blue flowers such as Virginia bluebells and woodland phlox. In shade gardens, grow it with epimediums, foamflowers, and pulmonarias.

How to Grow & Maintain: It prefers a moist, acidic to neutral soil in spring sun and summer shade. Plants spread slowly but rarely become invasive. It has no insect or disease problems, and once established, requires little or no care. Unfortunately, it tends to be a favorite of deer.

Beyond the Species: 'Sunbonnet' is a hard-to-find cultivar selected for its bigger, brighter flowers. Bellwort (*U. perfoliata*) is very similar but has smaller flowers. Zones 3 to 8. Pale bellwort (*U. sessilifolia*) is smaller, growing 4 to 12 inches tall, and more delicate and lighter yellow in flower. It has a greater tendency to spread and form a groundcover. Culture and use are the same, but it prefers a more acidic soil. 'Variegata' is a rare variegated form that is quite nice. Zones 3 to 8.

151

Uvularia grandiflora

Yucca filamentosa
Adam's Needle

Zones: 4 to 10
Size: 1 to 4 feet tall

Yucca filamentosa

Although actually a broadleaf evergreen shrub, Adam's needle looks more like a perennial and is usually used as one. It features a basal rosette of rigid, sword-shaped, spine-tipped green leaves with long curly threads along the margins. The leaves form a clump 2 to 3 feet tall. In late spring a flowering stalk rises from the center of each rosette, typically to 6 to 8 feet (infrequently to 12 feet), bearing a long terminal panicle of very showy, nodding, bell-shaped, creamy white flowers.

Pollinator & Wildlife Value: The yucca moth is completely dependent on this genus as a nectar source and egg-laying site. Flowers attract other butterflies too. The yucca giant skipper butterfly uses it as an egg-laying site and a larval food source.

How to Use: This is an interesting accent plant in borders, especially the variegated selections, and is perfect for xeriscaping. It is very tolerant of urban conditions such as poor soils, road salt, and pollution. Soften its bold texture by surrounding it with summer bloomers such as blanket flower, sages, prairie phlox,

Yucca filamentosa 'Color Guard'

Mexican hat, butterfly weed, and black-eyed Susans. Keep it well away from walkways and pathways.

How to Grow & Maintain: Adam's needle needs very well-drained soil. It tolerates, poor, sandy soils and some shade but does best in full sun. Choose a site carefully for this long-lived, difficult-to-transplant perennial. Water only during establishment; after that plants are very drought tolerant. Remove the unsightly flower stalk after flowers are done blooming for a better-looking plant. Remove older, brown leaves at their base in early spring (wear gloves). It has no insect or disease problems, and deer and rabbits avoid it.

Beyond the Species: A number of variegated cultivars have been selected. 'Color Guard' has bold center stripes of bright canary yellow. 'Bright Edge' has leaves edged in creamy white to yellow. Soap tree yucca (*Y. elata*) is native to deserts in the Southwestern part of the US. It forms a rounded ball of foliage 2 to 6 feet tall with creamy white to pinkish flowers. Zones 7 to 10. Soapweed yucca (*Y. glauca*) is smaller, growing 1 to 3 feet tall, and has narrower leaves. It is a long-lived, taprooted perennial that eventually spreads to form colonies. The foliage is the main attraction, since the greenish-white flowers only bloom for a short time from late spring to early summer. The stiff, narrow, blue-green leaves are covered in spines. Zones 4 to 10.

NATIVE BUZZ

Dragonflies
Odonata order

There are more than 5,000 known species of dragonflies. Most temperate-zone species live as adults less than a month, though some species can live as long as six months. They are valued as predators, since they help control populations of harmful insects. Dragonflies are expert fliers. They can fly straight, up and down, hover like a helicopter, and even mate mid-air. If they can't fly, they'll starve because they only eat prey they catch while flying.

Range: Highly variable, with some being widespread while others are highly local in their distribution.

Habitat: Immature dragonflies are born in bodies of freshwater, and they require nutrients derived exclusively from freshwater sources to survive. Upon maturing, however, adult dragonflies gravitate toward land, but still require adjacent bodies of freshwater for food and sustenance.

Larval Food: In their larval stage, which can last up to two years, dragonflies are aquatic and eat just about anything—tadpoles, mosquitoes, fish, other insect larvae, and even each other.

Adult Food: Mostly other flying insects, particularly midges and mosquitoes. They also eat butterflies, moths, and smaller dragonflies. They are a great control of the mosquito population. A single dragonfly can eat 30 to hundreds of mosquitoes per day.

Grasses & Sedges

Ornamental grasses bring both practical and aesthetic benefits to the landscape. On the practical side, they come as close as possible to being no maintenance and can be used as support for nearby perennials. On the aesthetic side, grasses come in a wide range of heights, colors, and textures and offer more than one season of interest.

154

Carex pensylvanica
Pennsylvania Sedge

Zones: 3 to 8
Size: 6 to 10 inches tall

Pennsylvania sedge is one of hundreds of native sedges. Sedges are not true grasses, but rather are in their own family, *Cyperaceae*. Several distinguishing characteristics set them apart from grasses, mainly in their flower structure. Most are not suitable for traditional garden use, but this species offers a lot. It is a cool-season plant that greens up very early in spring and forms a neat mound of bright green. It spreads by stolons and makes an elegant, fine-textured groundcover when massed. Brownish flower spikes appear mid- to late spring.

Pollinator & Wildlife Value: This sedge is food for several insects, including leafhoppers, grasshoppers, and butterfly caterpillars (Appalachian brown butterfly). Birds eat the seeds.

How to Use: Pennsylvania sedge makes a beautiful, soft-textured groundcover in partial sun to full shade. It provides a nice backdrop to spring wildflowers and early color in shade gardens. Plant it among spring ephemerals to fill in after they go dormant. It tolerates dry shade under large trees. Use it in place of traditional turfgrasses in shady areas where you don't need a tightly mown lawn. It withstands light foot traffic and periodic mowing. All sedges look nice planted near water features and work well in rain gardens.

Carex stricta

How to Grow & Maintain: This plant prefers an acidic, well-drained, average to dry soil in light to full shade, but will tolerate a wide range of conditions, including full sun if grown in moister soil. It's very easy to grow once established. Plants spread slowly so if you want a solid groundcover, place clumps as close together as you can. Plants can be divided anytime during the growing season to increase your numbers. Pennsylvania sedge can be mown two or three times during the growing season if desired. Cut back old foliage in very early spring before new growth emerges. It has no insect or disease problems, and deer avoid it.

Beyond the Species: Palm sedge (*C. muskingumensis*) grows 2 to 3 feet tall and has wider, straplike, light green leaves. Grow it in sun or shade in moist soil. The creeping rhizomes spread slowly to form an effective groundcover. 'Wachtposten' is more upright. Zones 4 to 9. Tussock sedge (*C. stricta*) forms a dense, 2- to 3-foot clump of long, slender leaves that arch outward, creating a symmetrical fountain-like effect. Attractive reddish-brown flowers appear in late spring. It grows in sun or shade in moist soil and eventually forms a large colony. It's an important host of the mulberry wing skipper butterfly. Zones 3 to 8.

Carex pensylvanica

Deschampsia caespitosa
Tufted Hair Grass

Zones: 2 to 7
Size: 3 to 4 feet

Deschampsia caespitosa

Tufted hair grass is a cool-season grass that offers beauty from late spring into fall. It is a well-mannered bunch grass that forms tight basal tufts that grow about 1 foot tall and eventually spread about 2 feet wide. During summer it produces large, open panicles of glistening silver-tinted flower heads that reach about 3 feet tall. They are especially effective when backlit or set off by a dark background. The panicles turn yellowish tan as the seed ripens and may remain attractive through much of winter.

Pollinator & Wildlife Value: It is a larval host and nectar source for some butterflies, including umber skipper. Birds eat the seeds.

How to Use: This is a wonderful grass for cooler climates, but it is not as well suited to southern areas. A tolerance for wet soils makes tufted hair grass useful for planting near water, and it's a good choice for rain and even bog gardens. However, it does quite well in areas with soil on the dry side. Use it in perennial borders, grass gardens, or for massing, where it offers the beauty of an ornamental grass long before any of the warm-season prairies grasses are showy. It can be grown in partial shade, though flowering will be slightly reduced. Tufted hair grass is one of the few native grasses that can also be used in containers. It is tolerant of black walnut trees and air pollution.

How to Grow & Maintain: Tufted hair grass prefers evenly moist soil in full sun to light shade but grows well in most garden soils. Avoid sunny, droughty conditions. Cut back plants in late fall or very early spring. Plants may self-sow in optimum conditions but rarely become a nuisance. They do not spread and have no insect or disease problems. Deer avoid it.

Beyond the Species: Several cultivars are available in the nursery trade, but their parentage is questionable and some or all may have European species in them. In any case, they don't really have any redeeming qualities that make them a better choice than the species. Wavy hair grass (*D. flexuosa*) is shorter, staying under 3 feet tall. It requires very well-drained soil. It is beautiful massed in dry, shady areas, if you can locate it in the nursery trade. Zones 2 to 7.

Panicum virgatum
Switchgrass

Zones: 3 to 9
Size: 4 to 7 feet tall

Panicum virgatum

A full-grown clump of switchgrass is a stately sight, especially in fall when the showy seedheads sway above the beautiful golden yellow to deep burgundy leaves. This warm-season clumping grass grows from a dense crown of congested rhizomes. The 1- to 2-foot-long green, blue-green, or silver leaves are sometimes tinged with red toward the tapering tip. The seeds are produced in open, billowy panicles in late summer. The dense foliage stands up well in winter and offers interest. There is a lot of natural variation in switchgrass, which has led to the large number of cultivars selected.

Pollinator & Wildlife Value: Insect feeders include leafhoppers and caterpillars of skippers and moths. Seeds are eaten by a variety of birds. Muskrats enjoy pondside plants. The upright foliage provides cover for birds and small mammals in winter. Spring-nesting birds use it for cover.

How to Use: Use switchgrass as a specimen or background plant in mixed borders with other late-summer prairie plants such as asters, goldenrods, coneflowers, and sneezeweed. It can be used as a large-scale groundcover or for screening. The open flower panicles look best when viewed against a dark background. Switchgrass tolerates poor conditions, including poor drainage and occasional flooding, making it a great choice for rain gardens. It is a good substitute for the nonnative, overused *Miscanthus* species. Dried flowers look good in arrangements.

How to Grow & Maintain: This grass is very adaptable, growing on a wide range of soil types, from moist to dry, in full sun. It is very drought tolerant once established. Plants are fairly slow to spread, but division will be needed every four years or so to keep plants under control in gardens. Allow 2 to 3 feet between plants, as clumps become large. Most cultivars do not produce a lot of seeds but the species self-sows on open, moist soils. It has no insect or disease problems. Deer usually avoid it.

Beyond the Species: There are many selections of switchgrass available, and they are usually better choices for garden use since they tend to reseed and spread at a much lower rate than the species. Choose a cultivar based on its fall color, the degree of blue in its foliage, its mature height, or its ability to resist lodging and stay upright. 'Amber Wave' stays less than 4 feet tall. 'Dallas Blues' has broad steel-blue to gray-green foliage and huge purple flower panicles. 'Heavy Metal' has metallic blue foliage that turns yellow in fall. 'Northwind' is very sturdy and upright. 'Rotstrahlbusch' has good red fall color. 'Shenandoah' has reddish-purple foliage color by midsummer and a distinct reddish cast to the 3- to 5-inch flower heads.

157

Schizachyrium scoparium
Little Bluestem

Zones: 3 to 9
Size: 2 to 4 feet tall

Schizachyrium scoparium

This attractive clump-forming, warm-season grass has light green to blue foliage in summer, turning golden to reddish brown in fall and remaining very showy all through winter. Flowering begins in late summer but the thin flower heads really aren't noticeable until they turn to attractive silvery white seedheads. These fluffy seedheads and crimson-colored foliage are extremely showy in fall landscapes. It is sometimes sold under the outdated name *Andropogon scoparius*.

Pollinator & Wildlife Value: This grass is the larval host of several skipper butterflies and food for many other insects. Plants provide cover, nesting material, and seed for birds and small mammals.

How to Use: Little bluestem is among the best native grasses for fall color, and its small size makes it easy to use in most landscapes. The blue-green foliage provides a great backdrop for summer prairie flowers such as prairie phlox, black-eyed Susan, coneflowers, monarda, blazing stars, and asters. Plant it in mixed borders, along walkways, and in foundation plantings, where it won't overwhelm nearby forbs. It is wonderful massed as a groundcover and can be used in rain gardens. It can even be used in large containers.

How to Grow & Maintain: It prefers well-drained sandy or loamy soil in full sun, but will grow in rocky soils and partial shade. Full sun is best for upright growth. Not recommended for heavy clay or damp soils. Shade, high fertility, and abundant moisture contribute to lax, floppy growth. Little bluestem is slow to emerge in spring and really doesn't look like much until late spring or even early summer. Cut back clumps in late winter. It will reseed but seedlings are easy to pull out. No insect or disease problems. It is highly resistant to deer feeding.

Beyond the Species: The species itself is quite attractive and well-behaved but there are some cultivars. 'The Blues' is the most popular, selected for its good blue-green foliage color. Blue Heaven ('MinnblueA') is noted for its blue-gray foliage, burgundy-red fall color, and narrow, upright plant form.

158

Sporobolus heterolepis
Prairie Dropseed

Zones: 3 to 9
Size: 2 to 3 feet tall

Sporobolus heterolepis

Prairie dropseed is a warm-season, clump-forming grass that slowly expands to form a fountainlike mound about 18 inches in diameter. It has very narrow individual blades that are bright green in summer, turning yellow and orange in fall. It blooms in late summer, producing many upright flower stalks topped with pale pink panicles. These flowers have a luscious scent.

Pollinator & Wildlife Value: Foliage is eaten by grasshoppers and leafhoppers. Seeds are an important fall and winter food source for ground-feeding birds.

How to Use: Prairie dropseed has an elegant, refined look that makes it easy to use in many areas of the landscape. Include it in perennial borders and foundation plantings. A mass planting is stunning. Plants usually stay upright all winter. Plant fine-textured prairie dropseed with butterfly milkweed, asters, coneflowers, and blazing stars or use it alone as a large-scale groundcover. It can be used around the edges of rain gardens and under black walnut trees.

How to Grow & Maintain: Prairie dropseed prefers a well-drained soil with moderate moisture levels and full sun, but it will tolerate drier conditions. Avoid constantly wet soils. Prairie dropseed is slow to grow from seeds; start with plants if possible. Once established, it is long-lived. Cut back in early spring before new foliage emerges. Dig and divide clumps in spring as needed. Give plants plenty of room to fully arch. Plants do not spread but they do set some seed. It has no insect or disease problems, and deer avoid it.

Beyond the Species: 'Tara' is a dwarf selection with a more upright growth habit and good fall color. The clumps grow about 12 inches tall with flowers rising to 2 feet.

Shrubs, Vines & Small Trees

Most homeowners relegate shrubs and vines to background roles in the landscape—foundation plantings, hedges, screens, and backdrops for showy flowerbeds. And while many of these plants fulfill these roles with style and grace, there are also many that deserve places of prominence in the landscape. Many of these plants, including highbush cranberry, have showy flowers, interesting bark, and colorful leaves and fruits.

NATIVE BUZZ

Mulberry Wing Skipper Butterfly
Poanes massasoit

Larry E. Swanson

Males patrol with a low, weak, meandering flight through marshes in search for receptive females. Normal flight is down in between the stems of sedges. It is a species of concern in some areas as wetland habitat disappears.

Range: New York and Massachusetts west across the Great Lakes states to southern Minnesota and North Dakota. A coastal population ranges from southern New Hampshire south to Maryland.

Habitat: Freshwater marshes, sedge meadows, wet roadsides, and bogs.

Larval Food: Tussock sedge (*Carex stricta*), and possibly others.

Adult Food: Flower nectar, including milkweeds, buttonbush (*Cephalanthus occidentalis*), and narrow-leaved mint (*Pycnanthemum tenuifolium*).

Aesculus pavia
Red Buckeye

Zones: 5 to 8
Size: 12 to 15 feet tall and wide

This clump-forming deciduous shrub or small tree has an irregular crown and is very amenable to shaping and pruning. Very showy red to orange tubular flowers appear mid- to late spring in long panicles. The shiny, dark green leaves are attractive in spring and early summer but usually begin to decline by late summer. The round seed capsules ripen in fall and are poisonous. The flaky bark is attractive in winter.

Pollinator & Wildlife Value: The flowers are tailor-made for hummingbirds, and they rely on it as an early nectar source. Butterflies also visit the flowers.

How to Use: Red buckeye can be pruned into an attractive specimen small tree or allowed to grow unpruned and used in natural gardens and as an informal hedge. It can be used in rain gardens. The ideal site is where you can showcase it in spring and then let it fade into the background later in summer.

How to Grow & Maintain: It prefers moist, fertile soil. Flowering is best in full sun, but it will still make a nice show in partial to even heavy shade. It tolerates heavy clay soil. It is not very drought tolerant, so any plants in drier soil should be mulched. Leaves may scorch in dry conditions. The fallen fruits may cause a litter problem. It has no serious insect or disease problems. Deer and rabbits avoid it.

Beyond the Species: Bottlebrush buckeye (*A. parviflora*) is a dense, mounded, suckering shrub that grows 8 to 12 feet tall and wide. It blooms in midsummer and has showy white flowers with red anthers. It tolerates quite a bit of shade. Fall leaf color is a nice yellow. It is good for naturalizing and in rain gardens. 'Rogers' was selected for its larger flowers and longer bloom time. Zones 5 to 8.

Aesculus pavia

Amelanchier species
Serviceberries, Juneberries

Zones: 2 to 8
Size: 20 to 30 feet tall by 6 to 25 feet wide

Amelanchier alnifolia 'Regent'

If attracting birds is one of your goals, serviceberries should be at the top of your plant list. And the good news is, these deciduous shrubs and small trees are just as attractive to our species as they are to birds! Serviceberries have showy five-petaled, slightly fragrant, white flowers in drooping clusters that appear in early spring with the just-emerging spring foliage. Flowers give way to small, round, edible berries that ripen to purplish black in June. Finely toothed leaves emerge in spring, mature to lustrous dark green in summer, and turn yellow to red-orange in fall. The silvery-gray bark is attractive all year.

Pollinator & Wildlife Value: This genus is right at the top of the list when it comes to value to wildlife. The nectar and pollen of the flowers attract bees, syrphid flies, beetles, and other insects. Leaves are a food source for the larval forms of several butterflies, including tigers, viceroys, admirals, and hairstreaks. It is one of the earliest native plants to set fruit, providing an early food source for birds. Regular visitors include robins, grosbeaks, gray catbirds, cedar waxwings, northern orioles, ruffed grouse, woodpeckers, and thrushes. Squirrels, chipmunks, and other mammals eat the fruits.

How to Use: Use these shade-tolerant shrubs as understory plants in woodland gardens, on the north side of buildings, or in the shade of larger trees. The tree forms are good for courtyards and patios, since birds devour the red fruits before they fall and become messy, and the strong wood is resilient in storms. A dark or shaded backdrop will set off the form, flowers, and fall color. The smooth bark is attractive in winter and in early spring wildflower gardens. With a little attention to pruning and shaping, most species can become striking small specimen trees that work well in entry gardens and mixed borders. Serviceberries are tolerant of air pollution, and they can be used in rain gardens. All are excellent for naturalized settings, where their fruits attract wildlife. The fruits, which get sweeter as they ripen, can also be used for jams, jellies, pies, and wine—if you can keep them from the birds!

How to Grow & Maintain: Serviceberries tolerate a wide range of soils, but prefer well-drained, slightly acidic, moist soils in part sun to shade. Most tolerate dry, poor conditions once established. Remove some of the older stems each year in late winter to keep plants vigorous and producing more fruits. Renew overgrown shrubs with hard pruning. Root suckers are common, and if not removed, will result in a shrubby growth habit. These plants rarely have any serious pest problems, but you may see rust, leaf spot, fire blight, powdery mildew, sawfly, leaf miner, borers, or scale. These cosmetic problems do not usually affect the overall health of serviceberry. Deer may browse on twigs.

Amelanchier x *grandiflora* 'Princess Diana'

Beyond the Species: Serviceberry (*A. arborea*) grows 20 to 25 feet tall and 15 to 20 feet wide. It has multiple narrow trunks, a rounded crown, and excellent fall color, and it makes a handsome single or multi-trunked small tree. Zones 3 to 9. Western serviceberry (*A. alnifolia*) grows 3 to 12 feet tall and 6 to 9 feet wide. It has nice green foliage; large white flowers in spring; and abundant, sweet, dark purple fruits in late summer, making it a good choice for edible landscaping. Shrubs are attractive in bloom and in fruit, but they sucker profusely. 'Regent', a popular cultivar growing about 5 feet tall and wide with good flowering, foliage, and fruiting, makes an excellent hedge plant. Zones 2 to 6. Allegheny serviceberry (*A. laevis*) grows 25 to 30 feet tall and 15 to 25 feet wide. The foliage emerges a bronzy purple color that sets off the flowers nicely. It is taller than most species. 'Cumulus' is a narrow, upright selection that is easily grown as a single-trunk tree. Zones 3 to 8. Apple serviceberry (*A.* x *grandiflora*) is a naturally occurring hybrid of *A. arborea* and *A. laevis*. It is an excellent small clumping or single-trunked tree growing about 25 feet tall and wide. Several cultivars have been selected for good fall color, interesting growth habit, and good disease resistance. Good choices include 'Autumn Brilliance', 'Robin Hill', 'Princess Diana', and 'Strata'. Zones 4 to 8.

163

Calycanthus floridus
Sweetshrub, Carolina Allspice, Strawberry Bush

Zones: 5 to 9
Size: 6 to 10 feet tall by 6 to 12 feet wide

Calycanthus floridus

Calycanthus floridus 'Athens'

Sweetshrub grows into a dense, rounded shrub. Its dark green leaves in summer sometimes turn a yellow shade in fall, but it's not a reliable asset from year to year. The magnolia-like flowers are dark reddish brown and up to 2 inches across when fully open in late spring to midsummer. Flowers are borne somewhat inside the outer layer of foliage so they are often obscured from view. The flowers have a fruity fragrance, which is quite pronounced. There can be great variation in the fragrance of different plants, so it is a good idea to smell individual plants at the nursery before purchasing. The wrinkly, balloon-shaped fruits persist into winter, adding some interest.

Pollinator & Wildlife Value: Beetles are the primary pollinators. They use the fragrant flowers to help them find a spot for feeding and to lay their eggs.

How to Use: Place this shrub where you can enjoy the strawberry-like fragrance of the flowers, which is most prevalent in the evening. It does great in mass or naturalized plantings, but can be used in mixed borders as well as in rain gardens. The fragrant flowers are nice for cutting.

How to Grow & Maintain: It does best in a deep, moist loam but tolerates heavy clay soil. It grows in shade or sun but does not get as tall in sun. Maintain consistently moist soil throughout the growing season, especially during the first two years of establishment. A mulch of wood chips or shredded bark helps maintain soil moisture and reduces competition from weeds. Prune right after flowering as needed to shape plants. Plants will spread from suckers, which can be removed. It has no insect or disease issues. Deer avoid it.

Beyond the Species: 'Athens' has an unusual form growing 6 feet tall with flowers that are yellow and very fragrant. Flowers may be produced after the initial late spring flush, often into midsummer. 'Edith Wilder' has reddish-brown, very fragrant flowers. Leaves are more rounded than typical. Fall color is a reasonably good yellow. It grows 10 feet tall. 'Michael Lindsey' has very fragrant red-brown flowers and excellent shiny, dark green foliage and golden yellow fall color.

Carpinus caroliniana
American Hornbeam, Blue Beech, Musclewood

Zones: 2 to 8
Size: 20 to 30 feet tall by 12 to 18 feet wide

Carpinus caroliniana

American hornbeam has ornamental characteristics throughout the growing season. This small tree or shrub has a spreading irregular crown and beautiful muscle-like bark that is bluish gray, smooth, and sometimes marked with dark brown horizontal bands. Slender brownish catkins dangle from branches in early spring when little else is showy in the landscape. The dark green leaves change to a beautiful orange to red to reddish purple in autumn. The small nutlets mature in late summer and hang in 3- to 4-inch-long clusters, adding interest in fall and winter and providing food for many birds.

Pollinator & Wildlife Value: Leaves provide food for the larval stages of swallowtail, purple, and hairstreak butterflies. Moths, beetles, plant bugs, and leafhoppers feed on the foliage and sap. The nutlets are food for many types of songbirds as well as turkeys, squirrels, and other mammals. Smaller birds such as chickadees and flycatchers use the small limbs and cavities for nesting.

How to Use: Left unpruned, American hornbeam can be used for screening, as a background planting, or in naturalized areas. It can be used in rain gardens. With a little effort it makes an excellent small tree. Plant it where you can enjoy the attractive bark, such as next to a deck or sitting area. It can be sheared into a tall hedge. Ambitious gardeners can even transform a row of this shrub into a tall formal hedge like its namesake, European beech (*Fagus sylvatica*), which is widely used for hedging in England.

How to Grow & Maintain: The plant prefers a moist, fertile, slightly acidic soil in part shade or sun but will tolerate full shade and drier conditions. American hornbeam can be somewhat difficult to transplant. You'll have the best success with early spring planting of nursery trees that have been properly root pruned. It can be a slow grower. Maintaining adequate moisture and fertilizing young trees each spring help them grow a little faster. Surround lawn trees with a ring of organic mulch 2 to 4 inches thick. Not only will this keep the weeds down, reduce competition from turfgrasses, and preserve moisture, it prevents lawn mowers and weed whippers from marring the beautiful trunk. If you want American hornbeam to grow as a small tree, do some selective pruning each year to form a single trunk, starting while the tree is still young. It can be pruned anytime, but the best time is when plants are dormant: you can see the silhouette better. It has no serious insect or disease problems but leaf spots, cankers, and twig blight may occur. Deer and rabbits may browse, but it is not a preferred food.

165

Chionanthus virginicus
Fringetree, Old Man's Beard

Zones: 4 to 9
Size: 12 to 20 feet tall and wide

Fringetree grows naturally with one or a few short trunks and a spreading, rounded crown. Its dark green glossy leaves are late to leaf out in spring. Very showy, pure white, sweetly fragrant blooms appear with the foliage in late spring for about two weeks, cascading downward like the white beard of a wise old man. Flowers are dioecious, meaning male and female flowers are on separate plants, but both flower types are showy. The fruits, which appear on female plants only, are blue-black and olive-like, held in clusters in late summer. Leaves turn yellow in fall.

Pollinator & Wildlife Value: Bees are the main pollinators. Larvae of several moths feed on the leaves, including fringetree sallow and several types of sphinx moths. Fruits are highly desired by cardinals, bluebirds, brown thrashers, mockingbirds, blue jays, woodpeckers, and turkeys. The hardened seeds are eaten by small rodents.

How to Use: Fringetree is an excellent choice anywhere a small tree is needed. Plant it as a specimen in the back of the shrub border, near a patio, or in an entry garden. It looks especially nice when planted against a dark backdrop. For fruits, make sure to purchase a female plant or plant several of these dioecious shrubs with the hope that at least one will be female. It is tolerant of wind, pollution, and other urban conditions, and it can be planted near buildings; consider it for a courtyard garden. The white flowers look especially stunning at night when illuminated by nearby lights. Keep the mature size in mind; it becomes quite wide as it matures. A mass planting is spectacular in bloom.

How to Grow & Maintain: Best growth is in deep, fertile soil in sun to partial shade but it is quite adaptable. Flowering is best in full sun. It does not transplant well, so choose sites carefully. Fringetrees have a strong branch structure and rarely need pruning, but prune right after flowering if shaping is required. It has no serious pest problems, but you may see scale or borers on dry sites. To reduce chances of powdery mildew, prune to open up the inside and increase air circulation. Deer may browse the foliage and twigs.

Chionanthus virginicus

Clethra alnifolia
Summersweet, Pepperbush

Zones: 4 to 9
Size: 3 to 8 feet tall by 4 to 6 feet wide

Clethra alnifolia 'Ruby Spice'

Summersweet is a slender, upright, slowly spreading deciduous shrub with fluffy, bottlebrush-like terminal spikes of extremely fragrant white to light pink flowers. It blooms on current season's growth for four to six weeks in mid- to late summer, when most flowering shrubs are taking a break. Flowers have a deliciously spicy sweet fragrance that permeates the air. The glossy green foliage is somewhat late to leaf out in spring. Leaves turn a striking yellow to golden brown in autumn, and flower spikes give way to spikes of dark brown seed capsules that persist into winter and even longer. It is one of the few summer-blooming shrubs that will grow in partial shade. Plants spread slowly by rhizomes.

Pollinator & Wildlife Value: Flowers are an important nectar source for butterflies and humming-birds, and many pollinating insects, including bees, visit the flowers as well. The fruits attract birds and other wildlife.

How to Use: Use summersweet as a specimen, in groupings, or in the middle or back of the shrub border. It is multistemmed and suckering and can form colonies with time, making it useful for screening or hedging. Plant it near a deck, patio, or window where the fragrant flowers can be appreciated. Smaller types can be used in the perennial border for midsummer color and fragrance, but remember that plants are slow to emerge in spring. Allow summersweet to naturalize along a stream or pond where its suckering will help control erosion. It can be used in rain gardens.

How to Grow & Maintain: It prefers moist, acidic soil. Avoid hot, dry sites. It does best in dappled shade but tolerates quite a bit of sun if the soil is moist. Even established plants will require watering during dry spells. Use an acidic fertilizer as needed. Pruning is generally not recommended during the first three years to control the size or shape, but you can remove any dead or damaged stems. Older plants can become leggy. Remove a few of the older branches each year over the course of three years. Plants can be cut back to the ground in late winter. Spider mites can be severe on plants in hot, dry locations.

Beyond the Species: There are several compact-growing cultivars available that are better choices for traditional landscape use. They are also more floriferous and some have pink or rose flowers. 'Hummingbird' is a dwarf cultivar that is more compact, growing 3 feet by 3 feet. 'Ruby Spice' has intense deep rose flowers that do not fade in the heat of summer. 'Rosea' has pink flowers that age to white.

Cornus florida
Flowering Dogwood

Zones: 5 to 9
Size: 12 to 30 feet tall by 8 to 15 feet wide

Cornus florida

Cornus alternifolia

This deciduous small tree has early spring color from the showy white, 2-inch bracts that surround the small true flower. They are effective for 10 to 14 days, opening before the leaves. Leaves are dark green, turning shades of red, orange, or purple in fall, and showy crimson berries appear in clusters on branch tips. The somewhat horizontal branching growth habit offers winter interest. Older trees develop a nicely textured gray bark that is quite ornamental.

Pollinator & Wildlife Value: Dogwood flowers attract small bees and flies seeking nectar and pollen. Leaves are a larval food source for moth and butterfly caterpillars, including spring azure, and many other insects. Songbirds love the high fat content of the fruits, especially the smaller fruits on the shrub types. Chipmunks, foxes, squirrels, deer, turkey, and grouse feed on the fruits, preferring the larger fruits of the tree types. Dogwood's branching pattern makes it a favorite nesting tree for the wood thrush. Thicket plantings of the shrub types provide nesting sites and cover for songbirds. Turtles are known to eat fallen leaves of some types.

How to Use: This small tree is excellent as a specimen, near a patio, at the corner of a building, and in groupings. It is especially effective when planted against dark evergreens or a dark building where the bracts are set off in spring and the branching habit can be seen in winter. Use it as an understory shrub in woodland gardens or in shrub borders. It can be used in rain gardens, and it grows under black walnut trees. It is not tolerant of stresses such as heat, drought, pollution, or road salt, and flower buds can be killed or injured by cold in Zone 5.

How to Grow & Maintain: To perform well, dogwoods require a cool, moist, acidic soil that contains organic matter. Dry soil can lead to leaf scorch and susceptibility to diseases. Landscape plants should be watered during dry periods. Full sun promotes the greatest flowering, but plants tolerate partial shade well. Keep roots cool with an organic mulch to avoid leaf and trunk scorch. Lawn mower damage to trunks provides almost certain entry for disease, so mulch is crucial for lawn trees. Use an acidifying fertilizer in spring, especially on stressed trees. Prune after flowering only if necessary to shape. Anthracnose (dogwood blight) can be a serious problem, but healthy trees grown in sunny areas with good air circulation and soil moisture are rarely killed.

Other problems include leaf spot, powdery mildew, and twig blight. These problems result in unattractive foliage in late summer but are usually not serious enough to kill plants. Reduce chances of infection by keeping plants well watered and pruned to increase air circulation. Cankers causing stem dieback are usually caused by lack of water brought about by improper soil conditions or planting site. Prune out infected stems several inches below the canker or at ground level. Stressed trees are susceptible to borers. Deer and rabbits like to browse on dogwoods.

Beyond the Species: Many cultivars have been selected for disease resistance as well as flower color and shape, foliage color, fruit color, hardiness, and growth habit. 'Cherokee Princess' is a reliable early-flowering selection. 'Ozark Spring' was selected for its winter hardiness. 'Aurora', 'Celestial', 'Constellation', 'Stardust', and 'Stellar Pink' show good disease resistance. Pagoda dogwood (*C. alternifolia*) is less showy, but it is much hardier, making it a better choice in colder areas. It grows 20 to 25 feet tall and up to 25 feet wide as a small tree or large shrub. It has attractive horizontal tiers of branches, giving it a layered appearance. The deep green leaves are heavily veined and turn reddish in fall. Small, creamy white, musk-scented flowers appear in 3- to 5-inch clusters from mid- to late spring. The fruit is green and berrylike, turning to white to blue to nearly black on red stalks. Pagoda dogwood does best in cool, moist, slightly acidic soils in partial shade. It thrives in mulched landscape beds and rain gardens, but will not do well as a lawn specimen. A little selective pruning in winter to encourage the horizontal branching habit will pay off in a lovely landscape specimen. Golden Shadows™ ('W. Stackman') is a variegated selection with leaves that display a broad lime-green to chartreuse central zone

Cornus sericea

surrounded by a well-defined, iridescent golden-yellow margin. Zones 3 to 8. Pacific dogwood (*C. nuttallii*) has a growth habit similar to flowering dogwood, growing 10 to 30 feet tall and up to 15 feet wide. It is a western species and better suited to that area. The fruits are orange-red and develop in clusters. Zones 7 to 9. Gray dogwood (*C. racemosa*) grows 8 to 12 feet tall and up to 10 feet wide. Attractive gray stems support creamy white flowers followed by showy white fruits borne on red pedicels in late summer. It has good red fall color, and the showy red pedicels persist to contrast nicely with snow. It grows best in moist, cool soils in full sun, but is tolerant of dry conditions and partial shade. It spreads slowly by underground stems and is excellent for naturalizing at the edges of woods or for hedging, but it is also successfully grown as a specimen tree with persistent pruning. It does well in rain gardens. Zones 3 to 8. Red-osier dogwood (*C. sericea*) grows 8 to 10 feet tall and almost as wide. It has deep red stems that are showy in winter, creamy white flowers in spring followed by attractive white fruits, and maroon fall leaves. It spreads by layering when the lower stems touch or lie along the ground and can form dense thickets in the right conditions. Younger stems have the brightest color, so prune out oldest stems each spring to encourage new growth. Overgrown plants can be cut back to about 6 inches in spring. It is the same plant as *C. stolonifera*. Cultivars selected for their good twig color and less-aggressive spreading are good choices for landscape use, including rain gardens. 'Cardinal' has bright cherry-red stems. 'Baileyi' and 'Isanti' have a more compact growth habit to about 6 feet tall and good stem color. 'Farrow' (Arctic Fire) stays under 4 feet and has good twig color. Zones 2 to 7.

Cornus racemosa

Fothergilla gardenii
Dwarf Fothergilla, Dwarf Witchalder

Zones: 5 to 9
Size: 2 to 3 feet tall and wide

Fothergilla 'Mt. Airy'

This compact, slow-growing, mounded deciduous shrub is covered with fragrant white flowers in spring before the leaves appear. Thick, blue-green to green leaves turn brilliant yellow to orange to scarlet in fall, often with a combination of colors in the same leaf. The small fruit capsule matures in fall but isn't very showy. Plants spread to form a dense colony.

Pollinator & Wildlife Value: Flowers are an early spring source of nectar for bees, butterflies, and other insects. Birds eat the seeds.

How to Use: Dwarf fothergilla is an attractive shrub for small spaces. Use it in foundation plantings, in mixed borders, and in masses where you can enjoy the fragrant spring flowers and beautiful fall foliage. It can be mixed with other shrubs in shrub borders; it does especially well with rhododendrons, sweetshrub, ferns, and other acid-loving plants. It can be pruned into a small hedge. Use it in rain gardens.

How to Grow & Maintain: It does best in an acidic, well-drained soil in partial shade but can take full sun, where flowering is best. It will not tolerate wet or alkaline soils. Amend soil before planting to provide the necessary acidic conditions. Water well during dry periods. Fertilize in spring with an acidic fertilizer. Little pruning is needed other than an occasional thinning of the older branches, but it will tolerate hard pruning. Plants spread slowly from suckers, which need to be removed if you don't want a large colony. No serious pest problems, but root diseases can be a problem in heavy soil. Deer usually avoid it.

Beyond the Species: 'Blue Mist' leaves are an attractive blue-green color, especially in light shade. 'Jane Platt' does very well in the Pacific Northwest, where the fall color is outstanding. 'Mt. Airy', likely a hybrid between the two native species, has dark blue-green foliage, consistent fall color, and can grow to 5 feet. Large fothergilla (*F. major*) is a larger pyramidal or rounded plant growing to 9 feet or more in height. It is a good choice for naturalistic woodland settings. Zones 4 to 8.

Hamamelis virginiana
Witch Hazel

Zones: 4 to 8
Size: 10 to 20 feet tall and wide

Hamamelis virginiana

This deciduous shrub is the last shrub to bloom in autumn, producing golden yellow flowers that are slightly fragrant and have petals that look like lemon zest. The flowers take a back seat, however, to the wonderful golden yellow fall leaf color. Fertilized flowers form fruit through winter and into the following growing season. Fruits start out green and become woody and brown with age. This open, multistemmed shrub has a tighter growth habit when grown in more light. Branches have a zigzag pattern.

Pollinator & Wildlife Value: The nectar and pollen of the flowers attract flies and wasps and sometimes bees, moths, flower bugs, and beetles. The larvae of the witch hazel dagger moth and other moths feed on leaves. Birds and some small mammals eat the small brown fruits.

How to Use: Witch hazel's coarse texture limits its formal garden use, but it's a good choice for the middle layer in woodland gardens. It is suitable for shrub borders, where other plants can add interest until fall, when witch hazel shines. Take advantage of its shade tolerance and use it as an understory shrub. Plant it in front of evergreens to set off the showy foliage. It can be pruned into a small, wide-spreading tree. It can be used in rain gardens. The branches can be cut and the fragrant flowers forced to bloom indoors.

How to Grow & Maintain: Witch hazel prefers a uniformly moist soil in sun or part shade but is tolerant of dry, shady conditions. It's fast growing when young. Plants grown in full sun may show leaf scorch in summer. Rejuvenate overgrown shrubs with heavy pruning in early spring. This shrub has no serious insect or disease problems, but deer may browse it.

Beyond the Species: 'Green Thumb' leaves emerge in spring with an irregular dark green center surrounded by pale green. 'Little Suzie' is a compact hybrid that stays 4 to 5 feet tall and wide. 'Mohonk Red' has red flowers. Vernal witch hazel (*H. vernalis*) grows 6 to 12 feet tall and up to 20 feet wide and has a shrubbier growth habit. The main difference from witch hazel is flower time. It blooms in late winter. The flowers are similar to witch hazel's, but smaller. Several cultivars have been selected, mainly for flower color and bloom time. 'Carnea' is a red-flowered form. 'Christmas Cheer' is noted for earlier bloom time and intensely fragrant yellow and red flowers. 'Lombart's Weeping' grows in a pendulous mound to 5 feet tall and up to 10 feet wide. 'Sandra' has emerging purple leaves, good flower color, and golden fall color but does best in cooler regions. Zones 4 to 8.

Hamamelis virginiana

Hydrangea quercifolia
Oakleaf Hydrangea

Zones: 5 to 9
Size: 6 to 8 feet tall and wide

Hydrangea quercifolia

Hydrangea arborescens

Pollinator & Wildlife Value: The fertile flowers provide nectar and pollen to bees, wasps, flies, and beetles. Foliage is eaten by moth caterpillars. Plants provide shelter and nesting sites for birds and small mammals.

How to Use: Mass or group it in a mixed shrub border or allow it to naturalize in a woodland garden. It may be used for background, accent, or specimen plantings and in foundation plantings or informal hedges. Hydrangeas work well in rain gardens. The flower heads dry easily and are nice in fall arrangements or can be left on the plant for winter interest.

How to Grow & Maintain: Prefers well-drained soil in full sun to partial shade. Young plants may need some winter protection (burlap wrap) in Zone 5. Hydrangeas bloom on old wood so do not prune them in spring if you want flowers. Little pruning is needed, but it can be done anytime after flowering, as needed. The heavy flower panicles may droop considerably, particularly when moistened by rain. It has no serious insect or disease problems, but there is some susceptibility to leaf blight and powdery mildew. Hydrangeas tend to be high on the list of deer favorites.

Beyond the Species: Many cultivars are available. The smaller compact types are good garden plants. 'Alice' has large flowers and good fall color. 'Pee Wee' and 'Sike's Dwarf' are smaller and do not sucker as much. 'Ruby Slippers' is a dwarf with pink flowers, and 'Munchkin', another dwarf, opens white and turns pink as it ages. Smooth hydrangea (*H. arborescens*) grows 3 to 5 feet tall and up to 8 feet wide. It has lacecap flowers arranged in symmetrical, rounded heads 4 to 6 inches across and dark green leaves. It blooms on the current season's wood off and on throughout the summer. In cold winter climates, it is perhaps best grown as an herbaceous perennial and cut back to the ground in late winter. It tolerates full sun in northern gardens but needs some shade in southern areas. 'Annabelle' is a popular selection that has much larger flowers than the species. Zones 4 to 9.

This beautiful shrub offers year-round interest. It has conical clusters of white flowers that start blooming in late spring and slowly turn pinkish-purple with age, showy well into summer. The distinctive, deeply lobed, oaklike leaves turn attractive shades of bronze, crimson, or purple in autumn. Mature stems exfoliate to reveal a rich brown inner bark that is attractive in winter. Plants are upright and spreading with a broad, rounded habit.

Ilex opaca
American Holly

Zones: 5 to 9
Size: 15 to 30 feet tall by 10 to 20 feet wide

This upright, pyramidal evergreen shrub or small tree resembles the traditional English holly, with spiny-toothed leaves and showy red berries. Plants are dioecious (male and female flowers on separate plants), and it is the pollinated female flowers that produce the red berries that ripen in fall and persist throughout winter. Insignificant greenish-white flowers appear in late spring.

Pollinator & Wildlife Value: Holly flowers are cross-pollinated by bees, flies, and wasps, and moths and butterflies may visit for nectar. Because they persist in good condition through winter, the berries are particularly important as a source of emergency bird food during winter. Visitors include cedar waxwings, northern mockingbirds, northern flicker, bobwhites, and turkeys. Mammals that eat holly fruits include mice, squirrels, and raccoons. Evergreen hollies provide cover and nesting sites for birds.

How to Use: Evergreen hollies work well for hedging and barriers. They are very tolerant of air pollution. Since berries are only produced on female plants, you need one male plant in close proximity (50 to 100 feet away) to three to five female plants to ensure good pollination and subsequent fruit set. Nurseries should label plants "male" or "female" so you know what you are buying. The berry-laden branches are very effective in holiday floral arrangements.

How to Grow & Maintain: Evergreen hollies perform best in full sun in acidic, organically enriched, moist to wet soil, but they are somewhat adaptable to soils that are occasionally dry, and they can take some shade.

Ilex glabra

Ilex opaca

Chlorosis and stunting occur in alkaline soils. Little pruning is needed. Young plants grow faster with annual applications of acidic fertilizer such as iron sulfate, cottonseed meal, or sulfur. The best time for any pruning is early spring. Spider mites can be a problem during hot, dry spells. Leaf spot and powdery mildew can be problems during rainy years. Other problems that may show up are leafminers, whiteflies, and scale. Deer and rabbits usually avoid the spiny leaves.

Beyond the Species: Many selections have been made that have good form and size and do well as hedges or foundation shrubs. Female cultivars with good fruit production include 'Delia Bradley', 'Greenleaf', 'Mae', 'McDonald', and 'Miss Helen'. Topal holly (*I. x attenuata*) is a hybrid of *I. opaca* and *I. cassine*, another native species. The resulting cultivars make nice garden plants that are narrower and have deep green, smaller leaves, and good fruit production. 'Fosteri', 'Savannah', and 'East Palatka' are good selections. Zones 6 to 9. Inkberry (*I. glabra*) is a slow-growing, upright-rounded, stoloniferous, broadleaf evergreen shrub. It typically matures to 5 to 8 feet tall and can spread by root suckers to form colonies. It has spineless, flat, glossy, dark green leaves with smooth margins with several marginal teeth near the apex. Leaves usually remain attractive in winter unless temperatures dip well below zero. Inconspicuous greenish-white flowers appear in spring. Pollinated female flowers give way to pea-sized, jet black, berrylike fruits that mature in early fall and persist through winter to early spring unless consumed by birds. Cultivars typically have better form (more compact, less open, less leggy, and less suckering) than the species. 'Shamrock', 'Compacta', and 'Nordic' are good choices. Zones 5 to 9. Yaupon (*I. vomitoria*) is a thicket-forming, broadleaf evergreen shrub or small tree that typically grows in an upright, irregularly branched form to 10 to 20 feet tall and up to 10 feet wide. The leathery, glossy, evergreen, dark green leaves have toothed margins. It is the best holly for gardeners in the southeast US. Some of the many cultivars available include 'Carolina Ruby', 'Nana', 'Jewel', 'Pride of Houston', and 'Schelling's Dwarf'. Zones 7 to 10.

Ilex verticillata
Winterberry

Zones: 3 to 9
Size: 6 to 15 feet tall by 6 to 10 feet wide

Ilex verticillata

Winterberry is deciduous, one of the few hollies to lose its leaves in winter. The attractive dark green, leathery leaves vary from flat to shiny on the upper surface. Plants are multistemmed, with grayish stems. Inconspicuous flowers appear mid- to late spring and are white or greenish. Autumn color is not especially showy, but from late fall through winter, winterberry steps into the spotlight by producing an outstanding display of bright red berries that persist on the branches after the leaves fall.

Pollinator & Wildlife Value: Holly flowers are cross-pollinated by bees, flies, and wasps, and moths and butterflies may visit for nectar. Because they persist in good condition through winter, the berries are a particularly important source of emergency bird food during winter. Visitors include cedar waxwings, northern mockingbirds, northern flicker, bobwhites, and turkeys. Mice, squirrels, and raccoons eat the fruits.

How to Use: Plant winterberry in groups or mix it with plants that lack winter interest. It can be used for hedging, screening, and foundation plantings. The red berries are extremely effective when contrasted against background snow or when reflected in nearby bodies of water. It does well in rain gardens. Since berries are only produced on female plants (plants are dioecious), plant one male in close proximity (50 to 100 feet away) to three to five female plants to ensure good pollination and subsequent fruit set. Nurseries should label plants "male" or "female" so you know what you are buying. The berry-laden branches are very effective in holiday floral arrangements.

How to Grow & Maintain: Winterberry performs best in full sun in acidic, organically enriched, moist to wet soil, but is somewhat adaptable to soils that are occasionally dry. Chlorosis and stunting will occur in alkaline soils. Plants in relatively dry soils will have better berry size (and subsequent ornamental appeal) with irrigation during dry periods. Young plants will grow faster with annual applications of an acidic fertilizer such as iron sulfate, cottonseed meal, or sulfur. Winterberry has an attractive natural form, and little pruning is needed. The best time to do any pruning is early spring. If the soil is too alkaline, leaves may turn yellow between the veins. This can be corrected by lowering the soil pH with acidic fertilizers. Because of their low palatability and mild toxicity, the leafy branches are not preferred as a food source by deer and rabbits. However, when little else is available, deer will browse them.

Beyond the Species: Several cultivars offer better fruiting and dwarfs, and these are better choices for landscape use. Most are females that require a male pollinator to set fruit; they have been sexed by the nursery trade so you know what you are getting. 'Afterglow' features smaller, glossy green leaves and large orange-red berries maturing to orange. 'Cacapon' stays at 6 feet and has bright red fruits. 'Red Sprite' (also known as 'Compacta') is a popular dwarf maturing to only 3 to 4 feet tall. 'Shaver' has large clusters of red-orange berries. Use 'Jim Dandy' to pollinate all four cultivars. 'Winter Red' has a good growth habit and profuse bright red fruits that consistently persist into winter; 'Southern Gentleman' is a good pollinator for 'Winter Red'. Possumhaw (*I. decidua*) is a similar deciduous species that does better in southern gardens. It grows 7 to 15 feet tall and the glossy, dark green leaves turn a dull purplish green to yellow in autumn. 'Council Fire', 'Warren's Red', and 'Sentry' are good female selections. Zones 6 to 9.

Juniperus communis
Common Juniper

Zones: 2 to 9
Size: 1 to 3 feet tall by 3 to 10 feet wide

Juniperus communis var. *depressa* 'AmiDak'

This spreading shrub has a sharp, angular form and a rather coarse texture. The dense, awl-shaped needles are green in summer and take on a purplish color in fall. Reddish-brown bark peels off in strips. There are many species and cultivars of junipers, with forms ranging from 6-inch-tall groundcovers to over 30-foot-tall pyramidal trees. They all have needlelike or scalelike foliage or a combination. Foliage colors range from bright green to gray-green to silvery blue. Junipers are dioecious; male and female cones are on separate plants. Female cones look like small round berries and range from brown to blue to blue-black, often with a whitish bloom on the surface.

Pollinator & Wildlife Value: The nutrient-rich, berrylike female cones and their seeds are eaten by many types of birds, including northern flicker, cedar waxwing, robins, grosbeaks, woodpeckers, sparrows, turkeys, and white-winged crossbill. Caterpillars of some butterflies and moths feed on the foliage. It is the primary host plant for juniper hairstreak butterflies, which mainly use Eastern red cedar but will also visit other junipers. The prickly foliage of junipers provides cover for birds and other wildlife. Owls and other birds may roost in the tree forms.

How to Use: Junipers are among the best evergreen shrubs for native landscapes. Use the coarser species for naturalizing or as groundcover. Many cultivars have been selected for wonderful textures, foliage colors, and a variety of shapes and forms, and they are better choices for use in shrub borders, foundation plantings, rock gardens, and specimen plantings. Avoid planting junipers under drip lines, where crashing snow can damage them. Junipers tolerate road salt better than most evergreens.

How to Grow & Maintain: Junipers prefer neutral to slightly acidic, well-drained soil in full sun. They tolerate drought and wind well. Foliage will be sparser in shade. Make sure plants are well watered going into winter to reduce chances of winter burn. Plants can easily outgrow their space. Pruning back overgrown plants is not effective. Regular pruning of the branch tips in late spring will keep them from becoming overgrown and needleless in the middle. Browned needles may need to be combed out from plants to keep them looking neat. Trimming upright forms so that the upper part is slightly narrower than the base will allow light to get to the lower foliage. Bagworms can defoliate plants. Remove and destroy all "bags" as

continued on next page

continued from previous page

soon as you see them. Spider mites can be a problem in hot, dry weather. Spray the foliage forcefully with water each day. Juniper blight can show up during wet springs, turning portions of the plant brownish. Snip off diseased parts. Some cultivars are resistant. Deer feed on junipers when other food sources are exhausted.

Beyond the Species: Var. *depressa* is a naturally low-growing form with erect branch tips. 'AmiDak' (Blueberry Delight™) was selected for its ability to produce prolific blue fruits when pollinated. 'Depressa Aurea' has new growth with a golden-yellow color. 'Repanda' is a compact, rounded form growing to 1 foot tall and spreading 6 feet wide. Creeping juniper (*J. horizontalis*) is a low, creeping shrub usually less than 1 foot tall and spreading 3 to 6 feet to form dense groundcover. Leaf color is bluish green to steel blue, taking on purplish tints in fall. 'Bar Harbor' spreads up to 10 feet wide and has trailing bluish-green branches that turn purple in fall. 'Blue Chip' is very low growing and has good blue color throughout the year. 'Hughes' is somewhat resistant to juniper blight. It has distinct radial branching and silvery blue leaves and spreads up to 10 feet. 'Wiltonii' is a low form (3 inches tall by 4 feet wide) with intense silvery blue color. Zones 2 to 8. Eastern red cedar (*J. virginiana*) grows 25 to 40 feet tall with a straight trunk and a broad, conical head. The thin, reddish-brown bark peels off in long strips. Leaves are dark green and scalelike; newer growth may be sharp-pointed and whitened underneath. Dark blue berrylike cones on female trees are a favorite winter food of wildlife, and trees provide winter shelter for birds. Eastern red cedar is the alternate host of cedar apple rust, a disease that causes strange-looking orange galls on trees. Snip off any plant parts infected with the galls and destroy them. Use this durable tree for screening, windbreaks, or in natural settings on tough sites. 'Canaertii' stays at 20 feet in height and spreads 8 feet. It has a dense, pyramidal form and dark green leaves. 'Gray Owl' is a spreading form with silvery-gray foliage. It grows 4 feet tall and 5 feet wide. Zones 4 to 9. Rocky Mountain juniper (*J. scopulorum*) is the western counterpart to Eastern red cedar, growing up to 25 feet tall and spreading 6 to 20 feet. It is a good choice in the western US. 'Wichita Blue' is a compact, conical male form that usually stays under 15 feet tall. It has nice blue-gray foliage. Zones 4 to 8.

Juniperus horizontalis **'Wiltonii'**

Kalmia latifolia
Mountian Laurel

Zones: 5 to 9
Size: 7 to 15 feet tall and wide

Kalmia latifolia

Mountain laurel is a gnarled, multistemmed, dense, rounded, broadleaf evergreen shrub or small tree. Showy flowers open in late spring or early summer and last two weeks or more. The normal color is pink and that fades to nearly white, but breeding has produced red-budded, cinnamon-banded, pure white, and deep pink and red forms. Foliage is dark green and glossy; in full sun it can be yellow-green.

Pollinator & Wildlife Value: Bumblebees are the primary pollinators. Plants are the larval host of laurel sphinx moth. Hummingbirds and butterflies visit the flowers for nectar. Plants provide year-round cover for wildlife.

How to Use: Use mountain laurel in foundation plantings and for massing and naturalizing. It does well in shrub borders with other acid-loving shrubs such as rhododendrons and azaleas, fothergilla, and summersweet.

How to Grow & Maintain: It needs an acidic, humusy soil in sun to partial shade. Though often listed as tolerant of heavy shade, plants under those conditions are very thin and open, and they bloom sparsely. Some exposure to sun is required for proper flower color development of red and pink cultivars. If necessary, amend soil to increase soil acidity. Avoid windswept sites and heavy, high pH soils. Foliar burn may occur on exposed sites. Use an acidic fertilizer every spring. No pruning is needed but flowers should be removed after they are done blooming. Some protection from winter sun and wind is suggested in colder areas. Lace bugs can cause speckling on leaves. Leaf spot can be troublesome on nonresistant cultivars. Avoid damaging plants with sharp gardening tools, as these wounds are common entry points for borers. Deer and rabbits usually avoid it.

Beyond the Species: 'Bullseye' has white flowers with a purple band. 'Elf' is a dwarf cultivar that stays under 3 feet with pink buds opening to pale pink flowers.'Pink Charm' has dark pink buds that open to rich pink flowers with a narrow dark pink band inside the flower. 'Raspberry Glow' has burgundy red buds open to pink flowers. 'Sarah' is a compact grower with red flower buds that open to pinkish-red flowers.

177

Lindera benzoin
Spicebush

Zones: 5 to 9
Size: 6 to 12 feet tall and wide

Spicebush is a multistemmed, deciduous, understory shrub or small tree grown mainly for its beautiful yellow fall foliage. In early spring, clusters of small yellow flowers hug the branches, giving a burst of color to the woods before most plants have leafed out. In fall, the leaves turn a brilliant yellow to gold color. The best color comes on plants grown in sun. Fruits on female plants are brilliant scarlet red in autumn, but they are small and must be viewed from close range. Birds also enjoy them, so they tend to disappear quickly. The plants are dioecious, so male plants must be nearby to get fruits on female plants. The common name comes from the scent given off when foliage or stems are bruised or crushed.

Pollinator & Wildlife Value: Bees and flies are the main pollinators. Flowers are a good early nectar source for butterflies. It is a preferred host of the very interesting spicebush swallowtail butterfly caterpillar. Birds, including flycatchers, catbirds, robins, and wood thrushes, eat the fruits and use shrubs for cover and nesting.

How to Use: Grow spicebush where you can enjoy the early spring flowers and bright yellow fall foliage. A dark background of evergreens will set this shrub off nicely. Spicebush is good for naturalizing or in the shrub border or woodland garden. It is an excellent choice for sites with moist soil and semi-shade, such as next to a stream or pond, and it does well in rain gardens.

How to Grow & Maintain: Does best in moist, well-drained soils in full sun or part shade. Plants grown in shade and dry conditions will be more open in form and the fall color will not be as pronounced. It will tolerate full sun if given adequate water. Plants can be difficult to transplant and are somewhat slow to establish. Mulch soil to help maintain an even moisture supply. Plants have a nice natural form and require little or no pruning. No serious pest problems. Deer avoid it.

Beyond the Species: 'Green Gold' is a nonfruiting form with large yellow blooms. 'Rubra' is also nonfruiting, with deep red-brown blooms. 'Xanthocarpa' has orange-yellow fruits.

Lindera benzoin

Physocarpus opulifolius
Ninebark

Zones: 2 to 8
Size: 6 to 9 feet tall and wide

This tough and hardy multistemmed shrub produces fast-growing shoots that arch out and away from the center. The five-petaled, white to pinkish flowers are grouped together in 2-inch, flat-topped clusters in late spring and are followed by somewhat showy reddish-brown fruits. Older stems are covered with attractive shaggy bark that sloughs off in long fibrous strips, but the foliage usually covers it. The nicely shaped foliage stays clean and attractive all season and can be shades of yellow or purple. Dried fruits vary from brown to bright red, depending on soil and weather.

Pollinator & Wildlife Value: Bees, wasps, flies, and butterflies seek nectar and pollen from the flowers. Caterpillars of moths and butterflies feed on foliage. It is one of the species preferred by spring azure butterfly caterpillars. Some birds eat the seeds, and they will use the plants for cover and nesting. There is research indicating that altered leaf chemistry of the purple-leaved types is not as attractive to the ninebark beetle, a native insect that relies on it for feeding.

How to Use: The species is good in naturalized settings, where it makes good cover for wildlife and can be used for screening. The cultivars are excellent landscape plants and can be used as hedges, foundation plantings, rain gardens, and in shrub and mixed borders. Keep in mind that pruned hedges will have reduced bloom.

How to Grow & Maintain: Ninebark grows best in full sun and can withstand windy sites once established. It tolerates a wide range of soils as long as they are well drained. Plants in southern states benefit from some afternoon shade. Ninebark, especially the cultivars, benefits from a spring application of an organic fertilizer. Shape plants as needed by pruning immediately after flowering. Overgrown plants can be cut back in late winter, but not every year. Space hedge plants 2 to 3 feet apart. As plants become more vigorous, prune more heavily. Consistent yearly pruning results in a thick, bushy hedge. Hedge plants may suffer from powdery mildew in wet years, but otherwise they're trouble-free. Deer will browse on ninebark.

Beyond the Species: Many cultivars have been developed that are better suited to more formal landscape situations. 'Dart's Gold' is a compact 4- to 6-foot-tall and -wide selection with good yellow foliage

Physocarpus 'Center Glow'

color. 'Center Glow' has nice red foliage. Diablo® ('Monlo') has leaves that emerge deep purple. It can be pruned harshly each spring to promote vigorous shoots with large, highly colored leaves. 'Nanus' stays about 5 feet tall and wide. 'Nugget' has deep golden yellow foliage and a dense habit to 6 feet tall and wide. 'Snowfall' is a compact selection with larger flowers. 'Summer Wine®' ('Seward') is a compact selection with fine, deeply cut dark red leaves and pinkish flowers. 'Tiny Wine' and 'Little Devil' both have wine-red foliage and stay under 4 feet.

Ptelea trifoliata
Hop Tree

Zones: 4 to 9
Size: 15 to 20 feet tall and wide

Ptelea trifoliata

wafer-like winged samara that resembles an elm seed, is probably this shrub's showiest attribute. The ornamental seeds are held on the tree well into winter most years.

Pollinator & Wildlife Value: The flowers attract small bees, wasps, flies, and ants that primarily feed on the nectar of the flowers, although some small bees also collect pollen. Caterpillars of the giant swallowtail and eastern swallowtail butterflies feed on the leaves, as do other moths. Birds and small mammals eat the seeds and use plants for shelter.

How to Use: Hop tree is a great understory tree in woodland gardens. It can be used for naturalizing, massing, or in small groups. When pruned correctly, it becomes a 20-foot small tree with a broad canopy over a slender gray trunk and looks nice as a specimen or in a mixed border. It also works well as an informal hedge.

How to Grow & Maintain: Hop tree prefers well-drained soils but adapts to various soils, in sun or shade. Established plants are drought tolerant. Suckers will need to be pruned out to maintain tree form. Avoid overpruning of branches: plants look best when they have a natural look. Hop tree does not have any significant insect or disease problems. Deer avoid the bitter-tasting leaves.

Beyond the Species: 'Aurea' is a yellow-leaved form with bright gold young leaves that fade to light yellow-green by the middle of summer. 'Glauca' has blue-green foliage. Both are difficult to locate in the nursery trade, but worth the effort.

Hop tree doesn't get any accolades for having an outstanding spring flower display or showy fall color. It does, however, look nice just about anytime and is very low maintenance. It's very amenable to pruning and tolerant of a wide range of sunlight conditions. It can become an attractive small tree in just about any landscape. This dense, rounded shrub has 4- to 6-inch leaves that are shiny and dark green on top and pale and hairy below. They turn yellow-green in fall. The inconspicuous greenish-white flowers appear in terminal, branched clusters in late spring. Some people find the scent reminiscent of orange blossoms, but others find it not so pleasant. The fruit, a conspicuous

Ptelea trifoliata fruits

Rhododendron species
Azaleas, Rhodondendrons

Zones: 5 to 9
Size: 3 to 20 feet tall and wide

Rhododendron austrinum

This large family of shrubs can be broken down into two major groups: azaleas, which form multistemmed, suckering, deciduous shrubs; and rhododendrons, which are usually evergreen, have larger leaves and flowers, and tend to grow in more of a clump. All types produce showy flowers in almost every color. Heaviest flowering occurs in spring, but there are some species that bloom into late summer and even early fall. Most have good fall color, and the evergreen types offer winter interest.

Pollinator & Wildlife Value: The greatest value to wildlife probably comes from the protective cover and nesting sites these shrubs offer to birds and small mammals. Many azaleas are pollinated by hummingbirds. Most types attract bees and butterflies.

How to Use: Use these shrubs as specimen plants, in mixed or shrub borders, in foundation plantings, and as a middle layer in shade and woodland gardens. Plants will slowly spread to naturalize. The branches make good cut flowers.

How to Grow & Maintain: In general, rhododendron types do best in cooler areas with higher rainfall. Azaleas are more adaptable and can tolerate drier soils and lower rainfall. Both types do best in a slightly acidic, organic soil that doesn't dry too quickly. Flowering is best with at least a few hours of sun, but the plants themselves grow fine in quite a bit of shade. Leaves may scorch in full sun. Organic mulch will make sure these shallow-rooted plants maintain the regular soil moisture they like. Plants are invigorated by an annual pruning of old or weakened branches. Azaleas and rhododendrons are susceptible to several insect and disease problems, including canker, crown rot, leaf spot, rust, powdery mildew, aphids, borers, scale, and spider mites. These problems do not usually become serious if plants are grown in the proper conditions. Deer usually avoid the plants.

Rhododendron canescens

continued on next page

Beyond the Species: Smooth azalea (*R. arborescens*) grows about 15 feet tall and wide. Flowers are white to light pink in late spring to early summer and very fragrant. Zones 5 to 8. Coast azalea (*R. atlanticum*) is among the smaller species, growing 2 to 5 feet tall and wide. It forms a dense mound of blue-green leaves that set off the fragrant, pinkish-white flowers. It needs damp soil and a bit of sun to do well. Zones 6 to 9. Florida azalea (*R. austrinum*) is an upright deciduous type growing 6 to 10 feet tall and 4 to 6 feet wide. It has yellow or orange flowers in dense clusters in early spring. Zones 6 to 9. Flame azalea (*R. calendulaceum*) grows 8 to 15 feet tall and 5 to 8 feet wide. It has very large, ruffled flowers in shades of orange, yellow, and apricot, sometimes red, in spring. Leaves turn a nice dark red most years. Zones 5 to 8. Mountain azalea (*R. canescens*) has an upright form, growing to 15 feet tall but staying under 6 feet wide. The white and pink flowers are lightly fragrant. 'Varnadoe's Pink' has abundant dark pink flowers and a nice upright growth habit. Zones 6 to 9. Catawba rhododendron (*R. catawbiense*) typically grows 6 to 10 feet tall and wide, but may get taller. The evergreen leaves are quite leathery and have no fall color. The very showy flowers are lilac-purple to magenta with speckled throats, and clusters can get up to 6 inches in diameter. It blooms mid-spring. Several cultivars are available: var. *album* has white flowers tinged with lilac; var. *compactum* usually stays about 3 feet tall. Zones 5 to 8. Rosebay (*R. maximum*) is an evergreen type growing 6 to 20 feet tall or more and up to 20 feet wide. It has pink blooms in late spring and early summer. It spreads to form large thickets if left unchecked. It blooms better in heavier shade than most types. Zones 5 to 7. Pinkshell azalea (*R. vaseyi*) has pink flowers in early spring, before the leaves fully unfold. It grows 4 to 8 feet tall and about as wide. It is not as susceptible to powdery mildew as some other species. It has good maroon red fall color. Zones 5 to 8. Swamp azalea (*R. viscosum*) is a loose, upright shrub growing 4 to 8 feet tall and up to 5 feet wide. It has white to pale pink flowers in late spring into summer, being one of the last native azaleas to flower. Fall color is yellow to orange to purple. Zones 5 to 9.

182

Rhododendron catawbiense

Rhododendron maximum

Rhus typhina
Staghorn Sumac

Zones: 3 to 8
Size: 10 to 25 feet tall by 10 to 15 feet wide

Staghorn sumac is a multiple-trunked, deciduous shrub with an interesting branching habit and dense, velvety hairs on the stems. The dark green compound leaves are up to 24 inches long and have a tropical look. They turn a vivid orange, purple, yellow, and red in fall. Flowers are greenish in dense, upright panicles 4 to 8 inches long in late summer. On female plants, they turn into scarlet, cone-shaped clusters in fall and persist into winter.

Pollinator & Wildlife Value: Flowers are visited by bees, wasps, and flies for pollen and nectar. Sumacs are the primary larval host for red-banded hairstreak butterfly, and spring/summer azure butterfly caterpillars also favor it. The persistent fruits are a good late-winter food source both for songbirds and game birds.

How to Use: This is one of the first plants to turn color, sometimes in mid-August, and this is its greatest asset. It spreads by suckers to form large colonies and is good for stabilizing slopes to prevent erosion. Suckers are removed by regular mowing, so it can be grown next to lawns. It is a good groundcover in contained areas. It tolerates both salt and drought and can be used along roadsides. The cultivars tend to be better behaved and can be used in landscapes, where the beautiful foliage offers great interest.

How to Grow & Maintain: This plant will grow in almost any soil except constantly wet or boggy sites. It takes full sun to partial shade. Sumacs spread quickly by underground roots that send up new trunks. Once established, it is hard to eradicate. Male and female flowers are on separate plants, so not all plants produce showy fruit clusters. Fall color will be poorer on rich sites, so avoid fertilization. Plants can be trained into

Rhus typhina Tiger Eyes®

interesting small trees. Choose a plant with a strong, straight leader and prune it annually to maintain shape. Suckers will need to be removed each spring to keep it from turning into a thicket. It has no serious insect or disease problems. Deer and rabbits will feed on plants.

Beyond the Species: Tiger Eyes® ('Bailtiger') is a beautiful newer selection that has very attractive, finely cut, chartreuse foliage. It is a dwarf form, staying about 6 feet tall, and does not sucker as profusely as the species so it makes an excellent landscape plant. 'Laciniata' is a female selection with very finely cut foliage and good orange color. 'Dissecta' has large, deeply dissected leaves. Fragrant sumac *(R. aromatica)* forms a dense mound of branches only getting 2 to 6 feet tall and covered with glossy leaves. Fuzzy, berrylike fruits form at the tips of some branches when grown in full sun. Fall color varies from red to yellow. It grows in full sun to partial shade, preferring slightly acidic soil. Its suckering growth habit and tolerance of poor soils makes it a good choice for covering slopes and rough terrain. 'Gro Low' is a less-aggressive selection, staying under 2 feet in height, good for use as a low-maintenance groundcover in landscapes. Zones 3 to 9.

Rhus aromatic 'Gro Low'

Viburnum dentatum
Arrowwood Viburnum

Zones: 4 to 8
Size: 6 to 12 feet tall by 6 to 10 feet wide

Viburnum dentatum

Viburnums are easy-care, fast-growing, deciduous shrubs that bring a lot to the landscape. White flowers appear in late spring, and plants have nice green summer foliage. Flowers give way to blue-black, or sometimes red, fruits that are quite attractive to birds and other wildlife. Variable fall color ranges from drab yellow to attractive shades of orange and red to purple, depending on the species. Arrowwood is a large, multistemmed shrub with leaves that color fairly early in fall, usually turning a nice yellow, red, or reddish purple before falling, and abundant blue-black fruits. European cranberry bush viburnum (*V. opulus*) and wayfaring bush (*V. lantana*), two popular nonnative landscape plants, are invading natural areas and should be avoided.

Pollinator & Wildlife Value: The flowers attract bees for both nectar and pollen. Flies, beetles, and butterflies may visit for nectar. Some butterfly (spring azure) and moth caterpillars feed on plants. The fruits are eaten by a variety of birds, including thrashers, mockingbirds, woodpeckers, vireos, thrushes, and turkeys. Mammals may also eat the fruits. Some birds use the shrubs for nesting.

How to Use: Viburnums can be used for massing, screening, and hedges. Most species sucker and spread so are best suited to a contained space or in naturalized situations. Cultivars are usually much less aggressive—good for garden use—and can be used in borders and foundation plantings. Some can be pruned into nice small trees. They are all good choices for rain gardens.

How to Grow & Maintain: The plant prefers a fertile, slightly acidic, well-drained soil in full sun to part shade but will tolerate less-than-ideal situations, even drought, when mature. Shrubs will not flower and fruit as well in partial shade. Plants tolerate at least moderate amounts of shade and road salt. Suckers may need to be pruned to keep plants from getting out of bounds. Viburnums do not require a lot of pruning, but you can prune right after flowering to shape them or reduce their overall height. It is a good idea to remove a few of the older stems every three years or so to encourage new growth from the base. Prune immediately after flowering since flower buds form in summer for the following year. Viburnums do not have any serious disease or insect problems, but leaf spots and powdery mildew may show up. Deer and rabbits will browse on plants.

Viburnum opulus var. trilobum

Beyond the Species: Blue Muffin® ('Christom') is a compact selection with exceptional fall fruiting. Autumn Jazz® ('Ralph Senior') and Chicago Lustre® ('Synnestvedt') are upright selections with good fall color. Northern Burgundy® ('Morton') was selected for good leaf color in summer and fall. Maple-leaved viburnum (*V. acerifolium*) grows about 6 feet tall and wide. The leaves resemble maple leaves and turn interesting shades of soft red to pink in autumn. Zones 3 to 8. Nannyberry (*V. lentago*) is a 10- to 20-foot upright shrub or single-stemmed tree with drooping branches and a rounded crown. It is easily pruned into a small tree and is a good choice where you want a shade-tolerant specimen tree. Zones 3 to 7. Witherod (*V. nudum*) grows 5 to 12 feet tall and wide. It has good fruit production and fall color. It does especially well in low areas or alongside ponds. Zones 5 to 9. Highbush cranberry (*V. opulus* var. *trilobum*) grows 10 to 12 feet tall and wide. It has lovely, white lace-cap flowers that grow up to 4 inches across, and the leaves turn beautiful shades of yellow-orange to red in fall. The showy, deep red fruits persist through winter. 'Compactum' and 'Alfredo' are compact selections. 'Hahs' has a neat, rounded growth habit and good flower and fruit display. 'Wentworth' and Redwing™ ('J.N. Select') were selected for heavy fruit production. Zones 2 to 7. Black haw (*V. prunifolium*) grows about 12 feet tall and wide and can be pruned as a small tree. It tolerates poor soils and drought but not shade. Zones 4 to 9. Downy arrowwood (*V. rafinesquianum*) is a very hardy, smaller species, growing 6 feet tall and wide. The leaves have an attractive reddish tint when young, and it produces lots of showy blue-black fruits. Zones 2 to 8. Rusty blackhaw (*V. rufidulum*) typically grows 10 to 20 feet tall and wide. Zones 5 to 9.

Thuja occidentalis
White Cedar, Arborvitae

Zones: 2 to 7
Size: 20 to 40 feet tall by 10 to 15 feet wide

Thuja occidentalis 'Lutea'

This upright, pyramidal, evergreen shrub or small tree has dense, scalelike, green to yellowish-green foliage arranged in flat, fanlike branches. On mature trees, the bark is gray to reddish brown, separating in long shreds, and the trunk is often twisted. Foliage and bark are aromatic. Foliage often looks slightly yellow, purple, or brown in winter but returns to green in summer.

Pollinator & Wildlife Value: The larvae of moths feed on trees, as well as many other insects. Plants provide excellent shelter for birds. Ruffed grouse, sparrows, pine siskin, redpoll, and juncos eat the seeds. Pileated woodpeckers visit white cedar looking for ants.

How to Use: The large size of the species limits its use to screening and windbreaks. The cultivars are good choices for hedging, specimen plants, foundation plantings, and as accents. White cedar is one of only a few evergreen conifers well suited to urban rain gardens.

How to Grow & Maintain: It does best in a moisture-retentive soil in full sun or partial shade.

In deep shade, plants are open and have sparse foliage. Avoid dry, windswept locations. Plants are slow-growing and long-lived. They are subject to winterburn, especially when planted on the south side of buildings; however, winterburn is easy to prune out in spring since it occurs on outside leaves. Water deeply in fall to help prevent winterburn. Do not confuse winterburn with the normal browning of inside leaves as plants age or the normal color change arborvitaes go through in winter. Prune just after new growth emerges in spring. Formal hedges can be pruned again later in the season, but do not prune in late fall. Plants are susceptible to damage from heavy snow or ice. Avoid planting this shrub under a roofline where snow drops onto plants and break branches. Possible insect problems include bagworm, leaf miner, and spider mites. Deer are a serious problem, often completely defoliating the lower parts of plants.

Beyond the Species: Many cultivars have been selected for their foliage color, resistance to winterburn, and growth habit, which can include dwarf and globe forms. 'Techny' is a popular cultivar growing only 10 to 15 feet tall, making it a good choice for hedging. It has excellent deep green foliage color and tends to resist winter burning. 'Lutea' is compact, narrow, and upright, typically growing 25 to 30 feet tall and 15 feet wide. 'Little Gem' is a good globe form growing to about 3 feet in height and width. 'Hetz Midget' is a globe form that doesn't need any pruning to stay at 2 to 3 feet. 'Woodwardii' is another natural globe that grows 3 to 5 feet. 'Sunkist' has gold-yellow foliage when grown in full sun. 'Holmstrup' is a tough, upright grower that stays under 8 feet tall. 'Wintergreen' and 'Wareana' grow to 15 feet tall and are good for mid-sized hedging. Western red cedar (*T. plicata*) grows much taller, to 40 to 60 feet. It is a beautiful evergreen tree where its size can be accommodated. There are many cultivars available that have interestingly colored or variegated foliage, grow slower, and stay smaller. They are nice additions to the landscape. 'Aurea' has yellow foliage. 'Cuprea' is a slow-growing dwarf that eventually matures at 4 to 5 feet tall and wide. 'Hogan' is a slow-growing columnar form. 'Whipcord' is a slow-growing dwarf that has pendulous foliage. 'Zebrina' is a variegated form. Zones 5 to 7.

Wisteria frutescens
American Wisteria

Zones: 5 to 9
Size: 15 to 30 feet tall by 4 to 8 feet wide

Wisteria 'Blue Moon'

This twining deciduous vine's main attraction is the fragrant, pendulous, violet-blue flowers that cover the plant from late spring to early summer. The flowers hang down in clusters 4 to 6 inches long. It has bright green foliage all season. Beanlike pods remain after the leaves fall but they are not particularly ornamental. Plants may take seven years or more to bloom, so be patient. It is just as beautiful and much less aggressive than Japanese (*W. floribunda*) and Chinese wisterias (*W. sinensis*), which have become invasive in natural areas and should not be planted.

Pollinator & Wildlife Value: Flowers are pollinated by bees. Wisteria provides nectar for bees, hummingbirds, and butterflies. It is the larval host of marine blue, zarucco duskywing, and long-tailed skipper butterflies.

How to Use: Plants can provide a beautiful "roof" over patios and decks. For best flower display, train vines horizontally on a structure that is 10 to 20 feet off the ground. Wisteria does not have the ability to cling to surfaces. Instead, its stem and side branches twist around a support. Without support, it will crawl along the ground. It is an excellent choice for large, freestanding arbors, pergolas, posts, trellises, or fences.

How to Grow & Maintain: Flowering is best in a slightly acidic, well-drained soil in full sun. Twining vines physically wrap themselves around supports; they will not grow on a solid wall without something for them to twine upon. Provide a sturdy, well-anchored support to handle the weight of mature vines, which can be very long-lived. Wisterias generally do not need supplemental fertilizer, and excessive nitrogen can reduce flower production. It blooms on new wood. Prune side branches back after flowering, always leaving at least six leaves per branch, to keep plants in bounds. Remove excess branches to improve light penetration and flowering. Seedpods can cause digestive problems if eaten. The plant has no serious pest problems. Deer avoid it.

Beyond the Species: 'Amethyst Falls' is a popular selection that has vivid lavender-purple flowers in 6- to 8-inch clusters. It typically offers repeat bloom mid- to late summer, and has a more compact growth form. 'Nivea' has white flowers. Kentucky wisteria (*W. macrostachya*) is not quite as vigorous and it has longer flower clusters, up to 12 inches. Some references consider it to be a variant of *W. frutescens* and not its own species. 'Blue Moon' is a popular cultivar that often reblooms in summer. Kentucky wisteria is hardier, surviving winters and flowering in Zone 4, and worth trying in Zone 3.

187

Trees

Large trees are valued for their beauty as well as for the cooling shade they provide. But they have a lot more to offer landscapes and gardens, including architectural shape and bark with interesting texture and color, as seen on this 'Heritage' river birch.

Larry E. Swanson

NATIVE BUZZ

Green Sweat Bee
Agapostemon species

. . . .

These brightly colored metallic green or blue bees are active late spring until fall. Females carry pollen on their hind legs. Females are relatively fast flying, but males are often seen flying slowly around flowers looking for females. Their common name comes from their landing on humans to feed on sweat for the salt.

Range: Abundant throughout North America.

Habitat: Ground nesting.

Nectar Source: A wide variety of open, shallow flowers. They are short tongued, so have difficulty extracting nectar from deep flowers.

Acer rubrum
Red Maple

Zones: 3 to 9
Size: 40 to 65 feet tall by 45 feet wide

Red maple is a medium-sized tree with a broadly rounded, symmetrical crown. The smooth, light gray bark on young stems turns dark gray and shaggy on older limbs. Leaves have three- to five-pointed, saw-toothed lobes. The upper surface is light green, the lower surface whitish and partly covered with pale down. The small red flowers give the bare branches a red glow for a week or so in early spring, before the leaves appear. It is the first of the native maples to turn color in fall. Fall color is usually a brilliant red, but it can also be orange or yellow. Fall color can be inconsistent; purchase trees in fall to see what their leaf color will be if you want to ensure good fall color.

Pollinator & Wildlife Value: Bees may collect pollen from some maples. Some adult butterflies will feed on the sap of maples, especially sugar maples. Maples are the preferred host of several moth caterpillars. Many other insects rely on maples for food and habitat, which in turn attracts woodpeckers and insect-eating songbirds. These insects are especially important for feeding young nestlings. Some birds, including nuthatches, finches, and evening grosbeaks, eat the seeds, as do squirrels and chipmunks. Yellow-bellied sapsuckers drill holes into the bark to feed on sap. Tree-roosting bats, squirrels, owls, wood ducks, and other birds use tree cavities for nesting. Branches provide ideal nesting sites for robins, vireos, orioles, and other birds.

How to Use: Red maple is a good shade, lawn, or street tree. Its ability to survive in heavy soils means it can tolerate the poorer, compacted soils of streets and parking areas. It is susceptible to drought and road salt, but tolerant of air pollution. Most maples do well in rain gardens. All have shallow roots and produce deep shade under which it can be difficult to grow grass. Maples are moderately fast growing.

How to Grow & Maintain: It prefers slightly acidic, well-drained, sandy loam soils in sun to light shade, but tolerates most conditions. It will not grow well on alkaline soils, but will tolerate moderately moist soils. It has a wide native range; stick with local seed strains and sources for best results. Avoid pruning trees in late winter when the sap flows. This "bleeding" sap does not harm the tree, but it is messy and unsightly. Winter wrap all young maple trees to protect them from sunscald. Provide a barrier against lawn mowers and

Acer x freemanii 'Jeffersred'

weed whippers, which can seriously damage the thin bark. Leaf scorch can be a problem during dry periods, especially on young trees. Maples have some insect and disease problems, but most are cosmetic and usually aren't serious enough to really hurt a tree. Deer and rabbits may feed on young trees.

Beyond the Species: 'Autumn Spire' was selected for its bright red fall color, columnar form, and hardiness. It does

continued on next page

Acer saccharum

well in Zone 3. 'Northwood' is fast growing, nicely shaped, and has good fall color. It also does well in Zone 3. 'Autumn Flame' is a fruitless selection. Red Sunset® has good fall color. Vine maple (*A. circinatum*) is well suited to gardens in the Pacific Northwest. It is a small tree or large shrub, growing only 15 to 25 feet tall. It prefers partial shade. Zones 6 to 8. Freeman maple (*A.* x *freemanii*) is a hybrid cross between red and silver maples, combining the best of both. Trees have good form, a faster growth rate, better drought tolerance, showy fall color, and tolerance for a wide range of conditions. Selections include 'Armstrong', Autumn Blaze®, and Firefall™. Rocky Mountain maple (*A. glabrum*) stays small, growing 10 to 20 feet tall. It does well in cooler, moist conditions and at higher elevations. Zones 4 to 7. Silver maple (*A. saccharinum*) is a fast-growing species with weak wood, which makes it a messy tree after windstorms. It is tolerant of a wide variety of landscape situations and is often used in areas where other maples don't do as well. The leaves are deeper cut than other maples and are whitish on the undersides. Fall color is usually pale yellow. It grows 80 feet tall or more so keep it away from small yards and buildings. Older bark peels in vertical strips. It produces many seeds, which can become weedy, and the shallow, invasive root system makes it difficult to garden under. It is best used on tough, open sites where quick shade is needed. Zones 3 to 9. Sugar maple (*A. saccharum*) is an excellent choice for sites where the soil conditions are right. It prefers heavy clay or loam soils that are moisture retentive and on a north-facing slope, but it will tolerate drier, sandier sites. Avoid compacted, alkaline soils. It is larger than the red maple, growing 50 to 80 feet with a nice round canopy. Its greatest attribute is the brilliant fall color, which ranges from yellow to orange to scarlet. It is slow growing when first transplanted. It is sensitive to salt damage, so avoid using it as a street tree. It is also susceptible to leaf scorching and tattering when planted on open, exposed sites, which can make the leaves somewhat unattractive in late summer. 'Legacy' was selected for its good fall color and resistance to leaf tatter. 'Green Mountain' and Fall Fiesta™ ('Bailsta') have tatter-resistant leaves. Zones 3 to 8.

Betula nigra
River Birch

Zones: 4 to 9
Size: 40 to 60 feet tall by 15 to 25 feet wide

Betula nigra

River birch is an upright deciduous tree with a rounded or irregularly spreading crown. It can be grown as single- or multitrunked. Colorful bark is the hallmark of birches. River birch's bark is shiny and varies in color from red-brown to cinnamon-brown with a touch of salmon pink. It peels off in large horizontal strips. On older trees, the bark is darker and corkier. The toothed leaves are roughly triangular, with a dark green upper surface and pale yellow-green underneath. Fall color is yellow to green; nice, but not as ornamental as other birches.

Pollinator & Wildlife Value: Many insects feed on birches, especially moth caterpillars. Mourning cloak butterfly caterpillars also feed on leaves. Seeds and catkins are eaten by songbirds, ruffed grouse, and greater prairie chicken. Squirrels eat seeds. Woodpeckers use cavities for nesting. Large trees are occasionally used for nesting by hawks.

How to Use: River birch offers landscape interest year-round thanks to its unique peeling bark. It is one of the few large trees that can be grown as a multitrunked tree. Use it as a shade or specimen tree. It is the most heat tolerant of the birches, making it the best choice for most landscape situations. It is usually used as a specimen tree, but its large size prevents it from being suitable in small landscapes. It can be messy, dropping flowers and seeds and losing twigs in windstorms, so keep it away from decks and patios.

How to Grow & Maintain: It prefers moist soils and tolerates wet soils, but will do well on upland sites if given supplemental water when young. River birch needs full sun and a soil pH below 6.5 to prevent chlorosis. Select plants from a local seed source for best results. No pruning needed other than removal of lower branches to enhance the appearance of the trunk. Prune in summer to avoid bleeding. The brittle, twiggy branches break easily in windstorms, and catkins dropping in late spring can be messy, but only for a short period. River birch is highly resistant to bronze birch borer and is rarely troubled by leaf miners, two common pests of birches. Deer and rabbits will browse young trees.

Beyond the Species: Heritage® ('Cully') is a popular cultivar with lighter-colored bark and larger, glossier, dark green leaves. It usually grows to only about 45 feet tall. Fox Valley® ('Little King') is an interesting dwarf selection that only grows 8 to 10 feet tall in ten years. Paper birch (*B. papyrifera*) grows 40 to 70 feet tall with a spread of 20 to 30 feet. It has attractive bright white bark that peels away in sheets to reveal salmon-colored underbark. Fall color is a good yellow. It is fast growing and rather short-lived, especially in the landscape. It likes full sun but requires adequate moisture and cool roots, a situation often difficult to find. It is susceptible to cankers, wood rots, leaf miner, birch skeletonizer, and bronze birch borer. To reduce problems with bronze birch borer, which can be devastating, plant it on cool north-facing sites where the roots are shaded. Spread a wide circle of organic mulch such as wood chips or shredded bark under the canopy and make sure it receives adequate water during dry periods. Avoid planting it in a sunny lawn or near hot pavement. Time any pruning for late summer to avoid attack by bronze birch borers. Zones 2 to 6.

Celtis occidentalis
Hackberry

Zones: 2 to 9
Size: 40 to 70 feet tall by 20 to 65 feet wide

Hackberry's form is determined by its growing conditions. Depending on how much room it has, it varies from a vase-shaped, upright tree to one with an open, wide-spreading crown. The lance-shaped leaves are bright green and rough on top, lighter green on the bottom. Fall color is yellow to greenish yellow; the best color is when severe weather is delayed. The small fruit turns orange-red to purple in September and often hangs on for much of winter, providing food for several wildlife species. Mature trees have interesting deep, corky bark with warty protrusions.

Celtis occidentalis

Pollinator & Wildlife Value: Hackberry is among the best food and shelter trees for wildlife. Leaves are the larval host for several moth and butterfly caterpillars, including mourning cloak, Eastern comma, American snout, question mark, hackberry emperor, and tawny emperor. Songbirds, especially robins and cedar waxwings, and some game birds eat the fruits. Fallen fruits are eaten by turkeys, squirrels, and chipmunks. The narrow limb crotches, numerous spur branches, and witches' brooms attract many nesting birds, including cedar waxwings and eastern kingbirds.

How to Use: Its adaptability to a wide range of conditions makes hackberry a good tree for shade, windbreaks, street use, and shelterbelts. It tolerates wind, full sun, and the dirt and grime of city conditions, and the rough bark offers protection along city streets. It should be considered as a replacement for the American elm. It can be used in rain gardens. The seeds can create a litter problem when they fall.

How to Grow & Maintain: Hackberry prefers moist, well-drained soil but will tolerate both wet and dry sites and a wide range of soil pH. It grows in full sun or partial shade. Hackberry transplants easily, but sometimes takes up to two years to really start growing after planting. After that, it is moderately fast growing, especially on fertile, moister soils. It is drought tolerant once established. A few cosmetic problems affect hackberry, but none are serious. Hackberry nipple gall is a wartlike growth on the lower sides of leaves caused by insects known as psyllids. Clusters of twiggy outgrowth called witches' brooms appear on some branches, caused by mite feeding and a powdery mildew fungus, but this condition is not harmful to a tree. Some people actually find these witches' broom growths interesting, and they seem to help birds locate their nests. It is low on the list for deer and rabbits but they may feed on young plants.

Beyond the Species: 'Prairie Pride' has thick, leathery, dark green foliage; a nice uniform, compact, oval crown; lower fruit set; and it does not develop witches' broom. 'Chicagoland' has a nice straight trunk. Ultra™ has bluish foliage. Sugarberry (*C. laevigata*) grows 60 to 80 feet tall and wide. It is very similar, but has less corky bark and narrower leaves. It has better resistance to witches' broom but is not as hardy. 'All Seasons' has good fall color and is a little hardier. Zones 6 to 9.

Cercis canadensis
Eastern Redbud

Zones: 4 to 9
Size: 20 to 30 feet tall by 25 to 35 feet wide

This small spreading tree has large (4-inch), heart-shaped leaves that start out reddish purple, turn bluish green in summer, and yellow in autumn. Very showy purple-pink flowers appear in early spring before the leaves. The leaves can appear tired and spotted by late summer, but turn a nice yellow in fall. Flat, peapod-like fruits appear in early autumn and persist through winter. Bark on mature trees is reddish brown to black and furrowed. Best flowering occurs on trees at least four years old.

Pollinator & Wildlife Value: Bees are the primary pollinators; they also seek nectar. Caterpillars of several moths and Henry's elfin butterfly feed on plants. Seeds are eaten by birds, including quail, cardinals, goldfinches, and rose-breasted grosbeak.

How to Use: This small tree is excellent in shrub or mixed borders to soften harsh corners, as an understory tree, as a grouping of three in a large lawn, or at the

Cercis canadensis 'Forest Pansy'

edge of a woodland garden. Try to plant it where a dark background will set off the flowers. It looks very nice as a clumping tree. Layered branches give trees architectural form. The zigzag branch pattern and persistent seedpods add winter interest. Zone 4 gardeners should only plant northern-grown strains in sheltered locations to ensure hardiness. Redbud is sensitive to salt, so site it away from salted walks and roads.

How to Grow & Maintain: Redbud prefers moderately moist soils high in organic matter but will grow in drier sites once established. It prefers partial shade, but tolerates full sun and even full shade. Plants resent being dug from fields as they get larger, so start with smaller trees. Their moderate growth rate will result in a nice specimen in a few years. Redbuds do not do well when stressed. Keep landscape plants mulched and well watered. A spring application of an organic fertilizer may be needed on poorer soils. No major pruning is needed. Canker is the most destructive problem of redbud, and it can lead to the death of a tree. Protect trunk and bark from damage from lawn mower or weed whipper injury by circling trees with mulch. Deer usually avoid it.

Beyond the Species: 'Alba' and 'Royal White' have white flowers. 'Forest Pansy' has scarlet new leaves maturing to maroon. 'Flame' has double pink flowers and seldom sets fruit. 'Silver Cloud' has pink and white variegated leaves and grows 12 feet tall and wide. Cultivars are only reliably hardy in Zone 5.

Cercis canadensis

Cladrastis kentukea
Yellowwood

Zones: 4 to 8
Size: 30 to 50 feet tall by 40 to 55 feet wide

This medium-sized deciduous tree has a short main trunk with major branches starting within 6 feet of the ground. The crown is spreading and rounded. Showy, heavily fragrant, white flowers resembling wisteria are borne in hanging chains in late spring. It doesn't bloom heavily every year, but when it does it is spectacular. Summer leaf color is bright green, almost with a tinge of blue. Fall color can be a clear yellow or sometimes a warm gold-orange. The zigzag branching pattern, seedpods, and smooth gray bark add a lot of winter interest. It is the same plant as *C. lutea*.

Pollinator & Wildlife Value: Not a lot is known about yellowwood's wildlife value. Flowers are pollinated by bees and possibly by moths, since flowers are most fragrant at night.

How to Use: This refined, medium-sized tree is good for spots where it has room to spread and develop its nice vase shape. Plant it in the rear corner of a backyard or use it as a shade tree on smaller properties. In larger areas it can be planted alongside small trees or larger shrubs to create a woodland setting. The flowers tend to be more fragrant at night, so a spot near an evening sitting area is nice. It has deep roots, so shade-tolerant groundcovers and lawn grasses will grow well beneath it. Keep in mind it may take several years to become established and produce flowers.

How to Grow & Maintain: It requires well-drained soil in full sun to flower well. It tolerates a wide soil pH range, and established trees are very drought tolerant. Corrective pruning is important when the tree is young to eliminate weak branch forks. Without pruning the branching structure can be weak, inviting storm damage and ultimately decay. Prune in summer to avoid excessive sap bleeding that occurs in winter and spring. While this bleeding does not harm trees, it is unsightly and messy. Young trees should be wrapped in winter to protect the thin bark from sunscald. It has no serious pest problems. Trees under stress are susceptible to verticillium wilt, a soil-borne fungal disease. Deer will browse on yellowwood.

Beyond the Species: 'Rosea' ('Perkins Peak') is a very fragrant, pink-flowered form. 'Sweetshade' has abundant white flowers.

Cladrastis kentukea

Gymnocladus dioicus
Kentucky Coffee Tree

Zones: 3 to 8
Size: 45 to 80 feet tall by 50 feet wide

Kentucky coffee tree has a picturesque, open-spreading crown. Its remarkably large, compound, bluish-green leaves appear late in spring. The greenish-white flowers that also appear in late spring are somewhat fragrant and attractive to pollinating insects. Fall color is inconsistent, but sometimes a good yellow. The 6- to 10-inch-long flat seedpods, deeply furrowed bark, and sparse branching add winter interest.

Pollinator & Wildlife Value: Bees, butterflies, and hummingbirds looking for nectar visit the flowers. Bees are the main pollinators. Some moth caterpillars feed on leaves.

How to Use: This excellent shade and street tree deserves to be planted more. It is a good replacement for the disease-prone (and often thorny) honey locust. The leaves cast very light shade (also known as filtered shade or dappled shade) that permits shade-tolerant turfgrasses and partial-shade perennials to grow underneath. It is tolerant of city conditions and offers good winter interest. Leaves appear late in spring and drop soon after first fall frost, so it's good where you want sunlight in spring and fall.

How to Grow & Maintain: It grows best in evenly moist, rich soil and needs full sun, but is tolerant of alkaline soils and drought. Kentucky coffee tree is slightly difficult to transplant because of the deep taproot. Plant smaller balled-and-burlapped or container-grown specimens in early spring. It is a moderate to slow grower. Encourage faster growth by fertilizing young trees in spring and providing supplemental water during dry periods. The large seedpods usually fall sporadically over a long period, but some people still consider them litter.

Caution: Seedpods are poisonous, so children should be discouraged from playing with them. Seed-free male selections are available. It is free of insect and disease problems. Deer do not like Kentucky coffee tree.

Beyond the Species: 'Espresso' is a fruitless male selection with upward-arching branches in a vaselike form. Prairie Titan® is an upright-spreading male selection with good summer leaf color and interesting winter architecture.

Gymnocladus dioicus

195

Halesia tetraptera
Carolina Silverbell, Mountain Silverbell

Zones: 5 to 8
Size: 30 to 40 feet tall by 20 to 35 feet wide

This medium-sized deciduous tree has clusters of bell-shaped white flowers in late spring. The flowers are very attractive when viewed from a short distance; they're best viewed by looking up into the canopy or at eye-level to achieve the maximum ornamental effect, since they are pendulous. Flowers emerge just before the foliage. Fall color is yellow to green. Fruits remain attractive in winter. Older trees develop deeply furrowed bark.

Pollinator & Wildlife Value: Flowers are pollinated by several types of bees. Leaves are eaten by moth caterpillars. Squirrels may eat the fruits. Carolina chickadees nest in dead trunks.

How to Use: Use it as a specimen near a patio or plant it in groups to naturalize a woodland edge. It grows well as a single or multi-trunked tree. It combines well with rhododendrons and other acid-loving plants. A background of evergreens or a dark fence will set off the flowers nicely. It is not urban-tolerant, especially of heat, drought, and poor soils, and may develop chlorotic foliage on alkaline soils. Silverbell is a good disease-free alternative to flowering dogwood and crabapples.

How to Grow & Maintain: Silverbells do best in a well-drained, acidic soil in full sun to partial shade. Trees require evenly moist soil throughout the growing season, until the ground freezes. Apply a 2- to 4-inch layer of pine needles or shredded pine bark to maintain soil moisture and soil acidity. Trees benefit from an annual spring application of an acid fertilizer. Trees can break easily in wind and snowstorms; selectively shape young trees to avoid weak, narrow crotch angles. Mature trees rarely need pruning; prune after flowering, if desired. No serious pest problems. Deer avoid it.

Beyond the Species: 'Rosea' and 'Arnold's Pink' are pink-flowered selections. 'Silver Splash' and 'Variegata' have green leaves streaked and splashed with white or yellow. Two-winged silverbell (*H. diptera*) is smaller, growing 14 to 25 feet tall and about 15 feet wide. It blooms about two weeks later than Carolina silverbell. Zones 5 to 8.

Halesia diptera

Magnolia acuminata
Cucumber Magnolia, Cucumbertree

Zones: 4 to 9
Size: 50 to 80 feet tall by 30 to 40 feet wide

Native magnolias are a diverse group, ranging from shrubby small trees to grand specimens over 100 feet tall. Flowers range in size from a couple of inches to over 16 inches across and can be quite showy. The petals unfurl to reveal a large center cone. Some species bloom very early in spring; others, in summer. They can be single- or multitrunked and most have nice smooth, gray bark. Most are deciduous but some are evergreen or semi-evergreen. Leaf buds are often fat and furry, ornamental on their own. Cucumber magnolia has slightly fragrant, greenish-yellow, tuliplike flowers that are 2 to 4 inches long. They are not as showy as some other species; it is grown more for its foliage and nice shape. It gets its common name from the seed cones, which resemble cucumbers. The fruits turn red in late summer. Unlike most magnolias, it develops gold fall color, which is a nice backdrop for the showy fruits.

Pollinator & Wildlife Value: Magnolia flowers are pollinated by sap beetles and other beetles. Some caterpillars feed on the leaves. Seeds are eaten by birds, including turkeys, and squirrels.

Magnolia acuminata

How to Use: Magnolias can be used as specimen, shade, or understory trees. They grow well in dappled shade under large shade trees. The large leaves can become a litter problem when they fall. Cucumber magnolia usually stays 40 to 50 feet tall in landscape situations. It has a nice form and isn't as messy as other species, so it makes a nice shade tree in the lawn.

How to Grow & Maintain: It grows best in moist, rich loamy soil in sun to light shade and does not like extremely wet or dry soil. Magnolias can be difficult to transplant. Trees may drop their leaves after transplanting, but they recover quickly. Late spring frosts may brown the flowers on early-flowering species, but this won't kill a tree. Prune after flowering only if necessary to shape the tree. Ice and snow can cause weak branches to fall. It has no serious pest problems but scales may cause yellowing of leaves; prune out badly infested branches. Deer may browse on plants.

Beyond the Species: Southern magnolia (*M. grandiflora*) grows 60 to 80 feet tall or more and up to 50 feet wide, so it is really only suitable as a specimen tree on large lots away from buildings. It is an evergreen species. It has fragrant, waxy, creamy white flowers from late spring to midsummer. 'Bracken's Brown Beauty' is a compact cultivar that typically grows to 30 feet tall with a dense, narrow crown. Flowers and leaves are about half the size of the species. 'Little Gem' grows 15 to 20 feet tall with an 8- to 10-foot spread. It flowers at a much younger age than the species. Zones 7 to 10. Bigleaf magnolia (*M. macrophylla*) grows 25 to 40 feet tall and 20 to 35 feet wide. It has very large leaves and large, sweetly fragrant flowers in spring. Zones 5 to 9. Umbrella magnolia (*M. tripetala*) grows 25 to 40 feet tall and 15 to 35 feet wide. It is a nicely shaped tree but the flowers are not as showy as other species. It is hardier than other native magnolias. Zones 4 to 9. Sweetbay magnolia (*M. virginiana*) grows 40 to 60 feet tall and is semi-evergreen or evergreen. It has a nice columnar form, only getting 10 to 20 feet wide, and can be grown as a clump tree. Leaves are whitish green on their undersides. Creamy white, lemon-scented, smallish flowers bloom for a month or so in late spring into summer. Moonglow ('Jim Wilson') is a vigorous upright selection with slightly larger flowers. Zones 5 to 10.

Ostrya virginiana
Ironwood, Hop Hornbeam

Zones: 3 to 9
Size: 20 to 40 feet tall by 15 to 30 feet wide

Ostrya virginiana

How to Use: This tough tree is well suited to smaller city landscapes and tight spaces where most shade trees grow too large. It can be grown as a clumping tree. Its clean, disease-free foliage provides good summer shade—dense if grown in sun and more open when grown in light shade. The wood is strong and resistant to ice and wind damage. The seedpods are eaten by birds or slowly disintegrate, so there is no litter. Its main drawback for use is its slow growth rate, but this can be somewhat overcome if it's given supplemental water and fertilizer when young. Use it as an understory tree in woodland gardens, where the slow growth is advantageous. Ironwood is not tolerant of salt or compacted soil, so it's not a good street tree.

How to Grow and Maintain: It prefers a cool, moist, well-drained, slightly acidic soil, but adapts to a wide range of landscape situations provided the soil is acidic and not waterlogged. It tolerates full sun, partial shade, and even heavy shade. Transplant balled-and-burlapped or container-grown trees in early spring. Trees are somewhat slow to establish after transplanting. Regular watering and fertilizing when trees are young will help plants come out of transplant shock quicker and become established. Apply a 2- to 4-inch layer of organic mulch such as pine needles, shredded oak leaves, or shredded pine bark to keep the soil evenly moist and maintain soil acidity. Prune in winter to remove dead or damaged branches and to shape trees, if needed. Trees may bleed sap in late winter. It has no serious insect or disease problems. Deer may browse it.

Ironwood is a handsome, small- to medium-sized, deciduous tree with many horizontal or drooping branches and a rounded outline. Dark green, birchlike leaves turn a mild yellow color in fall. The straight trunk and limbs are covered with interesting shaggy, gray bark. In late summer, the seeds ripen in flattened, papery pods that are strung together like fish scales or hops to form a little cone.

Pollinator & Wildlife Value: Moth caterpillars and beetles feed on foliage. Ruffed grouse, wild turkey, downy woodpecker, purple finch, and several other songbirds and small mammals eat the seeds. Ruffed grouse feed on overwintering buds and catkins.

Oxydendrum arboreum
Sourwood

Zones: 5 to 9
Size: 25 to 30 feet tall by 15 to 20 feet wide

This deciduous plant usually remains as a small tree in the landscape, but it can grow to 50 feet in its native habitats. Young trees have a somewhat irregular growth habit, but as they age they develop an attractive pyramidal outline with drooping branches. Foliage starts out light green in spring, turns a lustrous dark green in summer, and puts on a real show in fall, turning yellow, red, or purple, and sometimes all three colors on the same tree. White, fragrant flowers appear in early summer in 4- to 10-inch-long drooping racemes that hang from the tips of the branches and give the tree a weeping softness. They turn into yellowish fruits that hang on through winter. The fruits, along with the interesting grayish-brown, deeply furrowed bark, add winter interest.

Pollinator & Wildlife Value: It's highly valued by bees, which in turn produce renowned honey from its nectar. Small seeds are eaten by birds and mammals, and it is occasionally used for nesting by songbirds.

How to Use: This tree is usually used as a specimen so its many attractive attributes can be fully appreciated. Place it near a deck, patio, or terrace that can be viewed from indoors in winter. It also looks nice at the edge of a forest or natural area. Its narrow, upright growth habit makes it good for small spaces.

How to Grow & Maintain: Sourwood prefers acidic, well-drained soil in sun to light shade. Flowering and fall color is best in full sun. It likes an even supply of soil moisture and tolerates wet soils; water well during dry periods. Apply a 2- to 4-inch layer of an organic mulch such as pine needles, shredded oak leaves, or shredded pine bark to keep the soil evenly moist and to maintain soil acidity. Sourwood rarely needs pruning. Avoid cultivating around the shallow roots. It has no serious problems; leaf spot and twig blight can be minor. Deer will feed on leaves and twigs.

Oxydendrum arboreum

Picea glauca
White Spruce

Zones: 2 to 6
Size: 40 to 70 feet tall by 10 to 40 feet wide

This large evergreen tree is pyramidal when young, and it becomes narrower as it matures. Bark is scaly and dark gray or grayish brown. The stiff, grayish-green needles are crowded along branchlets. Slender, 2-inch cones mature in fall and hang from branches.

Pollinator & Wildlife Value: Spruces are the larval host of some moths. Birds and small rodents eat the seeds. The dense canopy provides excellent winter shelter and nesting spots for many birds.

How to Use: Spruces are vital to northern landscapes and long-lived if properly cared for. Their large size restricts their use, but they can be used for screening, windbreaks, and shelterbelts, as well as background plantings. They are tolerant of salt, heat, and drought. Don't plant a spruce if you want to mow right up to the trunk. Their natural shape is pyramidal, with branches all the way to the ground—it's not palm tree-like. They can be used for large-scale hedging. Dwarf and compact forms can be used in rock gardens or as specimens and accents in the landscape.

How to Grow & Maintain: Spruces do best on well-drained, slightly acidic soils in full sun. Foliage is thinner in shade. Trees do poorly in overly wet soils and in drought conditions. Give spruces plenty of space; crowded trees drop needles. Spruces require little or no pruning. If you want to shape a tree, trim a little in late spring just as the new growth is hardening, rather than a lot all in one year. If possible, keep snow off branches in winter to reduce branch breakage. Sawflies can leave bare spots on trees. Remove sawflies by hand as soon as you see them. Cankers show up as wounds on trees and branches and lead to defoliation. Prevent cankers by growing healthy trees. Once a tree is infected, there is little you can do. Deer avoid spruces.

Beyond the Species: 'Echiniformis' is a slow-growing dwarf cushion form that stays under 2 feet tall and wide. 'Little Globe' is a globular form about 2 feet tall and wide. Black Hills spruce (*P.* x *albertiana*) is a hybrid between *P. glauca* and *P. engelmannii* with very confused classification. It is also known as *P. glauca* var. *densata*, 'Densata', 'Conica', Black Hills spruce, and Alberta spruce. It is a dense, cone-shaped, slow-growing form of white spruce that stays 20 to 25 feet tall even after many years. It has brighter green needles and slightly smaller cones than white spruce. Whatever you find it sold as, it is a very nice plant for landscape use, and there are several interesting selections available. 'Cecelia' is a globose form with bluish needles that stays under 2 feet in height. Jean's Dilly™ is upright and perfectly conical, eventually reaching 5 feet in height. 'Sander's Blue' eventually reaches 20 feet in height and has soft blue-green needles. Zones 3 to 6. Engelmann spruce (*P. engelmannii*) grows 40 to 70 feet tall but only 15 to 30 feet wide, so it has a more columnar form and gray-green needles. 'Argentea' has silvery gray needles. 'Glauca' has bluish needles. Zones 3 to 5. Black spruce (*P. mariana*) usually stays at 20 to 30 feet, but can grow over 50 feet in favorable conditions. It has a narrow, pyramidal shape and widely spaced branches that are somewhat drooping, and bluish-green needles. It tolerates some shade. The species is not as readily available in the nursery trade, but there are some cultivars that make nice garden plants. 'Ericoides' is

Picea glauca

Picea x albertiana

Pinus strobus
Eastern White Pine

Zones: 3 to 8
Size: 50 to 80 feet tall by 20 to 40 feet wide

There's nothing like the scent of pine trees or the sound of wind whistling through their branches. Just about every area has at least one native species. These stately evergreens range from 12-foot scraggly small trees to giants towering over 100 feet tall. Eastern White Pine has a pyramidal shape and whorls of horizontal branches evenly spaced along the trunk. The bark is thin, smooth, and greenish gray on young trees, but thick, deeply furrowed, and grayish brown on older trees. The soft, flexible, gray-green needles are 2½ to 5 inches long and occur in clusters of five. Cones are 4 to 8 inches long, thick, and usually gummy.

Pollinator & Wildlife Value: Many insects visit pines, including caterpillars of butterflies and moths: western pine white butterfly and pine elfins are two. Seeds are an important food source for many birds and small mammals. The sap attracts woodpeckers. Birds that use trees for nesting include vireos, evening grosbeaks, warblers, eagles, owls, and hawks.

How to Use: This large conifer is best reserved for rural landscapes or large estates where it can to grow to its full height and width. A mature specimen is a beautiful sight. With diligent shearing, it can make a beautiful hedge. Large pines can be used as specimens in large landscapes, but are usually used for screening and windbreaks. They don't adapt well to urban conditions. There are many cultivars that stay smaller and do well in landscape situations.

How to Grow & Maintain: Pines grow best in fertile, acidic, well-drained soils in full sun. Plants will brown out and even die if planted near roads that are salted in winter. Pruning is not recommended for most tree species, including white pine, but it does help form more-compact growth on cultivars. Prune in spring when the candles are beginning to lengthen, pinching or cutting back no more than one-third to one-half of the candle. Trees tend to shed lower branches as they grow. Although native trees are susceptible to several insect and disease problems, landscape trees are usually not bothered. White pine blister rust shows up as powdery red rust on the bark. The alternate host for this rust is *Ribes* species (gooseberries and currants). Don't plant these where white pines are a priority. Pick off sawflies as soon as you see them. Scale insect damage shows up as whitish flecks on needles. For serious infestations,

continued on next page

201

a slow-growing dwarf that eventually becomes rounded and flat-topped. 'Nana' is a slow-growing, mounded cultivar growing 2 feet tall and 3 feet wide. Zones 3 to 5. Colorado blue spruce (*P. pungens*) grows 30 to 50 feet tall and up to 20 feet wide. As the name implies, the needles have a bluish cast. Many cultivars are available, some having bluer foliage, some with gold foliage, and some with globose or weeping forms. 'Fat Albert' grows about 15 feet tall and has a dense, upright, pyramidal form. 'Hoopsii' is a dense pyramidal selection with excellent slivery blue needles. Zones 3 to 7. Red spruce (*P. rubens*) grows 30 to 60 feet tall and about 20 feet wide. It is an eastern species very similar to white spruce that doesn't always adapt well to landscape use. Zones 3 to 5.

continued from previous page

you may need to spray plants with dormant oil or lime sulfur in late fall or early spring. Deer browsing can be a problem, and young trees can get winterburn on exposed sites. Needles in the center of trees brown before falling, and this change often confuses uneducated homeowners, who think their tree is dying. Deer and rabbits love young pines, and this can make it difficult to get plants established.

Beyond the Species: 'Blue Shag', 'Compacta', and 'Nana' are rounded, dense shrubs growing 6 to 8 feet tall and 6 feet wide; 'Compacta' has softer foliage than the species. 'Fastigiata' is a columnar form growing about 25 feet tall and 8 feet wide. 'Pendula' is a 10-foot weeping form that must be staked when young. It takes several years to really look nice. Bristlecone pine (*P. aristata*) grows 12 to 25 feet tall and 8 to 20 feet wide with a rounded, densely needled crown. Plants are quite picturesque in old age. Zones 4 to 7. Jack pine (*P. banksiana*) usually stays 20 to 40 feet tall in landscape situations. It is an open tree with many small dead branches that often remain on trees for many years. It is hardy and tolerant of poor, sandy soil and shade, thriving in sites unsuitable for other pines. It is fast growing when young, making it good for windbreaks and screening. Its stark, open growth habit can be adapted to landscape use, especially with modern architecture. 'Uncle Fogy' is an interesting selection with an irregular, often weeping, form. It

Pinus strobus

grows about 6 feet tall and 10 feet wide. Zones 2 to 7. Pinyon pine (*P. edulis*) grows 10 to 20 feet tall and 8 to 15 feet wide. It is shrubbier, slow growing, and drought tolerant. Zones 5 to 8. Limber pine (*P. flexilis*) is similar to white pine; it grows 40 to 50 feet tall and 20 to 30 feet wide. It is a rugged, low-maintenance tree, if it does not develop blister rust. Zones 4 to 6. Longleaf pine (*P. palustris*) grows 40 to 70 feet tall and up to 40 feet wide. It has soft needles up to 12 inches long and an open-branched crown. Zones 7 to 9. Ponderosa pine (*P. ponderosa*) grows quite large— 60 feet tall or more—and is a good choice in higher elevations. Zones 3 to 7. Red pine (*P. resinosa*) grows 50 to 100 feet tall or more and has an open, rounded, picturesque head. The stiff, 4- to 6-inch needles appear in clusters of two. Cones are about 2 inches long, light brown fading to gray in color, and free of resin. Red pine thrives on sandy loam and dry soils in full sun, and it is disease and insect resistant. Winter burn can be a problem on younger trees. 'Wissota' is a dwarf form that grows about 6 feet tall and wide. Zones 3 to 6. Pitch pine (*P. rigida*) grows 30 to 50 feet tall and 15 to 25 feet wide. It is a good choice for drought sites with poor soil. Zones 4 to 7. Loblolly pine (*P. taeda*) grows 70 to 100 feet or taller and 20 to 35 feet wide. It grows quickly and tolerates tough sites. Zones 6 to 9.

Pinus strobus 'Blue Shag'

Quercus species
Oaks

Zones: 3 to 10
Size: 25 to 80 feet tall and wide

A well-grown oak is an asset in any landscape, usually greatly increasing property value. Their stately presence is felt year-round. Leaves offer summer shade, fall color, and often persist into winter for added interest. A tree's strong, bold silhouette adds to the winter appeal. Oaks are divided into two general groups: white and red. The easiest way to differentiate is by leaf shape. Species in the white oak group tend to have rounded leaf lobes, and red oaks have sharp-tipped leaf lobes. Most oaks are deciduous, but some are evergreen. With many species of native oaks, it is best to select an oak that is native to your region and, if possible, from a local source. The main things to keep in mind, when choosing any landscape tree, are its mature size and its soil requirements.

Pollinator & Wildlife Value: Oaks provide food and habitat for a large number of beneficial insects, birds, and mammals. According to University of Delaware entomologist Douglas Tallamy, oaks support well over 500 different species of butterfly and moth caterpillars, which in turn provide food for many types of birds. The acorns are a valuable fall food source for many wildlife species, including turkeys, squirrels, prairie chickens, grouse, and chipmunks. Birds and small mammals nest in the branches and in tree cavities.

How to Use: These deciduous trees should be given a prominent place where they can grow to their full potential. Do not be put off by oaks' reputation of slow growth or susceptibility to oak wilt, which is not usually a problem in landscape situations. Most oaks do well in rain gardens, if you have the room. Some work well as street trees.

How to Grow & Maintain: Most oaks grow best in fertile, acidic soil in full sun, but some tolerate lighter, sandier soils and dry conditions. Most have taproots and are somewhat difficult to transplant, so it's best to start with a younger tree. Seedlings are fast-growing, so don't hesitate to plant an acorn where you want a tree. Plant it in fall (providing protection from digging squirrels), or store it in moist sand in a cool place over the winter and then plant it in spring. Oak roots are very sensitive to changes in soil level. Even a small change can kill roots, so avoid adding or removing soil around trees. Oak wilt, a fungal disease, can kill mature oaks; red oaks are more susceptible than white oaks. The oak wilt fungus enters trees via insects through wounds caused by pruning or by root damage during construction. The fungus can spread to nearby trees by root grafts. Oak wilt is mainly a problem on native stands; usually landscape specimens are isolated enough not to be at risk. Do not prune while insects are most active, from about April 1 to July 1. Deer and rabbits may browse on young trees.

Beyond the Species: White oak (*Q. alba*) grows 50 to 75 feet tall, with a spread of 40 to 60 feet and a broad, rounded top and irregularly spreading limbs. The leaves, which don't fully unfold until midspring, are deeply divided into five to nine fingerlike, rounded lobes. They are bright green in summer, turning deep red or violet-purple in fall. Zones 4 to 9. Swamp white oak (*Q. bicolor*) grows 40 to 65 feet tall and has an open, rounded crown. It is easier to transplant than some oaks, and it makes a handsome specimen or shade tree. It is also faster growing and more tolerant of tougher sites,

Quercus alba

continued on next page

Quercus bicolor

Quercus macrocarpa

but it doesn't like drought. Fall leaf color is an attractive bronze-brown. Zones 4 to 8. Scarlet oak (*Q. coccinea*) is a red oak type, growing 50 to 75 feet tall with an irregular open crown. Leaves are shiny dark green, turning scarlet to brownish red in fall. It tolerates dry, infertile soils but they must be acidic. It is a good landscape tree and has relatively fast growth, good form, and scarlet fall color. Zones 4 to 9.

Northern pin oak (*Q. ellipsoidalis*) is smaller, growing to only 45 to 65 feet and is a nice landscape plant in the right site. Fall color is a good deep red to reddish brown. It will suffer from chlorosis on soils with too high of a pH, but this problem is easily corrected by adding iron to the soil and lowering the pH. It is susceptible to oak wilt. Zones 3 to 7. Oregon white oak (*Q. garryana*) grows 25 to 60 feet tall or more and has a wide-spreading crown and brown fall color. Zones 7 to 9. Shingle oak (*Q. imbricaria*) grows 40 to 60 feet tall and has good resistance to pests. Zones 5 to 8. Laurel oak (*Q. laurifolia*) grows 40 to 60 feet tall, does well in urban areas, and has good resistance to pests. Zones 7 to 9. Bur oak (*Q. macrocarpa*) is a white-oak type with leaves shaped like bass fiddles. It grows 50 to 80 feet tall and makes an impressive specimen. It is adaptable to various soils and more tolerant of city conditions than other oaks, but it can be difficult to transplant. It is too large for most city landscapes, but it is a good choice for rural and large suburban sites. Zones 3 to 8. Chinkapin oak (*Q. muehlenbergii*) only grows 40 to 50 feet in height with an open, rounded crown. It tolerates drought and higher pH soils better

than most oaks and is more resistant to diseases and insect problems, making it a good landscape choice. Zones 5 to 8. Pin oak (*Q. palustris*) grows 65 feet tall or more with a spread of up to 50 feet. It is easier to transplant than most oaks, has outstanding fall color, and good pyramidal form, making it better adapted to landscape and street tree use. It requires acidic soil, however. Zones 4 to 8. Willow oak (*Q. phellos*) grows 40 to 60 feet tall and is fast-growing. The light green, willow-like leaves create dense shade and a graceful effect when they turn bright yellow before they fall. It prefers moist, rich, acidic, well-drained soil but tolerates clay, salt, poor drainage, and compacted soil and is one of the best oaks for street tree use. It can develop chlorosis in high pH soils. Zones 6 to 9. Red oak (*Q. rubra*) grows 50 to 80 feet tall and is faster growing than other oaks and easier to transplant. The dark green leaves turn shades of red in fall and persist into winter. It prefers sandy loam soils that are well drained and acidic; it will get iron chlorosis in high pH soils. It is tolerant of city conditions but is very susceptible to oak wilt. Zones 4 to 8. Shumard oak (*Q. shumardii*) usually grows 40 to 60 feet tall and requires a more acidic soil. Zones 5 to 9. Black oak (*Q. velutina*) grows about 60 feet tall and has an open crown. Fall color is dull red to orange-brown. It is worth seeking out in the nursery trade, especially where hardiness is a concern. Zone 3 to 9. Live oak (*Q. virginiana*) is a majestic, widespreading tree growing 40 to 80 feet tall with low branches and is often covered in Spanish moss. Zones 8 to 10.

Tilia americana
Basswood, Linden

Zones: 2 to 8
Size: 50 to 90 feet tall by 40 to 50 feet wide

Tilia americana

This large deciduous tree is stately and well-formed with a clean, straight trunk; broad, rounded crown; and large, heart-shaped, dark green leaves. Autumn color is a dull green to slightly yellow-green. The light gray, smooth bark becomes dark gray with age. The distinctive straplike leafy bracts support clusters of sweetly fragrant (but not very showy) creamy white flowers in summer that are very attractive to bees. The fruit is a rounded nutlike drupe that hangs onto the tree long into winter.

Pollinator & Wildlife Value: Flowers are visited by many types of bees, and the result is great honey. Butterfly and moth caterpillars feed on leaves, including tiger swallowtails. Many beetles, borers, and other types of insects feed on basswoods. Seeds are eaten by small birds and mammals, including chipmunks, squirrels, and mice. Woodpeckers and other cavity nesters use it.

How to Use: Basswood is a hardy, trouble-free tree that makes a good specimen or shade tree if you have room for its large size. It is fast growing and long-lived. It casts deep shade that is difficult to grow other plants under. It needs adequate root space and is not tolerant of soil compaction or air pollution, so it's not well suited to street-tree use. The more compact cultivars usually do better in typical landscape situations.

How to Grow & Maintain: Prefers moist, fertile, well-drained soils but will grow on drier, heavier soils in full sun or part shade. Basswood is easily transplanted in early spring. It is moderately fast growing and long-lived. Wrap young trees in winter to prevent sunscald. Prune out sprouts that develop at the base of the tree. Few insects or diseases bother it, but you may see Japanese beetles, spider mites, aphids, borers, leaf miners, or scale. Deer and rabbits may eat twigs and leaves.

Beyond the Species: Several cultivars have been selected for smaller size or more compact form, but some may not be as hardy as the species. 'Bailyard' (Frontyard®) has a broadly pyramidal shape and good yellow fall color; it grows to 70 feet in height. 'Boulevard' grows 60 feet tall and only about 35 feet wide with a more columnar shape. 'Sentry' has an upright branching habit. 'Redmond' has a uniform pyramidal habit and grows about 50 feet tall. Legend™ only grows about 40 feet tall and has a handsome pyramidal form.

Index

continued on next page

Meet Lynn Steiner

Lynn Steiner is one of the Upper Midwest's best-known garden writers and a frequent speaker at gardening and environmental events. She is the author and photographer of several books that advocate for the effective use of native plants in the typical home landscape. *Landscaping with Native Plants of Minnesota,* the first book designed to identify Minnesota's native plants and plant communities and to demonstrate how to use them effectively in a typical home landscape, was a finalist in the 2006 Minnesota Book Awards in the Science and Nature category.

Lynn is the author and photographer of several other books, including *Rain Gardens: Sustainable Landscaping for a Beautiful Yard and a Healthy World,* published in February 2012. Other titles include *Landscaping with Native Plants of Wisconsin*, published spring 2007, and *Landscaping with Native Plants of Michigan,* published in 2006 and named a Michigan Notable Book for 2007. She also helped develop, wrote, and provided photographs for *The Complete Guide to Gardening* series, ten regional gardening books published in 2012 by Cool Springs Press.

For fifteen years, Lynn was the editor of *Northern Gardener* magazine, the official publication of the Minnesota State Horticultural Society. Under her direction, *Northern Gardener* received several Overall Excellence awards from the Minnesota Magazine & Publication Association, and several individual contributors received Garden Writers Association Media awards. She now writes a column for the magazine titled "Northern Natives."

Lynn lives with her husband and two cats on a 115-year-old farmstead in northern Washington County, Minnesota, where she enjoys tending her gardens and watching the progress of her restored prairie, savanna, and oak woodland.